Idiots

How Identity Politics is Destroying
the Left

Katie Roche

First published in 2021 by Katie Roche

Copyright © 2021 Katie Roche

Printed by Ingram Spark

ISBN: 978-1-8380896-3-4

Contents

1. Introduction

Biological sex isn't real. All white people are inherently racist. Obesity is neither unhealthy, nor caused by lack of exercise and poor diet. For the average person, these statements sound crazy. No sane person would say something like that. But there's a place where these views would not only be accepted, but any opposition is regarded as bigotry. Welcome to the world of identity politics. A land where anything goes. It's a place where feelings trump facts. Where weakness is celebrated. And where identity is placed above all else. Frighteningly, it's taking over the left in both the UK and the USA.

Because of identity politics, the left now fetishizes victimhood. It obsesses over identity. And it treats wokeness as a competition. (Woke, as in 'woke up' or 'awoken', means to be aware of social issues. Metaphorically, a woke person is awake to the oppression in the world, while others sleep, unaware of what goes on around them). They call themselves socialists, but they're not. A more apt name for them would be 'fauxialists'. Because they have little interest in redistribution of wealth or other economic matters. Nor do they care about other topics, such as humanitarian issues. As Angela Nagle, the author of *Kill All Normies* points out, to be accepted by the left, you just have to be seen to be liberal, rather than actually be a liberal. Like Barack Obama, you can launch drone attacks but still be liberal because you support gay marriage (1). Many of us socialists are exasperated by these people. We hate watching the movement that is so

1

important to us being destroyed by lunatics. And it's terrible to see so many people reject the left because they think all we do is push bizarre narratives and overlook simple facts.

So how did the left go insane? This book will analyse the rise of identity politics in the UK and the USA from 2010 to the present day. It will look at how the current obsession with identity politics came to be. As well, the book will explore some examples of what social justice warriors believe and how they act. These examples illustrate how social justice warriors are self-serving and hypocritical. It will also explain why identity politics is damaging for the left and examine the big problems with identity politics. In addition, this book will make the case that the social justice warrior movement has caused lasting damage to the political landscape. And that the cultural left has ultimately undermined themselves.

What is Identity Politics?

Identity politics is where groups of people with a shared background campaign for their specific interests. Examples of identity politics movements include gay rights, civil rights and feminism (2). These movements aren't necessarily a bad thing. Throughout history, they have made some important contributions to social progress. However, there are many problems with identity politics.

The biggest issue as the Marxist historian Eric Hobsbawm said, is that:

"Identity groups are about themselves, for themselves, and nobody else. A coalition of such groups that is not held together by a single common set of aims or values, has only an ad hoc unity, rather like states temporarily allied in war against a common enemy. They break up when they are no longer so held together. In any case, as identity groups, they are not committed to the Left as such, but only to get support for their aims wherever they can." (3).

For the left today, it means that they are unconcerned with the abolition of the class system and economic inequalities.

The second problem with identity politics is that minority groups are just that- a minority. There are not enough minorities to secure an electoral victory. To succeed in enacting change, the left needs the support of people who aren't from minority groups. Politics- like it or not- is a popularity contest. Saying 'our party is for minorities' says to non-minorities 'our party is not for you'. That's a good way to lose votes. As a result, people who are sympathetic to left-wing views but aren't minorities become disenfranchised. They will not vote for left-wing parties. If you're a white, heterosexual, working-class man, and you're repeatedly hearing from left-wing parties "you're a bad person. You shouldn't vote for us"; you will vote for a right-wing party. And that costs left-wing parties elections.

These problems have been around for a while. And admittedly, they haven't destroyed the left. But more recently, identity politics has transformed into something toxic: the social justice warrior movement.

What is a Social Justice Warrior?

A social justice warrior is a follower of the social justice warrior movement. This movement is a fusion of identity politics and a self-help movement that began in the late 2000s on social media sites. Most social justice warriors are young, well-educated, middle-class adults. The movement has influenced older generations of left-wingers too.

The phrase 'social justice warrior' may be a play on the earlier phrase 'keyboard warrior', meaning someone who is very aggressive and argumentative online. This term is similar to an armchair activist, in that they complain a lot but do not get involved with actual campaigning (4). The word 'warrior' may have originally been used ironically, to indicate the trivial nature of the causes that keyboard warriors (and later social justice warriors) get involved with. However, social justice warriors aren't just online anymore. Its influence has spread to real world politics.

The main goal of the social justice warriors is to achieve equality of opportunity for certain social groups. These include groups traditionally represented in identity politics, such as lesbian, gay and bisexual people, ethnic minorities and the disabled. But it also includes newer identity groups (these will be explored in chapter 3). The idea behind the social justice warrior movement is that through being aware of issues affecting minorities, society can bring about equality. They believe that inequality is caused by various subtle forms of discrimination. People who are not minorities must be constantly aware of their privilege, and how to tame it's affects to bring about social equality. They must always be thinking about diversity and inclusion. And these people must make great efforts to ensure they are not subtly offending minorities.

In practice, there are very few people in the social justice warrior movement who don't identify as some type of minority. We'll see why that is in chapter three. This fixation with being a minority leads to is Oppression Olympics. Oppression Olympics is where different minority groups vie for the title of 'most oppressed'. As well as backstabbing, and squabbling (5). Everyone is fighting all the time. They fight to have their voice heard above all others. And over who's doing something 'wrong'. As Nagle points out, social justice warriors can be savagely competitive over who should be leading the movement (1). Indeed, a social justice hero can find themselves falling from grace at any point. See the story of Ira Grey. Grey was held as a paradigm of woke purity: transgender, queer, a person of colour, and mentally ill. He ticked all the boxes. He told stories of escaping his abusive family. Online, he spoke about issues affecting transgender people. He also taught classes on sexual consent. Then he was accused of rape by a former partner. Grey tried to rationalize this by saying that there is "no such thing as 100% good consent" (6). Fortunately, the rank and file social justice warriors saw through him and he is nowhere to be seen. (Gray now uses multiple names, including Ira Sanchez, Ira Bohm-Sanchez and Dalton Sanchez. This makes it difficult to find information on his recent activities).

It has been interesting to see how rapidly these new identities and causes have taken hold of the left. As Douglas Murray noted in his book, *The Madness of Crowds*, it took many years for mainstream society to embrace racial equality and gay rights. In contrast, more recent issues such as transgender rights have been accepted straight away (7). Why has the mainstream left been so quick to embrace these new identities? It's because the left has a fear of being on the 'wrong side of history'. People don't want to be seen in the way we see yesterday's homophobes and racists. Most people feel ashamed of slavery, segregation and other forms of discrimination that were permissible in the past. So, they have gone along with these new identities without much critical thought. The downside of this is that they do not see the contradictions in what they support, or ways that they are regressive. Nor do they see that in some cases, these new identities are old prejudices dressed up in woke clothing. For example, there are many conflicts between transgender rights and women's rights. The transgender movement also promotes regressive ideas about gender and sexuality. Yet those who raise concerns are dismissed as 'transphobic'.

The power that the social justice warrior movement holds over its followers has been compared to a religion. The

New York magazine journalist Andrew Sullivan identified many similarities between the social justice warrior movement and Christianity. These include the way that they aim to restrict speech, along with having no tolerance for alternative views (8). Further parallels include the way that it views whiteness, heterosexuality and masculinity as equivalent to the original sin (that humanity has been guilty of sin ever since Adam and Eve disobeyed God in the Garden of Eden). In the social justice warrior movement, a person with these characteristics must repeatedly state that they recognize their privilege. They are also held responsible for the actions of their ancestors. It is reminiscent of how Christians must regularly ask to be forgiven for the original sin. Another comparison between religion and the social justice warrior movement is their powerful dogma. They command an unquestioned following and unfaltering belief. They see dissenters as 'sinners'- even when those 'sinners' actually agree with some of what the social justice warrior movement says. And like with sinners in the church, these dissidents are to be ostracized. We must not see or hear anything they have to say, in case they lead people astray.

The Socio-Economic Background of the Social Justice Warrior

The circumstances in which social justice warriors were born into explain why the social justice warrior movement started when it did. The bulk of the social justice warriors were born in 1990s and early 2000s, falling into the late millennials and generation Z. The psychologist Jean Twenge refers to this age group as Generation Me (9).

Generation Me had a childhood that was idyllic in many ways. They grew up in affluent families with heavily involved 'helicopter' parents. Helicopter parents metaphorically hover over their children, monitoring everything they do. These parents were very anxious and protective about their children. They gave their children much less freedom and independence than prior generations. For instance, by not allowing them to play unsupervised in case they were injured or abducted (10). They also pushed their children to participate in many extra-curricular activities. And they emphasised academic attainment (11). These parents would also get involved in their child's life in more extreme ways. For example, phoning their child's school to dispute poor grades (12). Or contacting their child's summer camp because their child looked unhappy on a photograph (13). As a result, many members of Generation Me lived very infantilized lives into early adulthood. Parents were still involved in their adult child's life, as if it were a continuation of childhood. For example, by contacting their child's university and employers to resolve disputes (14).

Generation Me were also the first generation of children to be particularly wanted by their parents. Thanks to improvements in birth control, couples could postpone parenthood until they had established their careers (9). This had many advantages. Parents were prepared for the child's birth and were financially stable. The child was also unlikely to feel unwanted or neglected. However, this brought its own problems. Couples had to put a conscious effort into conceiving children, which is more difficult in older couples. Both men and women's fertility declines after the age of 30 (15,16). However, in-vitro fertilization (IVF) and other reproductive technologies became widely available in this period (17). In 1986, the first pregnancy resulting from a frozen egg was documented (18). This development led to social egg freezing where a woman freezes her eggs while she is young. This enables her to focus on her career and find a partner without worrying about being too old to conceive (19). While these treatments let people have children when they wouldn't have been able to otherwise, they came with many downsides. These include side effects, high failure rates and a high monetary cost. Having a child became much more difficult and expensive.

For that reason, kids were more precious to their parents than they had been in the past. Parents started off with high expectations for their children from before they'd even been conceived. These expectations continued throughout the child's upbringing and into early adulthood. Parents were also more protective of their children. Parents of children conceived via IVF report feeling that their child was more vulnerable than other children. They were also less confident than their parenting ability than parents who conceived naturally (20). This lack of confidence makes it harder to be assertive and set boundaries. For instance, if the child is told to do something they don't want to do (such as chores or eating a certain food). They become sad. The parent thinks 'I'm a bad parent' and backs down. This teaches the child that they can't cope with mildly unpleasant experiences and that acting sad gets them what they want. This is unhelpful for their development. Children often thrive when they are exposed to some controlled risks and when boundaries are set (21). But these precious bundles of joy were often doted on by their parents. Childhood was about happiness, not instilling discipline.

According to Twenge, another defining aspect of Generation Me was that they were raised in the self-esteem movement. Self-esteem is about perceived self-worth. High self-esteem is about thinking you're brilliant. At school and in extra-curricular activities, there was a heavy emphasis on making sure children's self-esteem wasn't damaged. For example, children would often receive a participation certificate for taking part in a competition when they didn't win. Generation Me is also known as the trophy generation for this reason (22). The idea was that their self-esteem wouldn't be dented and so they wouldn't be discouraged from continuing with the activity in the future. Children were also taught to think about how important and special they were. They were encouraged to value themselves based on the things they were good at and that made them unique from other children. For small children, this included singing songs about how they were special and making posters with the same message. Parents were encouraged not to criticize their children or point out when they weren't good at something. As a result, this generation learned to think highly of themselves. But the darker side of this is that Generation Me have high rates of narcissism (9).

The self-esteem movement was supposed to have many benefits. Low self-esteem was said to cause children to bully others. And when the children grew up, high self-esteem was supposed to prevent unemployment and criminality. However, evidence does not support that. Studies show that criminals, drug addicts and bullies have higher self-esteem than the general population (23). As well, focusing on self-esteem doesn't look at the structural issues that cause such problems. For instance, unemployment isn't just a matter of attitude. If there are more jobseekers than there are jobs, there will be unemployment. This implies that high self-esteem isn't the magical cure-all it has been touted to be.

Furthermore, self-esteem is more complex than the self-esteem movement claims. It relies to some extent on comparisons with others. Psychologist Mark Leary developed the sociometer theory of self-esteem (24). Leary argues that self-esteem is actually about what he terms "relational value". This is how much you feel you matter to other people. He proposes that personal successes, such as outperforming others in a competitive environment, raises self-esteem by making a person feel that they are important to those around them. In contrast, being rejected by our peers lowers our self-esteem. This suggests that self-esteem isn't simply about being 'special', but about being valued by others. He also raises the question of cause and effect. For instance, do shy people lack confidence because of low self-esteem, or do shy people have low self-esteem because their shyness means they are rejected in social situations? There are no answers to this. But it does imply that self-esteem might be the consequence of success, rather than the cause.

Another defining aspect of Generation Me was that they were the first digital natives. In 1995, companies such as AOL, CompuServe and Prodigy began providing home internet access. This has meant that Generation Me were the first generation to have had internet at home for their whole lives. They were also the first generation to grow up with social media. In the early 2000s, many popular social media platforms were founded. Facebook was launched in 2004 and Twitter started in 2006 (25). So, Generation Me has been using social media from an early age.

Social media provided fertile ground for affluent, liberal young people to socialize and share ideas. Many aspects of the social justice warrior movement were forged on Tumblr. Tumblr is a blogging site with social media features. For instance, users can follow other users and reblog posts as they can on a site such as Twitter or Facebook. However, it was unique in allowing people to post lengthy, expressive, and personal posts. This format facilitated discussions of complex ideas that were out of place on other social media platforms. It could also be used anonymously. Unlike other social media sites, people could use Tumblr without their friends and family knowing (6,26). As well, there was a culture of victimhood on the site. Many users used identity-related phenomenon to explain their personal issues. Young people would describe normal aspects of growing up as abuse or oppression. For example, having to do chores or getting in trouble at school were being described as forms of abuse or discrimination. Typical teenager problems were transformed into issues around identity. Feeling misunderstood could be from undiagnosed Autism, or from unrecognized mental health issues or being gender nonbinary. Rather than simply from being a teenager. Because these sites attract similar people, there is nobody to question what they are saying. This resulted in these communities descending into groupthink. These sites also enabled people to bond with others with similar identities from around the world, when they might not have otherwise met anyone else with that identity. Also, these sites enabled people to forge new identities by letting them experiment without their friends and family knowing.

The effect of internet access and social media is that Generation Me grew up in the filter bubble. The filter bubble occurs online, as we are increasingly only shown content that validates our perspectives. This is a result of personalized features on search engines and social media feeds. It means we don't see material that contradicts our views, so we don't learn how other people think, or see that others disagree with us. This exacerbates political polarization (27). We make our own filter bubbles to some extent. For instance, by following only people we agree with on social media. But the consequence of the filter bubble is that we now all live in our own little echo chambers. It can feel like everyone agrees with you and supports the parties and candidates you like. Even when that doesn't reflect reality.

More broadly, Generation Me are Thatcher's and Reagan's children. They grew up during the leadership of 'third way' politicians such as Bill Clinton and Tony

Blair. The political consensus was that society should embrace capitalism. Children were encouraged to compete. In the UK, gamification of public services was introduced. Competition was artificially created with the aim of improving public services. For instance, school league tables and parental choice in education began under Blair's leadership (28). New Labour also embraced the concept of Active citizenship. In Active Citizenship, the public were regarded as consumers of the welfare state rather than recipients (29). This has resulted in the left-wing version of 'no such thing as society'. In the left, the focus is on how an individual is oppressed, rather than on improving society.

A more troubling aspect of this focus on individuality is that Generation Me are more selfish than previous generations. Twenge says that many members of Generation Me report not feeling any obligation to help others. They perceive that it's an individual's responsibility to help themselves (9). They have been raised to be assertive and put themselves first. This is why the social justice warrior movement emphasizes lived experience. In the politics of the social justice warrior movement, the focus is about how other people need to help you. But never how you can help others. Outside of identity issues, they rarely show compassion toward others. The idea of helping someone less fortunate than themselves is moot- in their eyes, they are the world's least fortunate people! They don't need to help others. Others need to help them! The irony is that for a group of people so concerned with privilege, these people never check their own privilege.

For the future of socialism, this is a problem. Although socialists are often accused of being entitled, socialism is about giving what you can and only taking what you need. On the other hand, the social justice warrior movement is about taking what you can and giving only what you must. Socialism is about looking beyond your own life and making sacrifices. It's about putting others before yourself. Over the years, many people have died fighting for their rights. So many brave men and women have died fighting for the good of humanity. Sometimes you have to look after yourself so you can help others. We all know the oxygen mask on the plane metaphor. You have to put your own oxygen mask on before you help others put theirs on. But generally, if someone needs more than you, you should provide it. Socialism advocates that. The social justice warrior movement doesn't.

Overall, the way social justice warriors were raised resulted in the key traits that define them: individualistic, entitled, fragile. Each of these traits help explain why social justice warriors are how they are.

What is Social Justice?

Having discussed what a social justice warrior is, you might be wondering what social justice actually is. Social justice is branch of philosophy that looks at the way of achieving the most just society. It incorporates ideas from various philosophical traditions (30). Social justice considers issues such as the distribution of wealth and provision of public services, and rights.

Different thinkers have very different ideas on what a socially just world looks like. For example, is it an individual's responsibility to pay for their own healthcare? Some conditions are caused by personal choices. Should healthy people have to pay out of their taxes for that? On the other hand, does society have a responsibility to pay for healthcare? Nobody asks to get sick. And many people are born with illnesses at birth. In other cases, conditions develop through nobody's fault. And even with lifestyle related disorders, there are certain predisposing factors. Some people live a very unhealthy lifestyle and never get sick, while others are very cautious with their health and get sick anyway. This is the type of question a philosopher who specializes in social justice might look at.

Many big names in the field of social justice were left-wing, such as John Rawls, the author of *A Theory of Justice*. He makes the case for the concept of justice as fairness. He argues for the distribution of wealth, via income-linked taxation to alleviate social disadvantage. His rationale for this was that the resources we have are controlled by things that we do not have power over: our genes, where we are born and our social class, to name a few. Not everyone has the opportunity to become wealthy. And so, it's not fair to determine wealth based on these attributes (31).

However, social justice is not necessarily left-wing. For instance, Robert Nozick was another big name in the field of social justice. In the 1970s, Nozick worked alongside

Rawls. As a response to A Theory of Justice, he wrote a book called *Anarchy, State and Utopia*. Nozick argues for the concept of justice as a desert (32). Nozick's view was that the most just society is one where people are rewarded for their efforts and abilities. If someone is rich, it is because they deserve to be. The rich shouldn't have to give their hard-earned money to someone who is less wealthy. It's not their responsibility to help the poor. Nobody has the right to deprive someone else of what they are entitled to. He argues against aiming for equality of opportunity on the grounds that it was depriving someone else of what they deserved. What Nozick was arguing for was conservatism. In his view, life simply isn't fair. And it doesn't need to be. His views have very little in common with those of the social justice warriors. For example, it's very doubtful he would support affirmative action or other measures to help marginalized people. To many people, he promotes social injustice. Yet his work falls under the umbrella of social justice.

The problem with the term 'social justice warrior' is that it sets a false dichotomy. Social justice sounds like a good thing. We all want to live in a just society. For that reason, it sounds difficult to disagree with. You say you're against social justice warriors. Does that mean you're against social justice? Do you support injustice? Of course, nobody is against social justice. Even if you don't agree with what the social justice warriors say. For many left-wingers, it's difficult to resist going along with the perceived 'good guys'. In this sense, it is similar to the term 'pro-life' for people who oppose abortion. Nobody is anti-life. But many people don't feel that aborting a foetus is taking a life. And the term 'social justice' contributes to that. However, the reality is that social justice is much more nuanced than the social justice warrior movement makes it appear.

Therefore, the term 'social justice warrior' is a misnomer. The social justice warriors have a narrow view of what social justice is. This phrase overlooks that social justice means different things to different people.

A Note on Vocabulary and Grammar

This book will use the term 'ethnic minority' rather than 'person of colour' to describe people who are not white but who live in the USA or the UK. 'Person of colour' is a politically correct way of saying 'coloured person'. But 'coloured' is regarded as offensive because it implies whiteness is default. Which is why it fell out of use. But person of colour does the same thing. Nobody calls white people 'people of whiteness'. This is because whiteness is assumed to be the norm. It is as if white people do not have an ethnicity and being 'of colour' is something extra that a person has. For example, when we say, 'a person with a disability', we are acknowledging that most people don't have a disability. And when we say, 'person of colour', it gives the wrongful impression that being white is the default state of being (globally, most people are not white). Also, by lumping all people who aren't white in the category of 'of colour', it implies all non-white people are the same. This is not true. The term glosses over the vast social and cultural differences between ethnic groups. Furthermore, ethnic minorities can be white.

Ashkenazi Jews and Gypsy/Travellers are examples of people who are often regarded as white and also as ethnic minorities. Yet these people are excluded from the category of people of colour. It's not the skin colour that's the sole reason for discrimination.

When referring to ethnicity, the words black and white will not be capitalized. There has been a recent trend for style guides recommending capitalizing the word 'black' when used to refer to race. For instance, the *Seattle Times* style guide says that black should be capitalized because it "is a reflection of shared cultures and experiences". In contrast, the guide states that white should not be capitalized as "its use is a physical description of people whose backgrounds may spring from many different cultures" (33). Journalist Kwame Anthony Appiah points out that there are many issues with this. Writing in *The Atlantic*, he makes the point that nobody's skin is literally white or black (34). Therefore, it's inaccurate to say that white is a physical description and black isn't. There are also relatively light skinned people who identify as black, and quite dark-skinned people who are regarded as white. Appiah also argues that both white and black people's backgrounds are from different cultures. Isn't Africa as diverse as Europe? By saying all black people have a shared culture, this is what it implies.

Another problem with capitalizing black only that it implies that the white ethnicity is default and natural. As Appiah points out, proper nouns (which are spelt with a capital letter) are usually referring to something made or discovered by humans (such as people's names, the names of towns, cities and countries and companies). Whereas natural phenomenon such as colours, plant names and animal names are not proper nouns (34). Ethnicity to some extent is socially constructed. While it's a scientific fact that people have different colour skins, there are points where it is difficult to determine who is what ethnicity. The Antonio Banderas case illustrates this. Banderas, a Spanish actor has olive skin like many people from Spain. In 2020, after Banderas was nominated for an Oscar, some US news outlets described Banderas as a person of colour. The Spanish media was bemused by this, as most Spanish people consider themselves to be white (35). If Banderas had been from Mexico or another south American country, he would be regarded as a person of colour. But as a Spanish person, he is classed as white, even though his skin tone is identical to that of South American Hispanics. This shows how not all cultures see ethnicity in the same way. Having said that, other social groups aren't capitalized. For instance, we don't capitalize working-class, middle-class and upper-class. Therefore, black and white will not be capitalized.

This book will use a person's chosen gender pronouns. For instance, a person who was born male but who identifies as female will be called 'she' rather than 'he'. The main reason for this is to avoid being prosecuted under the UK's draconian hate speech laws. These laws have been used to prosecute people for 'misgendering' (referring to someone as the sex they were born as) (36).

The book is structured as follows: Chapter 2 will explore the ideological foundations of the social justice warrior movement. It will analyse the social and political theories that led to its formation. This includes the birth of the New Left in the 1960s, postmodernism, privilege theory and intersectionality. It will explain where each of these theories originated from and how they amalgamated in the social justice warrior movement.

Chapter 3 will look at the role of identity in the social justice warrior movement. These identities include nonbinary genders (where people identify as neither male or female), queer sexualities, neurodiversity, and being a member of an ethnic minority. It will explore how marginalized communities are revered by the social justice warrior movement. It will also assess the phenomenon of privilege laundering. This is where people who are not from marginalized communities identify as oppressed to gain respect and authority. It will also look at how social justice warriors focus on people's identity above all else.

Chapter 4 will assess how identity politics has caused the left to reduce its focus on social class. This chapter will explain why identity politics is a predominantly middle-class movement. It will also explore how the most privileged people are most able to advocate for themselves. This chapter will consider the impact that this has on society's most disadvantaged people. It will assess how social justice warriors have distracted policy makers from issues that matter to the working-class.

Chapter 5 will explore the role of mental health in the social justice warrior movement. It will argue that mental health has become politicized. Furthermore, this chapter will assess how mental health is viewed as being interchangeable with being a member of a marginalized community. As well, it will explore the implications of the politicization of mental illness. In addition, this chapter will explore how the need to protect mental health is used to justify many of the social justice warriors' actions. This chapter will examine the implications of this for healthy political debate. It will also look at how this affects people's mental wellbeing.

Chapter 6 will analyse the role of speech, language and violence in the social justice warrior movement. Social justice warriors censor many everyday words for fear of offending oppressed people. This chapter will explain why this is not helpful in achieving greater equality. Furthermore, this chapter will examine how social justice warriors treat language as violence. It will examine how this is used as a rationale for censoring views and speakers who don't agree with social justice warrior values. This chapter will also look at the phenomenon of metaphorical violence. It will examine how this concept has led to cases of physical retaliation.

Chapter 7 will look at how the social justice warrior movement has embraced capitalism. It will examine the ways in which companies have embraced social justice warrior causes for their own profit. For instance, by including identity politics-related themes in their advertising. It will also examine how social justice has become an industry in itself. This chapter will also examine the role of capitalism in feminism, and the effect this has on women.

Chapter 8 examines how social justice warriors distort scientific and historical facts. It will explore how social justice warriors believe that objective facts have been created to oppress marginalized people. For example, social justice warriors claim that certain historical facts are used to justify the marginalization of women. This chapter also will explore how social justice warriors treat knowledge discovered by white, western men as automatically untrue. This chapter will also analyse the implications of this.

Chapter 9 will assess the overall impact of the social justice warrior movement. It will explain why the public finds the social justice warrior movement distasteful. It will look at how the social justice warrior movement has split the left. This chapter will also explore how the movement has caused the public to overlook genuine instances of discrimination. In addition, this chapter will examine the woke backlash, where the public have begun to fight wokeness at all costs. This chapter will also argue that the social justice warrior movement has failed the oppressed people it claims to represent.

2. How the Left Went Crazy

This chapter will look at some theoretical concepts that explain the way the that the social justice warrior movement think. It will examine some of the theories used by the movement and explore how these influence them. It will also explore the circumstances of how these theories came to be adopted by the social justice warrior movement.

The Theories that Made the Social Justice Warriors

There are a number of academic theories and concepts that have influenced the social justice warrior movement. Here are the key ones:

The New Left

The roots of the current obsession with identity politics can be traced back to the New Left. The New Left refers to the left's shift from focusing on economics to concentrating on various social issues. It started in the 1960s and has been revived at various times. The New Left embodies what is now more commonly known as identity politics.

The New Left began with Herbert Marcuse, a philosopher and social theorist. Marcuse was a member of the Frankfurt School. The Frankfurt School were a group of Marxist philosophers. The group formed at the Goethe University Frankfurt in the 1920s. However, they had to flee Germany and move to the USA to escape the Nazis (37). This group applied Marxist ideas to other social movements.

Marcuse wrote the famous essay, *Repressive Tolerance*, which set out many of the principles followed by the New Left (38). The essay claimed that tolerance towards different viewpoints serves only privileged groups. As a consequence, people have learned to accept bad opinions. Because of tolerance, the majority of people have learned to not question institutions such as the police and the armed forces. For that reason, people cannot evaluate different viewpoints. So, letting people hear multiple positions and choose what they believe doesn't work. Therefore, for the good of society, certain views should no longer be accepted. He says that society can objectively determine which ideas should be tolerated. Only ideas that advance society by reducing poverty and oppression should be heard. The right to free speech and freedom of assembly should be withdrawn from those with views that are contradictory to those aims. Examples of opinions that shouldn't be voiced include opposition to expanding provision of social security and public healthcare. In the essay, he also says that the education system should explicitly support progressive values. Furthermore, Marcuse condemns peaceful protest, saying that it is complicit with oppression.

To many people, what Marcuse says is very chilling. The idea that a person can determine which views should and shouldn't be heard is alarming. The problem is that one person's objective determination of what perspectives should be accepted is different from another's. For example, if a Christian feels that discussing homosexuality openly should not be allowed because it is sinful, are they right? Should a homosexual speaker be no platformed for that reason? There are people who would say yes to this. And there are many others who would disagree. That's the situation that letting everyone have the freedom of speech and assembly is trying to avoid. One day, your good view might be deemed bad.

Marcuse's influence on the present-day left is clear to see. It is why only people with certain views are allowed to speak at events at universities. It is what gave rise to the liberal professor, who sees their job as not to educate, but to instil certain principles into their students. And it is why violent protest is so prevalent today. It is also partly why social justice warriors are so self-assured about their views and so confident in suppressing voices they disagree with.

Another major influence on the New Left were the Argentinian theorists Ernesto Laclau and Chantal Mouffe. In their book *Hegemony and Socialist Strategy*, which was published in 1985, they argue that the failings of communist countries put the viability of socialism into doubt. They also claim that the range of movements on issues, such as gay rights and anti-nuclearization, showed a different way of achieving a more equal society aside from achieving class equality. They further contend that these social movements proved that the working-class were not a unified block with similar political interests. Rather, the working-class are a diverse group with different needs. Instead of focusing on economic equality, they propose that the left should emphasize equality between different social groups (39). Again, we can see how Laclau and Mouffe have influenced today's left-wingers to concentrate on identity over class.

Postmodernism

Another major influence on the identity politics left is postmodernism. Postmodernism is a philosophical perspective that developed in France during the latter half of the 20th century. The term was first used in the 1970s in the book *The Postmodern Condition* by Jean-François Lyotard (40,41). It originated from literary theory. It's difficult to explain what postmodernism is. The term is used in many different fields and it is not well-defined (42). One thing that postmodernism argues reality is socially constructed. That includes physical phenomenon that are indisputably real, such as biology and physics, shape and size, and numbers- they are all socially constructed (41). Furthermore, in postmodernism, enlightenment ideas, such as empiricism and free speech, are made to oppress minorities.

Admittedly, many people misunderstand what socially constructed means. Socially constructed means made by people. It can be easy to forget such things are made by people and they can appear natural. As well, things that are socially constructed have changed throughout history and are varied amongst societies. For example, money is a social construct. Not every society has money and money hasn't always existed. At different times in history, there have been other things that function as money (for example, trading livestock). This doesn't mean money isn't real. But it does mean that money isn't found in nature, in the way we would find a plant or an animal or a geographic feature. With some matters, it's disputed whether they are a social construct- this is the old 'nature vs nurture' debate. An example of this is gender roles. Some people think gender roles are innate- from birth, baby boys behave in a more masculine way than baby girls, and vice versa (43). Others think gender roles are learned- we teach boys to be masculine and girls to be feminine (44). There might never be a definitive answer to the question of where gender roles come from. But it does help illustrate what is meant when something is described as socially constructed.

Another common misconception is that postmodernism is a form of Marxism. Unlike postmodernists, Marxists are pro-rationality and pro-science (45). Most Marxists think that some things are socially constructed, but others are not. Furthermore, Marx was anti-censorship, (46). He was also anti-identity politics. He criticized "bourgeoisie socialism", which shares many elements with identity politics. He claimed it was intended to preserve capitalism (47). He was against prostitution (48) and held many other views that are antithetical to postmodernism and the New Left.

Postmodernists are also very dogmatic. Pluckrose and Lindsay argue that postmodern academics act as if their theories on the causes of inequality and bigotry are absolute, verifiable truths. It is as if they are comparable to scientific discoveries such as germ theory. These academics overlook that postmodernism is an unprovable theory (as almost all theories in the social sciences are) (49). This type of thinking informs the social justice warrior's activism. Social justice warriors see it as their duty to combat the issues that postmodernist theory has identified.

If postmodernism sounds crazy, that's because it is. Postmodernism has some interesting ideas and imaginative interpretations of the world. But what makes an interesting essay, book, paper or dissertation isn't necessarily what works well in real life. As the social critic Camille Paglia said: "French theory is like those how-to tapes that guaranteed to make you a real estate millionaire overnight. Gain power by attacking power! Call this number in Paris now!" (50). Like those motivational tapes, postmodernism doesn't work. It offers a simple-sounding solution, but it does not deliver. It is over-simplistic to say that all inequalities are caused by reality being socially constructed in a way that upholds them. Postmodernism is not the solution to social issues. Furthermore, Pluckrose makes the apt point that post modernism has become everything it professes to hate. In its attempts to destroy all-encompassing power structures, it has become one itself (41).

You'd expect academia to have rejected postmodernism by now. After all, academics are clever people. So why do they believe in postmodernism? There are several reasons. Firstly, postmodern texts are written in impenetrable prose that makes little sense. They often feature lengthy passages with confusing detours, complex sentences and obscure vocabulary. For example, Judith Butler, an American philosopher who specializes in gender and sexuality, wrote *Gender Trouble*. This book applies postmodern theory to gender and argues that biological sex is a social construct. Here is one example of a sentence from that book (51):

> *"If one 'is' a woman, that is surely not*
> *all one is; the term fails to be*
> *exhaustive, not because a pregendered*
> *'person' transcends the specific*
> *paraphernalia of its gender, but*
> *because gender is not always*
> *constituted coherently or consistently*
> *in different historical contexts, and*
> *because gender intersects with racial,*
> *class, ethnic, sexual, and regional*
> *modalities of discursively constituted*
> *identities."*

From this passage, we might be able to deduce that Butler is saying that the concept of being a woman varies in different cultures. At 60 words, this sentence is far too long. It's not very clear either. Furthermore, she uses obscure words. For instance, "pregendered" is not a word in the dictionary. Furthermore, Butler never says what a pregendered person is. It is up to the reader to assume what she means. The problem is the whole book is written like this. Between going off to look up obscure words and having to re-read lengthy passages, it gets too exhausting to read. It's not just Butler's books that are poorly written. Most postmodern books use a similar style of writing.

But here's the twist: even postmodern scholars themselves have little understanding of what they are writing about. In 1996, the physicist Alan Sokal submitted a paper to a high-profile academic journal that argued that gravity is a social construct. He deliberately misused scientific and mathematical language, so that the paper made no sense. It was accepted for publication in a high-profile academic journal (52). Sokal quickly revealed that the paper was a hoax. This proved that postmodern academics would publish something that fitted their views, even when it was actually nonsense.

Sokal expanded on this point in his later book, *Fashionable Nonsense* (53). This book argues that most of the texts written by postmodern philosophers were actually meaningless. The book shows how authors use mathematical and scientific terms incorrectly. It demonstrates that to a reader familiar with mathematics and science, the passages actually make no sense. For instance, several postmodern theorists include algebraic-style formulas in their work. But Sokal and Bricmont explain what the mathematical symbols in the formulas mean. They prove that these formulas did not make any points. They propose that this misuse of scientific terminology is done to impress and intimidate readers, who are unlikely to be familiar with such terminology. It also hides that there is no substance behind their points. They note that postmodern theorists say that they are using these terms metaphorically. But Sokal and Bricmont point out that most metaphors are linked to familiar examples that the reader can relate to.

Conversely, postmodern writers use scientific and mathematical metaphors that the reader is unlikely to be familiar with.

After the Sokal hoax, you might expect that academics had learned their lesson regarding postmodernism. But they haven't. In 2017, an article named 'The Conceptual Penis' was published in *Cogent Social Science* journal. The paper argues that the penis is a social construct, and that this construct is driving climate change. Like Sokal's paper, it was intentionally poorly written so that it made no meaningful points. In spite of this, it was published in a peer-reviewed journal. This suggests the peer reviewers had not examined the paper closely. It appears they published it because they agreed with its ideological position (54). But it didn't stop there. The same team published several other papers in other peer-reviewed journals. These articles also used postmodern philosophy and were deliberately nonsensical. These include a paper comprising of passages from Adolf Hitler's autobiography *Mein Kampf*, interspersed with social justice jargon and citations from various postmodern sources (55).

The fear of challenging postmodernism has carried to all levels of the academy. In many universities, postmodernism is great. If you don't get it, you must be either too stupid to understand it, or too lazy to read it properly. That's why it has so many believers- nobody will admit that it makes no sense to them. There is an emperor's new clothes effect. Everyone seemingly thinks postmodernism is wonderful. Nobody else admits that they struggle to understand it. And nobody realizes that it makes no sense. So, it goes unquestioned.

In the past, postmodernism was confined to the humanities and social science departments of universities. But now, it's come out into the wider world, and it's influencing how we think about social and political issues. For instance, Judith Butler's work on gender performativity and queering has been an enormous influence on the current transgender movement.

Privilege Theory

Another key aspect of the current identity politics movement is privilege theory. Privilege theory posits that people from certain backgrounds have unwarranted advantages over others. The term originally related to white privilege. But the concept is now applied to many other oppressed groups, including gender, disability and sexuality. It has also been applied to groups that haven't traditionally been considered oppressed, such as thin privilege (privilege over fat people). In left-wing circles, the phrase 'check your privilege' is commonly used. It means you should be aware of your social position when you do or say something. The idea is that being aware of your privilege makes you more understanding of oppression.

The term originates from Peggy McIntosh's essay, *White Privilege: Unpacking the Invisible Knapsack* (56). In this essay, McIntosh lists ways in which she is privileged as a white person. The major failing with this essay is that it conflates economic privilege with racial privilege. For example, point three is "If I should need to move, I can be pretty sure of renting or purchasing housing in an area which I can afford and in which I would want to live." Few people of any ethnicity can say this. She can afford a house because of her economic privilege, not her race. Furthermore, point 37 is "I can be pretty sure of finding people who would be willing to talk with me and advise me about my next steps, professionally". Again, this relies on her socio-economic privilege. She has connections with people who can give advice on her career because of her wealth, rather than the colour of her skin. Many white people are affected by these problems too. When reading this list, bear in mind that McIntosh herself is a very privileged woman. She was born to a rich family. Her father held a high position at Bell Laboratories when they were working on early developments in computing. He held many patents on technologies that are still in use today. She attended elite universities and earns a six figure salary (57). Her experiences are not representative of the average white woman. Also, many things McIntosh mentions are trivial. For example, that certain rude behaviours don't reflect badly on her race. Are these really the worst things non-white people face?

Another major problem was is that privilege theory describes the symptoms rather than the cause of class inequalities. For example, being well-educated happens because of class privilege. It is not a privilege in itself (58). By focusing on the end result of privilege, rather than the cause, privilege theory fails to understand the origins of inequality. Therefore, privilege theory cannot tackle the underlying inequalities that create the privileges.

Furthermore, we cannot neatly divide people into oppressors and the oppressed. As we all have multiple identities, a person can be oppressed in some senses and not in others (59). This makes it difficult for all minorities to work together. For instance, a devout Muslim Asian woman may have few shared political interests with a black gay man. Even though they are both from oppressed groups. Perhaps the woman is homophobic, or the man is misogynistic. They might have different views. For that reason, these two people might not be interested in working together. Think of this happening repeatedly with all different identity groups. They all have different views and needs. This makes it difficult for these groups to form political coalitions.

As well, privilege theory ignores class inequalities. The social justice warrior movement talk as if all white people are all swimming in cash and never have a single worry in the world. white people do have advantages over other ethnicities. But white people still face class-based oppression. Which can be worse than any other form of oppression. Is a well-educated, affluent black man more oppressed than an impoverished white man? In this case, the white man is more oppressed. He might not suffer racial discrimination or 'micro-aggressions', but he will suffer from poor material conditions. He might have a bad house (or no house), limited food, and fewer life opportunities. He might also lack money for other essentials and have difficulty accessing healthcare. And you can see why this white man is angry. His poor material conditions are ignored, while people focus on identity.

Furthermore, freedom from oppression is not a privilege (60). To be privileged is to have something above others. For example, Donald Trump is a privileged person. He has much more money and material goods than most people. He has enjoyed a private education funded by his parents, as well as business connections and money from his father. If we said: 'everyone should live like Donald Trump', most people would regard that as ludicrous. He lives a lavish life of excessive consumption. It is not sustainable for everyone to live as Trump does. Privilege is something luxury afforded to the select few. It is something that nobody actually needs. On the other hand, to not be oppressed or discriminated against is a right that should be afforded to everyone. By saying that not experiencing discrimination is an unearned privilege, it implies that some people deserve to be discriminated against. It gives the impression that you must earn the right to be treated equally to others.

Privilege theory is also about using someone's non-minority status to exclude them from progressive causes. Nowadays, an idea or belief can be dismissed because of who is saying it. If an opinion is being expressed by someone who is from a privileged group, it can be discounted for that reason. For instance, being gender critical (a branch of feminism which focuses on sex-based rights and protections) is often derisively called 'white feminism'. Even though this branch of feminism has nothing to do with ethnicity and it has followers from many different ethnic groups. By describing gender critical feminism as white feminism, it's saying 'well, they're white, so they're wrong'. Instead of putting forward a case for gender critical feminists being wrong, a woman described as a white feminist is automatically wrong because of the colour of her skin.

Intersectionality

Another key idea that has taken hold within left-wing circles is intersectionality. Intersectionality looks at the overlap between different marginalized identities. Kimberlé Crenshaw, a legal scholar coined the term, after examining legal cases of black women being discriminated against at work. In these cases, the claimants alleged that they had been discriminated against because they were black women. One case Crenshaw analysed was the case of DeGraffenreid vs General Motors. In this case, the claimant showed that the company had not employed any black women for many years. In addition, they had laid off all the black women in senior management positions. However, because they still employed black men, the court ruled that General Motors had not racially discriminated against the claimant. And because the company employed women, it was not regarded a sex discrimination issue either. As a result, these cases fell neither into racial nor sexist discrimination legislation (61). In other words, there is a form of oppression that is unique to black women and that can't be understood by looking solely from the prism of racism or sexism.

Other concepts within intersectionality derive from earlier work on black feminism. Black feminism is a branch of feminism that focuses on black women. For example, the book *Ain't I a Woman* by bell hooks (she does not use capital letters in her name) argues that women are overlooked by the racial equality movements. She claims that race activists tend to focus on matters relating to black men. For example, she describes how the history of slavery concentrates on male slaves. It does not mention the trials experienced by female slaves, such as childbirth while being transported (she states that pregnant women were often captured, presumably so that the baby could be enslaved). Meanwhile, the issue of race is ignored by feminists, who focus on issues that affect white women. She describes racism within the feminist movement. For instance, where black women were not allowed to speak at feminist events. As a result, black women are not represented by either of these movements (62). Looking at oppression and discrimination in this way isn't necessarily a bad thing. It is true that some people are overlooked by these movements. And Crenshaw's work does highlight a gap in the law. Indeed, we aren't all one identity. The law should recognise that.

But intersectionality has gotten out of control. Even Crenshaw herself says that intersectionality has had its original meaning twisted. In an interview in Time magazine, Crenshaw said of intersectionality "It's not identity politics on steroids. It is not a mechanism to turn white men into the new pariahs" (63). Intersectionality is no longer about recognising the compound effect of being part of multiple oppressed groups. It is now about the idea that all people from marginalized groups belong to one homogenous block with shared political views and interests.

Intersectionality is also used to exclude certain campaigners. There's a common saying amongst social justice warriors: 'if you're feminism (or whatever else you're campaigning for) doesn't include transgender/disabled/people of colour, it's not feminism'. And being accused of not being intersectional enough is a serious charge in the social justice warrior movement. It's also a good way to bring other social justice warriors down. If a certain activist is getting more attention than you, simply tell everyone that person's activism isn't intersectional. And now they're 'problematic' and banished from the movement. But realistically, there's only so much a person can campaign for. Proper campaigning (not just posting on Twitter or signing the odd e-petition) is hard work. It takes up a lot of time. It's difficult to have a campaign that includes everyone and that is also successful. Indeed, the narrower a campaign's aims, the more likely it is to succeed. Also, being an activist is optional. It's disheartening to be told that your campaign is wrong by people who you'd hope would be sympathetic to the cause. Apart from discouraging people, it's hard to see what condemning activists for not being perfect is achieving.

The reality is that all these identities don't always go well together. It's not a case that everyone who is a minority will automatically sympathize and agree with one another. Indeed, different minority groups may have competing interests. For example, many disabled people are against aborting disabled foetuses. Their view is that a disabled foetus should be treated equally to a non-disabled foetus (64). But most feminists are pro-abortion. If you are a disabled feminist, what should you think? That aborting a foetus with a disability is abhorrent, or that women have the right to abortion? Disabled activists would say that it's wrong to abort the foetus because it's a presumption that disability is bad. Some even go as far as to equate it to genocide. Women say they have the right to choose what happens to their body, and that the baby is part of that body until it is born. Also, it's the woman who must care for the baby. In the case of a disabled baby, this will involve extra work. The responsibility could be lifelong. So, it's not the case that all oppressed people have the same political views and interests.

Furthermore, even people in the same minority group don't necessarily have unified interests. For instance, non-white people are lumped together under the label of 'people of colour'. But different ethnic minority groups can have very different political interests and views. An example that illustrates this is from California, who hold referenda on a regular basis on many policies. In these referenda, black people tend to vote in favour of anti-immigration policies. For example, they voted in favour of making English the state's official language and preventing illegal immigrants from receiving public benefits. This is similar to the voting patterns for white people. On the other hand, Hispanics were more supportive of immigrants, and voted against these propositions (65). This shows that ethnic minorities aren't always unified by their minority status.

Therefore, intersectionality is not a bad idea. But the way the concept has been applied by the social justice warrior movement has been reductive and divisive. It takes the position that the world can be divided into oppressed people and the oppressor.

The Birth of the Social Justice Warrior

At this point, you might have noticed that the theories discussed in this chapter began before most social justice warriors were born. So why have they come into political discourse now? The answer is that socio-economic circumstances have made Generation Me more receptive to these theories. Firstly, expanding higher education has meant more people are exposed to these theories. Liberals who learned about these theories at university are applying them to social issues. Now, illogical ideas about oppression have moved from academia to mainstream political discourse.

Secondly, all these theories play into the social justice warrior's fixation with themselves. You'll remember from the introduction that Generation Me were raised to be narcissistic, individualistic and fragile. And many of those characteristics are reflected by the social justice warrior movement's priorities. The focus on identity and themselves plays into their self-obsession. The social justice warriors focus on the things that matter to them as middle-class students and professionals. The New Left, along with postmodernism, privilege theory and intersectionality, allow them to do this. As identity is the only type of oppression, they have personal experience with, this is all they concentrate on. Furthermore, their naval gazing enables them to forge new oppressed identities. The way they were parented means they have stuck at the misunderstood teenager phase well into adulthood. But they look at their perceived misunderstoodness through the prism of oppression. We'll learn more about those new identities in the next chapter.

Luxury Belief Theory

So far, we've looked at theories that inform the social justice warrior's beliefs. And we've looked at the circumstances which primed social justice warriors to think as they do. But what we haven't looked at is why they adopt these particular views. Why are the woke so... woke? They believe things that to the average person, don't seem workable in real life. It feels like a competition for who can come up with the most farfetched ideas for how society should work. The reason for this can be explained by looking at luxury belief theory. Luxury belief theory postulates that certain political beliefs have become middle class status symbols. But these beliefs don't actually affect the people who espouse them very much. For instance, middle-class people are more likely to say that having children out of wedlock is fine. But they are less likely to have children out of wedlock themselves. Likewise, they are more critical of organized religion. However, they do not depend on religious institutions as much as the working-class do (66). This is why the cultural left is so out of touch with the people they say they represent. Their views are just for show. And it's much easier to support something that doesn't affect you personally.

The current movement to defund or abolish the police is a prime example of a luxury belief. The death of George Floyd was outrageous. As was the shooting of Jacob Blake, leaving him paralyzed. These were two of many unjustified shootings of black people by the police. These tragedies have led to calls to abolish or defund the police on the grounds that the police force is inherently racist. However, those who support this movement are least likely to require help from the police. A YouGov poll found that people with an annual income over $50,000 per year were more likely to support defunding the police than those with lower incomes (67). But rich people are much less likely to be a victim of a crime than poor people. For instance, 40% of victims of violent crime in the USA in 2018 had an income of less than $25,000 per year. In contrast, 16% of violent crime victims had an income over $200,000 (68). Therefore, the wealthy are less likely to have ever had any interactions with police, so the police feel irrelevant to their lives. They don't rely as much on the police to protect them as poorer people do. Also, if there were no police, affluent people could afford other means of protecting themselves from crime. For example, they could hire private security guards or live in gated communities. Thus, abolishing or defunding the police won't affect the middle-class as much as it would affect less affluent people. Which is why poorer people are less likely to support abolishing the police.

This chapter has explored how the social justice warrior reasons and why they think the way they do. It has done this by looking at the theories that have influenced them. In some ways, it is positive that people are more aware of political issues than they were in the past. But is this awareness truly benefiting society's most disadvantaged? Or are these woke people only concerned for themselves?

From this chapter, we can see how all these theories and social circumstances have melded together to form a toxic combination. Bad ideas have twisted together to form something terrible. And a generation of young people raised to be fragile and self-centred has made it worse. The subsequent chapters of this book will examine the influence of the social justice warriors on the left and on politics as a whole.

3. Identity and the Social Justice Warrior

Identity is an enormous aspect of the social justice warrior movement. The left now focuses on equality for various identity groups rather than economic equality. For instance, the left is more concerned about issues such as allowing transgender people to change their birth certificate. Or police brutality toward black people. Rather than concentrating on more wide-reaching issues, such as economic inequalities or lack of access to healthcare. This chapter will examine the role of identity in the social justice warrior movement. It will explore how identity has become so important in the left. This chapter will assess how marginalized groups are deified within the social justice warrior movement. It will also assess how this worship of minorities has led to many people forging an oppressed identity to gain credence within the left.

Privileged People are Bad, Marginalized People are Good

Marginalized voices are what the left is all about right now. As the philosopher Coleman Hughes says, there's a perception that minorities are more moral people than the rest of us (7,69). As such, nearly everyone in the social justice warrior movement has multiple oppressed identities. These include being queer, a person of colour, transgender and disabled. Such people are placed on a pedestal in the social justice warrior movement (6).

On social media, people will list their marginalized identities in their biographies. A common example would be:

@username

Nonbinary pansexual Autistic Fibro (they/them)

Their entire identity is a list of ways in which they are marginalized. Not explaining who they are in other ways-for instance, what job they do, what hobbies they enjoy, where they live or any other aspect of their identity. The way they are marginalized is all that matters.

Meanwhile, people who aren't from marginalized communities are considered pariahs. This is regardless of how sympathetic they are to marginalized communities. The terms 'white man' or 'cis-het' (cis is short for cisgender, meaning not transgender, and het is short for heterosexual) are virtually insults. Here's an example of a tweet showing the negative attitude toward cishets: "if u r cishet that is so embarrassing stay away from me [sic]" (70). This isn't an isolated example. Search 'cishet' on Twitter and you'll see thousands of tweets like this. Does this mean it's bad to be a 'cishet'? Ordinarily, most people would say that being a 'cishet' is neither a good thing nor a bad thing. Not being transgender and heterosexual are equal to being homosexual or transgender. Neither is better than another. But now, it's not acceptable to merely support marginalized people. You must be a marginalized person and despise everyone who isn't part of a minority group.

Grievance Studies

Another representation of the value of identity in the left is the growth of 'grievance studies' disciplines in universities. These are also referred to as 'victim studies' or 'identity studies'. Grievance studies subjects focus on studying a particular marginalized social group. Examples include black studies and gender studies. The problem is that these 'grievance studies' disciplines are not about critical examination of a topic, as most academic disciplines are. Rather, they are about promoting a certain narrow viewpoint. Most academic disciplines encompass a broad range of subjects and teach multiple ideological views, different theoretical perspectives, research methods, and approaches. But grievance studies disciplines do not do this. A student studying gender studies will look at everything through the framework of feminism. Everyone else on the course will also see things from a feminist point of view. Nobody can give an opposing viewpoint that makes the other students question their beliefs. Nor are they allowed to say how their experience is different from what the lecturer or the set texts are saying. There is no analysis of certain views and perspectives. Author and critic Bruce Bawer argues that these disciplines turn graduates into the Thought Police. They are busy ensuring everyone only believes the 'right' things, unaware that they are emulating Stalinism or other oppressive regimes. They know little apart from the areas of oppression they have studied. And so, they don't have the ability to question what they have learned. Nor do they understand the danger of their totalitarianism (71).

As with the broader identity politics movement, class is also overlooked by grievance studies. A person who is white, male, cisgender, heterosexual and non-disabled is unimportant; they are the epitome of privilege. Even if that person lives in serious poverty. As the sociologist Zygmunt Bauman argues, the introduction of these academic disciplines represents the left's move away from economics to cultural issues (72).

Self-Identity

The focus on the self in the social justice warrior movement manifests in many ways, but one key way is through identity. For many social justice warriors, the emphasis on having a unique identity began from the child's birth. Twenge found that there was a steep decline in children being named one of the top 10 names for their year of birth. This implies that parents want their children to be more distinct from others (9). Furthermore, she describes how Generation Me was taught that the key to confidence was 'being yourself'. In the social justice warrior movement, this focus on identity now manifests in the idea of 'living authentically'. Living authentically takes 'being yourself' a step further. It is the idea that you need to discover a kind of true self that is hidden within yourself. And discovering that self will bring fulfilment and satisfaction. For many social justice warriors, this has manifested by identifying as a minority.

Furthermore, in the social justice warrior movement, you need to be a minority to have any credence. If you are not a member of a marginalized group, you are privileged. And so, you are expected to give way to less privileged people. Understandably, people not happy about losing their power in the left. So, the solution is to self-identify as minority; known as privilege laundering. It can be used to identify out of being an oppressor. Which is a handy manoeuvre for these people, who are often some of the most privileged people in society. This is how intersectionality really works- privileged people at the top of the social tree find a way to identify out of their privilege. In effect, they have their cake and eat it. They have the advantages of privilege (well-educated, wealthy, no discrimination). This often makes it easier to get a platform and share their views. But in left-wing spaces, they can be oppressed when this counts. Most actually oppressed people don't have that option. There are many ways in which someone can identify as a minority. Here are some examples:

Gender

In my previous book, *2+2=5*, I wrote about how many people -most of which are members of Generation Me- now identify as neither male nor female, known as gender nonbinary. Nonbinary is also sometimes referred to as NB or enby. This is not the same as intersex, where a person is born with physical features of both sexes or they are born wish missing sex organs. It is people who are clearly a certain biological gender who say they do not feel male or female. Examples of nonbinary genders include:

- Bigender: someone who feels both female and male
- Agender: someone who feels they don't have a gender
- Demiboy or demigirl: someone who feels they are mostly male or female, but not fully male or female).

These are just a few examples. There are hundreds of nonbinary genders. To reflect their nonbinary status, many change their name or androgynously. Others using alternative gender pronouns such as 'they' or 'ze' instead of 'he' or 'she'. I argue that many people identify as nonbinary to try to erase their privilege, especially men (73).

However, it's not just gender where social justice warriors identify their way out of privilege. Generation Me do this with other aspects of their identity too.

Sexuality

Many members of Generation Me also identify as 'queer'. In one survey of young people in the UK and the USA, 57 percent of people aged 13 to 26 didn't identify as heterosexual (74). However, queer no longer means gay. Instead it is a vague catch-all that includes anyone who sees themselves as not strictly heterosexual. Although it is unclear what this actually means anymore. So many 'queer' people seem to be in typical, heterosexual relationships. So, what makes someone queer? According to The Trevor Project, an LGBT mental health charity, "anyone who feels queer is queer" (75). What does it mean to feel 'queer' if it doesn't mean attracted to members of the same sex? The definition of sexual orientation has been broadened so that it no longer covers the sex of the person typically attracted to. It now includes other attributes such as the speed in which someone feels attracted to someone, or the number of partners a person is attracted to. A number of new sexual orientations have been invented to describe these aspects of sexuality. These include:

- Sapiosexual: attraction to intelligence
- Polysexual: attracted to multiple people at the same time
- Pansexual: attracted to all genders (not just male and female, but also 'nonbinary' people).
- Demisexual: only attracted to people they have close connection with (arguably, this is normal) (76).

There are many more of these new sexualities. So many that it would take up the whole book to list them all. And new ones are being invented every day. These sexualities are vague and encompass traits that many people find attractive in a partner. For instance, intelligence is widely considered to be an attractive trait. A person could easily be heterosexual and also attracted to intelligence or the close connection with a person. As well, many people are attracted to multiple people at the same time. Its why people have affairs or cheat in relationships. These new sexualities are therefore not valid sexual orientations.

These new sexualities and genders are included in the ever-increasing umbrella of the LGBT movement. The LGBT acronym is ever-expanding. It now includes Q (for questioning or for queer). Or I (for intersex). And sometimes A (for asexual, meaning someone who has little interest in having a sexual relationship). Sometimes called LGBTQIA, LGBT+ (for all the other identities). The problem is, it's getting to a point where nobody is plain old straight anymore.

Indeed, you can be someone who has never been in a non-heterosexual relationship and still be 'queer'. Comedian and social justice warrior identity tick-sheet Sofie Hagen identifies as pansexual. Hagen is also biologically female but identifies as nonbinary and uses they/them pronouns. Even though they have never had a romantic relationship with a woman, they insist they are queer. Writing about doubts over their sexuality in the *Metro*, Hagen wrote "Of course, you are queer. You don't have to prove your queerness to anyone. You don't have to sleep with anyone to be queer!" (77). Based on what Hagen says, queer looks very much like being straight. Hagen doesn't have to prove their sexuality. But then again, what makes Hagen think she is queer?

So, what is the LGBT+ movement for anymore? In the past, would have been obvious that were campaigning for the needs of people who were sexually attracted to others of the same sex. These included appropriate sexual healthcare, same-sex marriage and protection from discrimination. But now the queer label that represents people with little in common that they no longer have a unified cause. So, it's harder to fight for 'queer' people's rights. For instance, what does a sapiosexual person need to be accommodated in society? Are they ever under pressure to date unintelligent people? Do they have people trying to turn them, so they are attracted to unintelligent people? Does only having sex with intelligent people carry additional risks that aren't found from having sex with unintelligent people? Do they ever get discriminated against because of their attraction to intelligent people? If everyone is queer, then nobody is queer: the thing that differentiates straight people from LGB people is lost. Consequently, the group becomes so diverse they have nothing in common anymore.

Sexuality is influenced by social justice warriors in other ways too. Social justice warriors make many demands on a person's sexuality. Firstly, a person must be unconcerned with the biological sex of their romantic interests. Instead, they must focus only on their potential mate's gender identity. This includes being willing to have sex with transgender people. For instance, a heterosexual man should be willing to have sex with a person who is biologically male but identifies as female. Even if they still have a penis.

Riley Dennis, a trans-identified male and transgender rights activist, made a video for *Everyday Feminism* on this matter. She argues that genital preferences are transphobic because the transgender person is being perceived as their biological sex rather than their gender identity (78). In other words, people must somehow find a way to overlook that they are not interested in having sex with someone with a penis or a vulva. Instead, they must find the way they identify as male or female as attractive. A related concept is the cotton ceiling. This is when a trans-identified male (a person who is biologically male but identifies as a woman) is perceived by a woman in all domains of life except in romantic relationships (79). This shows how identity trumps the biological reality of the romantic partner's sex. You must somehow modify your sexual tastes. This undermines the argument that gay people have made for many years that being gay isn't a choice. If you can become attracted to a different type of genitalia at will, why can't you become heterosexual?

Furthermore, followers of the social justice warrior movement must also overlook physically unattractive elements of person, such as obesity. Sonalee Rashatwar, who describes herself as a fat sex therapist, has devoted her career to encouraging people to have sex with obese people. She attributes the reluctance to have sex with obese people to fatphobia (80). Instead of being attracted to a person's physical features, you must be attracted to some kind of nebulous characteristic. In addition, kink-shaming, where someone's sexual fetish is criticized or mocked- it not acceptable (81). The social justice warrior movement demands inclusion, to such an extreme extent, that even sex is not off limits from their authoritarianism. The way that social justice warriors control the most intimate aspects of a person's life shows how much they seek to control society. It's not enough to tolerate somebody. You must find a way to see their identity as reality. You must make your sexual preferences fit with the goals of the social justice warrior movement.

Neurodiversity

Another popular form of privilege laundering is to identify as being neurodivergent. Neurodiversity refers to people with neuro-psychiatric disorders. The term encompasses neurodevelopmental disorders such as Autism, ADHD, Dyslexia, Dyspraxia, Tourette's Syndrome and other related conditions (82). These disorders frequently occur together and have some symptoms in common, which is why they are grouped together. That's not to say they're all the same. A person with mild Dyslexia would have very different challenges to someone with severe Autism. Nonetheless, these conditions are legitimate disabilities. But many people are now self-diagnosing these disorders and describing themselves as neurodivergent (83).

Now, given these conditions are typically identified in childhood, it might be surprising that adults self-diagnose with these disorders. But some people claim that they are able to conceal their symptoms so well that a doctor cannot identify them (84). And so, the disorder goes undetected throughout childhood. People do go undiagnosed or are misdiagnosed due to various reasons. For instance, they grew up in a time before such disorders were widely known about. Or their family couldn't afford to pay for a professional evaluation. Or the difficulties were attributed to some other cause, such as being a 'slow learner'. For that reason, there are clinics who evaluate adults for developmental disorders. However, it's a stretch to say a child can totally conceal a developmental disorder until they reach adulthood.

But in many cases, these people are refusing to undergo professional assessment. In some instances, they have been professionally assessed and found not to have any disorder. For example, teacher and neurodiversity activist Rakshita Shekhar visited nine different psychiatrists to be tested for Autism. All the doctors said she was not Autistic. She then diagnosed herself and condemned the doctors for failing to identify her condition (85). To most people, having been told by nine doctors that you are not Autistic would be a very strong confirmation that you are not Autistic. Indeed, most people would feel uncomfortable about saying they have Autism when many doctors have told them they don't have it. But not the social justice warriors. Their view is that only you know yourself, and if you think you are neurodiverse, you don't need a doctor to validate this. Lydia X.Y. Brown, an academic and neurodiversity activist who has self-diagnosed with Autism, supports this view (49,86). This is a common sentiment amongst neurodiversity activists. The phrases 'self-diagnosis is valid' and 'if you think you are Autistic, you are Autistic' appear frequently in social justice warrior spaces. Many -including Rakshita Shekhar- even describe having a formal diagnosis as a privilege (87). Pluckrose and Lindsay link this trend of self-diagnosis and rejection of medical input to postmodernism (49).

Furthermore, some people deliberately perform Autistic traits to signal that they are disabled. Brown describes how she makes a point of flapping her hands in public to signal that she has Autism. Hand-flapping is a trait found in some people with Autism, but Brown says she never developed this symptom (49,86). Deliberately performing Autistic behaviours is supposed to be helpful for a person's mental health. Again, it relates to the idea of being your 'most authentic self'. But if you are forcing yourself to do something to show you have Autism, it's not a symptom of Autism. You are putting on an act. As Pluckrose and Lindsay point out, Brown's performance is unhelpful to anyone. Her deliberately acting strangely will not benefit anyone with Autism.

The problem with self-diagnosis for an individual is that in the real world, self-diagnosis is meaningless. You are not protected from discrimination in the eyes of the law. You can't claim social security benefits. You can't get adjustments made in education or at work. You can't get other state services such as social care. And you can't get medications. The only thing you can do with a self-diagnosis is tell your friends and family. Self-diagnosis is only valid in contexts where it doesn't actually matter. For these social justice warriors, this type of disability is something they can do when they please. Like a game. Real Autism and other neurodevelopmental disorders are difficult and stressful. There are no days off. You can't stop being Autistic when the situation calls for it. It's not all about playing with toys and posting videos of yourself behaving in a stereotypically neurodivergent manner. But that's all that it is to social justice warriors.

The problem for everyone else is that self-diagnosis trivializes these conditions. Neurodevelopmental disorders can be very disabling. Even people with high-functioning or mild cases often require additional support throughout their lives. But self-diagnosed people rarely have any significant difficulties. Yet these self-diagnosed people are often very active in neurodiversity communities. Which drowns out the voices of those who face more significant difficulties. Online, neurodiversity is portrayed as cutesy. People post pictures of weighted blankets and stim toys (stim, meaning stimulation, are items which are designed to stimulate the senses. They usually involve a repetitive action, such as fidget spinners and reversable sequins. Many people find them soothing). Many also have 'stimmy hair'- hair usually dyed an unnatural colour and styled in an unconventional fashion. They never speak of the kind of problems that actual people with these disabilities experience. They don't talk of struggling to understand why nobody wants to be your friend. Or saying something you think is innocuous, but then finding that people are upset with you. Or breaking down in tears because the supermarket has run out of your favourite cereal. Yet these are the type of things that people with neurodevelopmental disorders battle against.

This also distorts the public perception of these disorders. There's a great deal of scepticism about the existence of neurodevelopmental disorders. There's a sizeable minority of people who don't think these disorders exist or that they are over diagnosed. Self-diagnosed people don't help this. Self-diagnosed people can give the impression that these disorders are medicalizing aspects of the human condition. Everyone is forgetful sometimes, or makes spelling mistakes, or says the wrong thing in a social situation. These are the type of difficulties that self-diagnosed people will often describe. But people who actually have these disorders have these issues to a more extreme extent. The view that these disorders aren't disabling or can even be a gift weakens the case for public support. Why would a person with ADHD need to claim social security on the grounds of disability if another person says that ADHD is a gift that made them highly successful? Isn't it simply a case that a person who is struggling simply isn't trying hard enough? That's the implicit message. This feeds into public scepticism about these conditions.

Ethnicity

Identifying as an ethnic minority is also a common type of privilege laundering in social justice warrior circles. It's less popular than other forms of privilege laundering, but it still occurs. The idea of claiming that you are an ethnic minority when you're not, might seem a bit odd. After all, you can't change the colour of your skin. But what you can do is an ethnicity DNA test, such as those offered by consumer DNA testing companies 23andMe or Ancestry.com. These tests show the geographic origins of a person's DNA. They almost always show that a person has DNA originating from a diverse range of places. As a consequence, white people have started describing themselves as people of colour after finding a small amount of non-white ancestry in their DNA (88). Senator

Elizabeth Warren did this when she claimed to be Native American. Warren does have some very distant Native American ancestry in her bloodline. She is somewhere between 1/64 to 1/1028 Native American (89). Aside from this, she is almost completely of European descent (90).

This begs the question: if Warren has some Native American DNA, isn't she entitled to identify as Native American? Many of her supporters have said this. But actually, Warren's situation isn't uncommon. 23andMe report that European-Americans have an average of 98.6% European ancestry (91). That means most white people have around 1.4% of their DNA from outside of Europe. Does that make them people of colour? It seems disingenuous for a person with 98.6% European DNA to describe themselves as an ethnic minority based on a small percentage of non-white DNA. It harks back to the US's 'One Drop' rule, where someone with any non-white ancestry was classed as coloured. Except unlike with the 'One Drop' rule, which was used to discriminate, these people are doing it for their advantage. Warren's spent many years trumpeting that she was the only ethnic minority in her department when she was a law professor at Harvard University. Her bar registration card also identified her ethnicity as American Indian (92). Warren acted unethically by claiming to be Native American. She cannot represent the needs of the Native American community. Nor has she faced discrimination or prejudice on account of her ethnicity. She has also given the wrongful impression that the Harvard law department was more diverse than it actually was.

A small number of white people have taken identifying as an ethnic minority even further. They identify as transracial- where someone lives as a different race than they were born as. This may include using cosmetics to appear closer to their identified ethnicity. Fortunately, the social justice warrior movement haven't accepted transracialism. Although that doesn't stop some social justice warriors from trying. A prominent example of this was Rachel Dolezal. In 2015, Dolezal was working as a black studies professor. She regularly referred to herself as black. She was also involved in a number of race-related campaign groups. But in a television interview, her parents revealed she was white, and showed pictures of her when she was younger, with pale skin and straight, blonde hair. She used fake tan and died and curled her hair, so she appeared to be mixed race. Once her true ethnicity was revealed, she faced condemnation and lost her job as a result of the outcry (93). There have been other instances of this, including Jessica Krug and CV Vitolo-Haddad, who were also academics who pretended to be black. Their cases sparked similar outrage (94). It's right that these people were condemned. But this highlights a contradiction with social justice warrior ideology. Why can you identify as you please, except with race? If Rachel Dolezal had been born a man who lived as a woman, she would be praised for her bravery. Nobody would be allowed to say she was really a man. But being a white woman who lives as a black woman is unacceptable. It shows that on some level, social justice warriors are aware that you can't identify out of biological realities.

Woke Segregation

Another way that social justice warriors put marginalized people on a pedestal is through flagging up minorities. Or to develop special spaces reserved for minorities. If this sounds like segregation in the USA, apartheid in South Africa, or the way Hitler treated Jews, socialists and gay men during the Holocaust, you're not alone.

Google has started tagging black-owned businesses in its search results (95). Although the intent is to help promote black-owned businesses, marking out these businesses is reminiscent of Coincidence Detector, a Google Chrome extension (a small piece of software that could be added to the web browser). Coincidence Detector would place a triple parenthesis around Jewish names in web pages. For instance, the surname Cohen would appear as ((((Cohen))). Google banned this extension because it was racist (96). It's hard to see why Google marking out black-owned businesses isn't racist but marking out Jewish names is. In both cases, it could increase the risk that the person or company being identified could be targeted for racial discrimination.

Another example of this woke segregation is the face mask exemption for 'people of colour' in Lincoln County in Oregon. This was done because many black and Latino people were concerned they would be perceived as criminals if they covered their faces (97). Given that non-white people are more likely to die of COVID-19 (98), allowing non-white people not to wear masks heightens their risk of catching the virus and dying. Which was the very thing the masks were supposed to prevent.

A further instance of this is opening special dormitories and halls of residence at universities for certain minority groups. In 2016, the University of Connecticut opened SCHOLARS house in 2016. SCHOLARS House is described as a "living and learning community" exclusively for black male students. The aim of this is to reduce the number of black males dropping out of university (99). And in 2018, Washington University in St. Louis turned a former fraternity house into a black-only residence and 'safe space' (100). Part of the issue with black-only dormitories is that they don't fix the underlying reason for the students dropping out. Writing in *The Intercept*, Briahna Gray points out that the biggest obstacle to graduation for black students is money. Black students tend to be from less affluent backgrounds than white students. Hence, they are often forced to drop out because they cannot afford to complete their degree (101). It's not just race that universities are having separate living quarters for. In the UK, the University of Sheffield opened LGBT-only halls in 2018 (102). In all these cases, special dormitories increase the risk that students will be identified and discriminated against. Also, it takes away the opportunity for students to bond with those from different backgrounds. For many, this is a key part of the university experience.

Sometimes it's necessary to highlight that someone is different. An example of this is the blind people's symbol cane. This is a short version of the white cane. Unlike a normal white cane, it is not used for navigation. Instead, it is intended to alert others that a person is blind. In this case, people need to know so that they can take care to avoid bumping into them, be more patient with them, and help with tasks that require vision. But most of the time, we don't need to concentrate on how people are different from us. And that's precisely what these initiatives are doing. In the Holocaust, Hitler made Jews wear Star of David badges on their clothes. The Nazis did this to mark out Jews as different from other Germans. Won't all these things have a similar effect of making people feel that they are not the same as others? Bringing back segregation is not the answer. Did these people not learn from the first time when there was segregation, when 'separate but equal' resulted in 'separate and unequal'?

This is an example of social justice warriors not thinking things through. They have started doing something that sounds woke. But they haven't thought about how this could go wrong. People could use it as an opportunity to discriminate. It could also exacerbate divisions between different groups. It shows that they have failed to consider the underlying causes of these inequalities. Instead, social justice warriors have found something that feels like a quick, easy, satisfying fix.

'Validity'

You might be thinking that these are just some isolated examples of crazy individuals who are rejected by the rest of the left. Are these people even taken seriously by the social justice warrior movement? The answer is yes. In fact, you're not to question someone's identity. Invalidating a person's identity is one of the worst things you can do in the social justice warrior world. For instance, saying Sofie Hagen isn't really queer invalidates their identity as a pansexual person. Or saying that Rakshita Shekhar isn't really Autistic because numerous medical professionals have told her otherwise is invalidating her Autistic identity.

An example of this thinking in action was when *Everyday Feminism* published an article entitled '5 Ways to Maintain Your Queer Identity in a Relationship People Read as Straight'. Miri Mogilevsky, the author of the piece, writes "Being a queer person in a relationship that's read as straight by others can be painful and invalidating, no matter how healthy and empowering the relationship itself is" (103). In the above example, if Mogilevsky truly feels she is queer, why does it bother her to be perceived as straight? Could she have some doubts about her sexuality?

This fear of invalidation suggests that social justice warriors who identify as minorities aren't secure in their identity. Most people are confident of their identity. You know if you are a man or a woman. You know what race you are. You know what your sexuality is. You know if you have a disability. If someone said you weren't what you thought you were, it wouldn't have a big impact on you. For example, if you were a woman who found yourself being mistaken for a man, you might be slightly offended, but it wouldn't be greatly distressing. However, it hits a nerve with these people because they themselves don't completely believe in their identity. Hence, they rely on others to validate them. So, they are upset when this doesn't happen. Social media posts frequently proclaim 'you are valid' in relation to various identities. It is as if to assure themselves and other social justice warriors that those questioning them are wrong. But as much it is to ward off their own doubts about the identity.

So, if you see someone who describes themselves as a person of colour, queer, disabled and transgender or nonbinary, they might actually be none of those things. As social justice warriors are largely part of a generation that were taught that they can be anything they want to be, that's precisely what they do. If you are a man who wants to be a woman, just declare that you are a woman!

This chapter has shown the ways in which identity is taking over the left. It also has demonstrated that the left's concern with giving a voice to marginalized people isn't as egalitarian as it first appears. Instead, it has given a platform to a group of people who are not oppressed but have found a way to make themselves appear oppressed. This comes at the expense of genuinely marginalized people. Unlike genuinely oppressed people, these self-identified minorities are able to use their privilege to find a wide audience for their views. Thus, marginalized people are overshadowed by these self-identified minorities.

4. Class and the Social Justice Warrior

Many Marxists and other socialists believe that capitalism and the class system is the root cause of many forms of oppression. This chapter will look at how class has been forgotten about by the woke left. This includes how class-related concerns are often dismissed and left-wingers are instead encouraged to focus on identity issues. The chapter also examines the impact that ignoring class has had on working-class people.

The cultural left's emphasis on identity means that other ways that people are oppressed are overlooked. Class is biggest way that people are oppressed, by a system that is made completely by humans. People who suffer poverty experience lack of access to suitable housing, healthcare, education and other things. These are much worse than being called by the wrong name or being asked where you're 'really' from. With poverty comes coldness, pain, fear, confusion, hunger, and embarrassment.

Class reductionism is an insult levelled at socialists who focus on economics rather than identity. Something this book will almost certainly be accused of. Usually, this criticism takes the form of saying 'instead of talking about class, we should really be talking about race, gender, gay rights or some other branch of identity politics'. For instance, Robin DiAngelo, diversity trainer an author of the bestselling book, *White Fragility* says that raising the issue of class is a form of "channel-switching". It is designed to avoid discussing race (104). Other times when left-wingers have been accused of class reductionism include when Bernie Sanders said he opposed paying reparations to black people. Instead, he called for universalist policies, such as Medicare for All (105). Campaigns for free college tuition have also been regarded as class reductionist. As has the minimum wage (101).

There have been issues with universalist policies failing to include certain groups. For instance, many housing developments financed by the 1949 GI Bill did not allow black people to purchase housing. Thus, the GI Bill primarily benefitted white people (106). Anything like this should not be allowed to happen again. However, it's wrong to say that there's no point in fighting for class equality because it might hurt minorities. That claim is patently false and wrongly pits minorities against poor people. Of course, the white working-class aren't a separate group from ethnic minority working-class people.

Dismissing the economic left's policy ideas as class reductionist is problematic for several reasons. Firstly, class isn't separate from other issues. The working-class is comprised of people who are disproportionately from minority groups. Gray makes the point that class issues are also race issues. For instance, Hispanics are more likely to not have health insurance than people of other ethnicities. One in three Hispanic people don't have health insurance, but only one in 10 are undocumented migrants. So healthcare is a bigger issue for Hispanics than immigration reform. In addition, there are more black people in poverty than there are in prison (101). Indeed, most oppressed groups experience economic oppression. According to the pressure group Poverty USA, one in four Native Americans, one in five black people and just over one in six Hispanics are in poverty. In contrast, only one in 10 white people and Asian people are in poverty. In addition, Poverty USA reports that women are more likely to be in poverty than men, although this difference is not as stark as with other oppressed groups. Furthermore, 25% of people with a disability were also in poverty (107). This rises to 50% for disabled people of working age (108). Many members of the LGBT community also experience high rates of poverty. According to research from the Williams Institute, almost 30% of bisexual women and transgender people are in poverty. As are nearly 20% of bisexual men. (Although gay men and lesbian women experience similar rate of poverty to their heterosexual counterparts) (109).

Furthermore, poverty drives many other issues. For instance, poor health is related to poverty in several ways. First, in the USA, difficulty affording healthcare leads to poorer health. So many people die because they can't afford the care they need. For instance, people with Diabetes often must pay up to $900 per month for insulin. And many are dying prematurely because they can't afford it (110). As well, poorer people have less access to preventative healthcare. They are much less likely to have Cancer screenings than wealthier people (111). This leads to them developing more serious health issues.

As well, poorer people often have less access to a healthy lifestyle. This means that poorer people are more likely to experience obesity. US states with a low median income, such as Mississippi, Alabama and West Virginia, have the highest rates of obesity. Conversely, states with the highest median incomes, such as Colorado, California and Massachusetts have much lower rates of obesity (112). Now, it might seem strange that poorer people are more likely to be obese. After all, if they struggle to pay for food, how can they afford to eat so much? But the truth is, many poorer people have little choice but to live an unhealthy lifestyle. For instance, 12.8% of Americans live in food deserts. These are areas where few shops stock affordable, fresh foods. This forces people to purchase unhealthy tinned and frozen foods (113). This regular consumption of high calorie food naturally leads to weight gain and obesity.

In addition, many working-class occupations involve dangerous activities, such as lifting heavy objects, working with machinery, and exposure to fumes and harmful chemicals. This means that these workers are more likely to suffer from an industrial illness or injury. As a result of all these factors, there are huge health disparities between the rich and the poor. On average, a man in the USA whose income falls in the bottom 1% dies 14.6 years before a man in the top 1% of earners (114).

Crime is also often related to poverty. One example described by Larry Krasner, Philadelphia's district attorney, is the case of the narcotics trade. Many people start taking drugs as a form of escapism, to help them cope with the psychological burden of living in poverty. In addition, high unemployment pushes people to turn to unlawful ways of making money, such as dealing drugs. Furthermore, having a criminal conviction makes getting a job more difficult. Hence, a person comes to rely on the money they make from drug dealing or other unlawful sources. As a result, violent turf wars erupt between competing dealers. This leads to people experiencing serious emotional trauma from the loss of loved ones and from serious injuries. It also makes people feel unsafe. This in turn leads to more drug-taking and exacerbates the issue (115).

Gender inequality is another area affected by economic factors. A big reason for women's inequality is money. Women often can't work full-time because of childcare responsibilities, so they have less money than men. As well, money can force women to rely on men. A woman is dependent on her husband if she is a housewife, where she must submit to him or else risk losing her financial security. Indeed, the second-wave feminists campaigned for a universal basic income to liberate women from financial dependence on men (116). There are numerous other examples of how economic factors influence other forms of oppression. But as you can see, class has a huge influence on almost all types of oppression.

Class and Political Activism

Class influences political participation. The rich are the most politically active group. The richer a person is, the more likely they are to vote in elections (117). They are also much more likely to participate in other political activities too, including volunteering for a political party or campaigning online (118). It's not just class that adversely affects political participation. Ethnic minority people are also less likely to vote than white people (119). As a result, many working-class people feel that politics is not important to them. In a piece printed in 2016 in the *New York Times*, many poor black voters in Milwaukee said they didn't vote because it didn't matter who the president was. They said that politicians didn't care about them, so there was no point in voting (120). Furthermore, practical barriers to voting such as difficulty reaching the polling station, not having the correct voter identification, being busy at work or with other responsibilities also make it more difficult for working-class people to vote.

But social justice warriors don't get this. They claim that having little involvement in politics is a privilege. They argue that people from oppressed backgrounds can't afford to be apolitical (121). This is one of many ways in which the social justice warrior movement is out of touch with the working-class. They misunderstand why people aren't politically active. Which shows how little they understand working-class people. And by condemning people for being politically inactive, it comes across as arrogant. If you don't take much interest in politics, and you see a Facebook post saying that being apolitical is a privilege, it's reinforcing the view that the political class are out of touch with people like you. Also, these activists are missing out on a key tactic for improving social conditions. They could work on increasing voter turnout amongst minority groups. In turn, this should get politicians to take more notice of minorities.

As well, oppression itself can make it harder to participate in political processes. The most oppressed people in society aren't necessarily on Twitter or Tumblr talking about how difficult their lives are. Internet access is correlated with income. Poorer people are less likely to have an internet connection at home (122). And they are less likely to own devices through which they can access the internet (123). These people don't have a voice online. They can't talk about their lived experience in the same way that shouty middle-class people can. And these loud people drown out the voices of more oppressed.

Furthermore, America has low voter turn-out. Although US saw unprecedently high turnout in 2020, (currently estimated to be around 64%) (124) this is not the norm. In the 2016 presidential election, only 55%- slightly more than one in two adults- voted (125). The USA's voter turn-out is amongst the lowest of developed countries. The Pew Research Center ranked the US's voter turnout 31 out of the 35 economically developed democracies it studied (126). Worryingly, low voter-turnout tends to favour right-wing parties and politicians. Except for Hawaii and New York, all the states with the lowest turn-out are solidly Republican (127). This too entrenches inequalities.

While the needs of working-class voters being overlooked by politicians has been an issue for many years, the growth of identity politics has exacerbated this issue.

73

Most social justice warriors are from well-to-do backgrounds. There is no formal data on this, but it can be observed. Most are either college students, or young graduates in professional careers. They often attended private schools as children. When they talk about their parents, they too usually have professional class jobs. The reason this is especially concerning is because of the social justice warrior's focus on lived experience. Their lived experience isn't representative of most people's experience. Even when they are a member of a minority group. For instance, the lived experience of a black college-educated person from an affluent family isn't the same as the lived experience of a black high school drop-out from an impoverished family.

The way that poorer people are excluded from politics is a vicious circle. Politicians take no interest in the lives of the working-class. As a result, the working-class aren't interested in politics. So, middle-class and upper-class people are more well-represented politically, because they are the ones who vote and yield the power.

How Social Justice Warriors See the Working-class

The cosmopolitan, liberal elite have long held a sneering attitude toward the working-class. And as such, the left can be very unkind to the poor.

'Educate yourself' is a common refrain to any misunderstanding or disagreement with liberal ideas. Social justice warriors assume that everyone has been to college, studied liberal arts, the humanities or social sciences, and should be familiar with various postmodern and neo-Marxist theories of oppression. And that having read and understood these theories, we should agree with their perspectives. Or that everyone has the time or ability to read complex academic texts about social issues (many of which are written in a deliberately inaccessible style and require several years of study to understand). For instance, that everyone should be familiar with the difference between sex and gender. Or theories about the role of language in shaping thought. Or all about micro-aggression theory. It has a sneering subtext, as if they only reason someone would disagree is because they are too stupid to understand you. It comes across as incredibly arrogant.

New slurs against working-class and lower middle-class white woman have also started to crop up. The most notable of which is 'Karen'. A 'Karen' is a middle-aged working-class or lower-middle class white woman. She is perceived as rude and entitled, which stems from her white privilege. She exhibits behaviours such as demanding to speak to an establishment's manager over trivial matters and speaking rudely to service staff. She is ignorant about race and other social issues, which manifests in casual racism and homophobia (128).

According to the social justice warriors, Karen can't be a slur because it's against white women, and white people aren't oppressed. They claim that only people who are oppressed can be slurred against (129). This is wrong for two reasons. First, the word 'slur' simply means an insult.

The Oxford English Dictionary, which is regarded as the authority on the English language, defines it as such (130). Second, even if the term slur only did apply to oppressed groups, then it's still a slur because women are oppressed. Interestingly, there is no equivalent term for a male 'Karen'. It's only white women who are demonized. Misogyny is at play here. But social justice warriors think white women should just take these insults. It's as if their whiteness is some kind of shield against sexism. Of course, this is not right. Many white men use Karen as a slur. Do those white men think they are more oppressed than white women? Or is it just that these men don't like white working-class women and what to dress this distain up as social justice? Describing women as a Karen or similar terms such as 'Becky', (meaning a young white working-class or lower middle-class woman who also knows little about social justice) (131), is a crafty way of being misogynistic and classist without anyone caring. Given how tolerant the social justice warriors profess to be, they can be incredibly prejudiced.

So why do social justice warriors care so much about identity and so little about class? This hatred of identity-related 'privilege' comes from identity politics' capitalist focus. Capitalism claims to be a meritocracy. Those who are at the top are there because they work hard and are superior to everyone else: they deserve what they have. Identity politics doesn't question this notion. It merely suggests that some people are not getting their deserved wealth because of prejudice, while other people have undeserved wealth because of their identity. This isn't even remotely Marxist or socialist. It is not about achieving equality. It is merely about achieving a society where there are still class inequalities, but where people from minority backgrounds are not disadvantaged by their backgrounds.

Indeed, within the social justice warrior movement, there is little care given to any matters around economics. The average social justice warrior can't say much about what the government should do for economic policy. They don't have a view on subjects like nationalization, co-operative ownership or such like. They don't even have thoughts on job creation, taxation or welfare systems. They rarely talk about practical policy ideas for achieving the equality they obsess over so much. After all, why would these things matter to them? They aren't affected by them.

The biggest victims of the social justice warrior movement are the working-class. Wokeness doesn't include these people. Instead, it's all about making the middle-class marginally more equal. You can see why Democrats lost so many blue-collar voters in 2016. Or why they failed to win the Senate in 2020. Bear in mind that part of the reason that Trump won in 2016 was because he promised to defeat political correctness (132). Why would you vote for a party who seem so far away from what matters to you? The social justice warrior's lives and priorities are so distant from that of the average blue-collar worker's that they might as well be aliens from another planet.

Ignoring Issues that Matter to the Working-Classes

In contrast, identity is primarily a middle-class concern. Bauman explains that identity politics results from a cosmopolitan elite who are obsessed with the identity issues that dominate their lives, which is why identity issues have overtaken class. Bauman argues that we live in a globalized, individualistic world. This world is great for the cosmopolitan elite, but terrible for many others. The cosmopolitan elite have the money and other resources to jet across the world. They integrate with other members of the cosmopolitan elite in other countries. Consequently, class doesn't affect them much. But identity does (72). And the social justice warrior movement reflects that in their fixation with identity. For example, in the social justice warrior movement, immigrants are an oppressed group. But class can be a major effect on the way immigrants experience life in the USA or the UK. For instance, is a wealthy white British person who chooses to move to New York and gets a visa as a skilled immigrant, in the same position as an impoverished Mexican family moving to Texas in the hope of making enough money to live on? Yet they would both be described as oppressed by social justice warriors.

Furthermore, working-class people don't have time to luxuriate on pondering their identity. Unlike middle-class social justice warriors, they are busy. Busy with working hard and demanding jobs. Busy looking after their children and grandchildren. And busy with housework. They can't sit around thinking about whether they fit neatly into the category of 'man' or 'woman' or if they might have undiagnosed ADHD. They don't have time to look at Tumblr all day long and contemplate whether they're demisexual or some other form of 'queer'. Or to obsess over if a certain action constitutes a micro-aggression. They have actual problems to deal with. The consequence of this is that we now have a left that has no concern with class-related issues. While there is a lot of fuss over identity-related issues, matters that are more salient to many less affluent people are overlooked. For instance:

Worker's Rights

The USA has terrible worker's rights. In a survey conducted by the International Trade Union Congress, the USA was ranked as the worst developed economy for worker's rights (133). The USA is one of the few economically developed countries with no federal right to paid sick leave (134,135). They also have no federal paid maternity leave (136). Furthermore, under the Trump administration many health and safety regulations were rolled back (137). These include allowing mine inspections to take place while the miners work. Under Obama, these had to take place before the start of a shift, to prevent injuries occurring when mining was taking place. The Trump administration also raised the speed limits in meat processing plants (138). Consequently, workers are now exposed to greater danger.

But when it comes to being woke, worker's rights don't matter. Even when a company claims to champion inclusivity. Look at the case of Voltage, a video games company. Voltage hired workers exclusively from LGBT backgrounds. But they were only hired on a freelance basis, so they didn't have the same benefits and job security as workers with a permanent contract. As well, they were paid half of the industry average. Furthermore, 21 workers were fired when they attempted to unionize (139). It's fair to say that Voltage don't care about their employees. It looks good to say they have an inclusive workforce. But actually, treating their inclusive workforce well doesn't matter.

As well, in the UK worker's rights have been eroded over the past 10 years. In 2012, the period where a person had to work for an employer before gaining protection from unfair dismissal doubled from one year to two years (140). Many public sector workers have also had their right to strike greatly limited. Under the Trade Union Act 2016, for a strike to be allowed to take place, 50% of union members must have participated in the ballot. For those working in 'important public services', such as teachers and bus and train drivers for Transport for London (141), at least 40% of members who are entitled to vote must have supported the strike. Again, this damage to worker's rights has mostly gone unnoticed by the woke left.

Housing

The USA has a very high rate of people living in poor quality housing. Over one in 20 people live in trailers (142). Trailers are not suitable for permanent housing.

They are made of materials that are poor insulators, which makes them difficult to heat up (143). They also have poor ventilation, making them prone to damp (144). These homes are easily damaged by hurricanes too (145). Many others live in overcrowded houses and apartments. So many families struggle to afford their rent and pay for daily essentials (146).

Add to that, there is little government protection from homelessness; just two percent of the US's housing stock is public housing (147). If you can't afford to buy or rent a home, you are on your own. This is a problem that's getting worse. Public housing is being demolished and not replaced. And the housing that still stands is often in a poor state of repair. But conservatives perceive that it's not the government's responsibility to house people. Ben Carson, the Secretary of Housing and Urban Development, has even said that his goal is to eliminate public housing (148). What do liberals have to say on the matter? Not much. The slow death of public housing hasn't had much attention in the media.

The UK does better than the USA, but they too are struggling with housing. 8.4 million people in England are affected by housing problems, including difficulty paying their rent or mortgage, low-quality housing, overcrowding or homelessness (149). Furthermore, many social housing buildings are unsafe. The Grenfell Tower fire in 2017 demonstrated this. This fire was in a local authority tower block in North Kensington, in London. During a refurbishment several years prior, the building had been clad with flammable panels (150). This caused a small fire in one flat to spread rapidly to the entire building (151). The fire killed 72 people and left many others homeless (152). It has highlighted the lack of concern that the local authority showed for the residents. They could have prevented the fire spreading by not using the cladding. Grenfell Tower wasn't the only building to be affected by this issue. As of 2020, approximately 2000 buildings still have similar flammable cladding on them (153). Again, social justice warriors don't care. Housing isn't woke.

Welfare

The US social security system is another area where the USA seriously lags behind other countries. The USA has a very low-quality welfare system that leaves many struggling. Gaps in the welfare system mean a person can find themselves in a situation where they are not eligible for any money, but they aren't able to earn any money either. The system consists of numerous programs, and there are variations in each state.

The US gives many people food stamps via the Supplementary Nutritional Assistance Program (SNAP) instead of actual money. This is a big issue because people need to buy things that aren't food. Food stamps can't be used to pay for many essential items. These include clothes, personal hygiene items, household products and appliances, school supplies for children and for transport (154). Furthermore, under the Trump administration, people who are classified as able-bodied adults without any dependents (ABAWD) are no longer eligible for

SNAP (155). As a result, 700,000 people have lost their SNAP provisions (156).

Other benefits aren't any more generous either. For instance, SSI (Supplemental Social Income) is only for the elderly, blind people and other disabled people. This is strictly means-tested. Claimants are not allowed to save up money beyond a certain point (157). A single person can only have $2000 in savings, rising to $3000 for couples. These limits have not increased since 1989 (158). These limits create a welfare trap where a person can't try to get out of poverty without finding themselves in worse poverty.

The situation in the UK is also a problem. The UK has a proud history of a strong welfare state. But that is slowly being destroyed. There have been numerous cuts in the past 10 years. An entire book could be written about the cuts to welfare in Britain (indeed, many books have been). But some examples include the benefit cap which was introduced in 2013. This put a limit on how much total benefit a family could receive (159). As well as this, there is the minimum income floor for self-employed Universal Credit claimants. Universal Credit is a benefit that is paid to people who are on a low income. It includes people who are unemployed, too disabled to work, or have a low-paid job. But if you are self-employed and on a low income, Universal Credit is calculated as if you work full time on the minimum wage. It won't top up income beyond that point (160). Even though the government claimed the aim of Universal Credit was to make work pay, the minimum income floor penalizes people for working.

The USA is the richest country in the world. They could easily afford to tackle all these issues through a strong welfare state. But they don't. They are certainly not short of money to spend on more frivolous things. For example, the budget for NASA in the 2019/2020 financial year was $22.6 billion (161). Space exploration is all very well and good, but wouldn't it be better to put the welfare of the country's own people first? Think how far that $22.6 billion could go toward a better welfare system, universal healthcare, free college tuition, new public housing or so many other things. The UK is also a very affluent country. They too could afford to provide the support the welfare state needs.

Do the social justice warriors care? Not one bit. The woke float in a bubble of privilege, untouched by these issues. Look at a liberal-leaning news website like *Vox* or *Bustle*. You'll find none of these issues mentioned. Yet topics like 'The queering of Taylor Swift' (162) or 'Student activists want change — and they're starting in the classroom' (163) are covered. The woke left are great at demanding that people check their privilege. But they never check their own privilege. Which is why they show no concern for the issues that affect so many people. On the other hand, they do support policies that actively hurt the working-class.

Immigration

On the flip side, the social justice warrior movement spends a lot of time campaigning on issues which are great for capitalism but are bad for poorer people. One example of such an issue is immigration. The left is now very pro-immigration. Any opposition to open boarders makes someone a 'nativist'. (A nativist is someone who is vehemently prejudiced against immigrants) (164). This fits with Bauman's description of the middle-class globetrotters who make up the bulk of the liberal left (72).

For many years, open boarders have been championed by free-market organizations such as the Cato Institute (165). That's because they're great for business. Rich multi-national corporations can simply get foreigners who are overjoyed at the prospect of living in America or the UK to do jobs for less pay than the local workforce. As a result, poor people are more heavily hit by high immigration. It you rely on low-paid work, and you're regularly being undercut by immigrants, you're not going to be happy with people who say high immigration is fine. Nagle points out that even Marx was critical of immigration. He said that immigration forces down wages by creating more competition for jobs. He also said it fostered divides between working-class people of different nationalities (164). Admittedly, going after the immigrants isn't the best solution to this problem. After all, they are often escaping worse poverty from their home countries. And nobody chooses what country they're born in. But open boarders aren't as wonderful as the liberal left believe them to be. A better solution would be to explore ways of reducing global inequalities so that fewer people feel the need to leave their home countries.

As well, immigration is bad for the countries where the immigrants are coming from. For countries with high levels of emigration, there is an issue with human capital flight, also known as brain drain. This is when many of a country's bright, young, skilled workers move abroad to more affluent countries. As a result, employers in these countries can't fill skilled positions. This has a devastating effect on poorer countries. For instance, in Kenya, an estimated 30 to 40% of doctors emigrate after completing their training. This leaves the Kenyan healthcare system desperately short of medical professionals (166). Therefore, for helping eliminate global poverty, open boarders aren't so marvellous.

A much more serious issue is illegal immigration (or, if you prefer 'undocumented immigration'. Social justice warriors often say that 'nobody is illegal'). The liberals claim that illegal immigration is great. Any opposition to illegal immigration-including support for the Mexican border wall- is racist. According to an article published on *Bustle*, even dressing up as The Wall for a Halloween party should be avoided. It could be upsetting for party attendees who have family and friends who wish to cross the Mexican border (167). Although, most illegal immigrants do not cross the Mexican border. Instead, they enter the USA legally but stay after their visa has expired (168). It goes to show how little these progressive wokies know about the cause that they supposedly care about so deeply.

Social justice warriors argue that illegal immigration is beneficial for the host country. They cite lower prices on agricultural products as evidence that illegal immigration is good for the economy (169). But illegal immigration, like legal immigration undercuts wages. And the people who are employing illegal immigrants are exploiting them. Bosses can take on illegal immigrants, pay them less than the minimum wage and provide substandard working conditions. They know there's nothing illegal immigrants can do about it. Illegal immigrants are also more likely to work in dangerous jobs and are typically paid less than legal immigrants or residents (170). If it weren't like that, then they wouldn't hire illegal immigrants. Furthermore, many people die or are seriously injured when crossing boarders illegally. Since 2014, over 33,000 people globally have died trying to migrate to other countries (171).

Look at the case of the Morecambe Bay cockle pickers. Morecambe Bay is a former seaside resort in the north west of England. If you look at the beach at Morcombe bay, you'll see sand caked in thick, shiny mud, with large puddles and lakes interspersed within the sand. You'll see large, imposing signs warning tourists not to go on the beach because of the quicksand. The beach seems to go on forever. The sea is so far away it looks like it would never come in. But it does. It is said to come in so fast that a horse could not outrun it (172).

In 2004, a group of Chinese illegal immigrants were employed by two British businessmen to collect cockles from Morecambe Bay beach. They obtained fake documentation to enable them to work. The group were paid £5 (around £7.77 in today's money, or $10) per 25 kilograms of cockles (55 lbs). Which was much less than the rate normally paid to cockle pickers (173). The cockle pickers work at low tide, when the cockles are easier to find. But one night, while the cockle pickers were working, the tide suddenly came in. It came in much too fast for the workers to escape. They were stranded on the beach. The workers could not speak or read much English. Hence, they could not read the warning signs. One worker phoned the emergency services and frantically screamed "sinking water! Sinking water!" in an attempt to get help. Unfortunately, the operator did not understand what he was saying and cut off the call (174). The tide continued to come in. By the time help arrived, it was too late. Only one person was rescued. In total, 23 people drowned. Lin Liang Ren, the gang master who ran the operation, was convicted of 21 counts of manslaughter. However, the businessmen who hired the cockle pickers were not convicted of anything (175). While this happened before the social justice warrior movement, it illustrates the dangers of illegal immigration.

Despite the hazards of illegal immigration, social justice warriors consider deportations to be cruel. Even the House Speaker, Nancy Pelosi, has agreed with this sentiment (176). Admittedly, the idea of someone being dragged away from the place they've made home certainly isn't pleasant. But sometimes, you have to be cruel to be kind. It's better to be deported than to die while trying to enter the country through an unsafe route. Or to be seriously injured at a workplace that doesn't follow health and safety regulations. If the UK and US governments were routinely turning a blind eye to illegal immigration, how many other cases like the Morcombe Bay tragedy would happen? The government has a duty to protect illegal immigrants as much as it has a duty to protect its own citizens. Letting people be exploited is not progressive in any way.

This chapter has shown that the social justice warrior movement's disregard of social class hurts many people. The left no longer stands for the working-class. It is for middle-class liberal free marketeers. This lack of concern for class is stopping the left from making progress. By ignoring the working-class, the left has become divided into small identity groups with contradictory aims.

5. Mental Health in Identity Politics

This chapter will explore the role of mental health in the social justice warrior movement. Social justice warriors have unprecedentedly high levels of mental illness. But they have come to weaponize this fragility and fetishize vulnerability too. This is known as being a virtuous victim. While mental illness is nothing to be ashamed of, the social justice warriors use it to manipulate people. As well, this chapter will examine how social justice warriors treat being part of a minority group as a mental illness in itself.

Why Are Social Justice Warriors So Unhappy?

Over the past 20 years, there has been a huge rise in young people with mental illnesses. Depression rates in teens increased by 59% between 2007 and 2017 (177). In addition, there has been a big growth in students with mental health problems accessing college counselling services. Furthermore, many college students struggle to cope with small difficulties. At one college, many students sought counselling after receiving B and C grades. They perceived this to be a devastating failure. Other students sought counselling after arguments with their roommates. Or in one case, after seeing a mouse in their dormitory (178). Most people would love it if their biggest problems in life were mediocre grades or seeing a mouse. So why is the generation that as everything so distressed?

Individualism and entitlement have helped contribute to another defining characteristic of the social justice warrior: fragility. Generation Me haven't been raised to cope well with adult life. Sadly, 'you can be whatever you want to be' doesn't work in the real world. It has set them up to be disappointed by life. This has resulted in high rates of dissatisfaction with life and in some cases, mental illness. For instance, Twenge says that millennials had unrealistically high expectations for life. She cites a survey which found that three out of four US college freshmen (first-years) aspired to do a PhD, MD or other advance degree. Of course, the vast majority never make it, thus starting their career off with a tinge of disappointment (9). In addition, perfectionism is higher amongst millennials than in previous generations (179). This perfectionism causes poor mental health. People cannot live up to the expectations they set for themselves, and so they become depressed. Furthermore, they put a lot of pressure on themselves, which causes them to feel stressed and anxious (180). Indeed, according to a study into perfectionism between 1989 and 2016, "American, Canadian, and British cultures have become more individualistic, materialistic, and socially antagonistic over this period, with young people now facing more competitive environments, more unrealistic expectations, and more anxious and controlling parents than generations before" (179). This explains why Generation Me has so much difficulty coping with everyday life. Furthermore, the focus on having everyone be a winner meant that social justice warriors never learned how to cope with failure. Generation Me has not developed the skills and resilience needed for adult life. Which is why they fall apart so easily.

Growing up in the Therapy Culture

A further influence on social justice warriors has been therapy culture. The term 'therapy culture' was coined by sociologist Frank Furedi. It refers to the way that society thinks about socio-political phenomena in terms of emotional well-being. For instance, attributing crime to low self-esteem or racial inequalities to poor mental health. It is a society which encourages open displays of emotion and utilization of psychiatric therapy for issues a person would previously have dealt with alone or through support from family and friends. Therapy culture is a product of a more individualistic society. It represents a shift from looking at problems from a society-wide perspective to an individual perspective (181). However, most of what therapy culture preaches has little to do with actual psychiatric practice.

The left has thoroughly embraced therapy culture in its practices. Its fetishization of mental illness is a celebration of weakness. The social justice warrior movement has a culture where the more oppressed and vulnerable you are, the better. On the left, people compete over who is the weakest. For social justice warriors, the left-right split in politics is not about economic and social progress vs economic and social conservatism. But instead, it is a war of the oppressed vs the oppressors. And in that war, you need people to firmly understand that you are the oppressed. Big displays of upset are normal in left-wing spaces. People should be slaves to their emotions! They shouldn't suck it up! Every feeling they have is valid, and people around them need to know how they feel!

Furthermore, the saying 'your feelings are valid' has become a slogan of the social justice warrior movement. Your feelings are valid means that it's wrong to question your emotions, or to try and stop feeling the way you do. As with many facets of therapy culture, this is the opposite of what most therapists teach (182). Most therapists aim to gently show patients why their feelings are not valid. A popular method of doing this is through Cognitive Behavioural Therapy (CBT). For example, a person with Social Anxiety might feel that everyone is judging them. The aim of CBT would be to make the patient realize that this is unlikely to be true. CBT looks at distorted thinking and using evidence to test assumptions. In this case, the patient might be encouraged to observe what people are actually doing in public, so that they realize that most people are too busy to take any notice of them. This would help the patient understand why they are wrong to think that everyone is judging them. Which demonstrates why social justice warriors are wrong to claim that emotions are always valid.

The social justice warrior movement also uses their vulnerability to shut out uncomfortable opposition. This is part of their rationale for ardent censorship. They refuse to learn anything about the right. For instance, many will block right-wing social media accounts. Others refuse to read right-wing publications, on the grounds that such things could be damaging to their mental health. This is a problem because if you can't understand voters, you can't win them over.

Self-Care, Self-Love and Radical Kindness

In accordance with the social justice warrior's focus on the self, mental health is about yourself. It's about loving yourself, caring only about yourself and ignoring others. Self-care is a big part of this. Self-care means engaging in activities that a person finds relaxing or enjoyable. This concept comes from a quote from black feminist poet Audre Lorde, who famously wrote: "Caring for myself is not self-indulgence. It is self-preservation, and that is an act of political warfare" (183). Self-care often involves indulgent activities that are unhealthy, such as eating cake or other unhealthy foods (6), or spending a lot of money. The trouble is this 'self-care' isn't actually healthy. The odd treat now and then won't kill you but encouraging people to do it all the time will hurt them in the long run. Also, some behaviours can form a vicious cycle. For example, a person in debt is depressed about their financial situation. They spend money to cheer themselves up, which helps temporarily. But as a result of the spending, the debt gets worse, so they feel worse. Self-care is partly based on the view that mental health is equal to physical health. So, eating fatty food is healthy because it helps your mental health, in spite of the harms to your physical health (184). In reality, being temporarily cheered up by food is not good for a person's physical or mental health. This highlights the flaws in the concept of self-care.

Another popular concept in the social justice warrior movement is radical kindness (adding the word 'radical' to a concept makes it left-wing). This concept is vague and ill-defined, but the foremost idea is to be kind to yourself (185). Something which most social justice warriors don't find difficult. Once you've been kind to yourself, the next priority is being kind to marginalized groups. However, you don't need to be kind to people you disagree with. In fact, social justice warriors make a point of saying radical kindness is only intended for marginalized people. There's a popular meme saying "Ps [sic]: radical kindness doesn't extend to racists, homophobes, or fatphobes radical kindness is meant to benefit marginalized members of our online and local communities" (186). There's nothing wrong with being kind. But being kind to people you like is easy. Being kind to people you don't like is much harder. But the people who need you to be kind the most are often the least kind people. They are as they are because they have been raised without love and kindness. So, making a point of not being kind to bigots is not helpful. If anything, it gives them more reason to be bigoted.

Another popular act of self-love is cutting out 'toxic' people from your life. For instance, the liberal-leaning publication *Bustle* published an article which recommends readers cut out controlling friends, negative friends, and friends who take advantage (187). While some of these are not good traits in a friendship, others sound like they need the support of a friend. Labelling someone as toxic and cutting them off might be good for your mental health. But what about them and their mental health? Someone who is negative might have undiagnosed Depression. On this matter, the article says, "you can't work harder at improving your friend's mental health than they are". Similarly, a controlling friend might be anxious. Simply cutting people off when they have too many issues of their own because they don't make you feel good is unkind and selfish. It will validate many of their bad thoughts and feelings. If you're depressed and your friend stops speaking to you because you're too much work to be around, how would that make you feel? But that's exactly what the social justice warrior movement says people should do. All that self-love is about is justifying selfishness.

The Politicization of Mental Health and Emotions

Mental health has become politicized. It is now deeply associated with the left and with marginalized groups.

Social justice warriors treat one another as vulnerable victims. For instance, many were devastated at Trump winning the 2016 election. *Everyday Feminism* published articles that treated Trump's victory as if some huge tragedy had occurred. One included a resource list suggesting self-care activities and other articles to help the reader "process" the election result. At the top of the article, there is a large picture of a woman crying. Beneath that, the opening paragraph mentions that most of the staff at the website had taken the day off to cope with the result (188). There is no sense that this type of response is disproportionate to what has happened. It gives the impression that being so distraught is a perfectly reasonable response to the party you support losing an election.

Donald Trump's presidency itself was also framed as triggering. When Trump won the election, several universities put on additional support for students who were upset by his victory. At Virginia Tech, students were sent an email assuring them that "they are loved" in spite of Trump's election win. It included a list of places where students could receive mental health support (189). As well, many people use trigger warnings for posts mentioning Trump on social media (190). Trump's policies are regarded as a trauma trigger too. *Huffington Post* published an article on self-care to cope "if your mental health is affected by Donald Trump's constant downplaying of COVID-19." One of these self-care tips is to become involved in political campaigning (191). While the COVID-19 crisis has been difficult for most people, it's extreme to find Trump's behaviour so upsetting. Trump has handled the pandemic poorly and being infected has not taught him any lessons. It is frustrating that he acts the way he does. But not liking the president isn't a mental health problem.

Furthermore, social justice warriors don't realize that conservatives are actually more anxious than liberals. Many psychological and neurological studies have proven this. One study showed that the amygdala (the part of the brain that processes emotion) is larger in conservatives than in liberals (192). Another study found that they show a more pronounced response to frightening stimuli (193).

Also, conservatives own more cleaning products and other items associated with maintaining order. This is thought to suggest a fear of uncertainty (194).

The idea of conservatives being very anxious might seem strange at first, but when you think about it, it makes so much sense. Conservatism is all about fear. They are afraid of terrorism, crime, and social disorder. And that reflects in their priorities. This is why conservative politicians talk so much about those issues. For example, most conservatives are in favour of a strong defence system. This is because they are afraid of the potential threat of war. They are scared of the unknown, which is why they are anti-immigration. Immigration brings in new people from different cultures. And conservatives find that frightening. They are also against social change, such as gay marriage or a new economic system, because they find change scary.

Other policies positions are influenced by fear too. Take the US gun lobby. These people are terrified of being a victim of crime. They spend their lives thinking 'what if someone breaks in my house and tries to shoot me'. Or 'what if someone shoots me in the street'. Or 'what if someone tries to shoot my child at school?' Their solution is to think: 'I need to be armed. I need a gun at home. I need to carry a gun with me all the time. My child's teacher needs to be armed'. They're not completely wrong. It is possible that someone would break in your house and shoot you. Yes, there's nothing the police could realistically do to prevent that situation. Someone could shoot you in the street. And someone could shoot your child in school. But a liberal can look at guns in a calmer, more reasoned way. Firstly, the chances of being shot in an unprovoked attack are incredibly slim. And having a gun won't necessarily help. The fewer guns there are, the less likely it is that someone will shoot you. Or that it's more likely another member of your household would shoot you. Therefore, most liberals would conclude that on balance, you don't need to carry a gun or have one at home for protection. Nor does your child's teacher need a gun.

Furthermore, people turn to conspiracy theories because the truth is too difficult to cope with. The psychologist John M. Grohol describes how conspiracy theorists have a high rate of fear and anxiety. They also had other psychological issues, such as narcissism and feeling alienated from society (195). So, they use conspiracy theories to cope with their anxiety and unhappiness. Take climate change as an example. The idea of the Earth being destroyed is terrifying. Most left-wingers look at pragmatic solutions to stop further damage from occurring. Whereas many conservatives appear to have decided that climate change is too bad to be true. They can't cope with the truth. So, they decide it can't be real and that scientists and other authority figures must be lying to them.

As well, the focus on mental health in the left has meant that right-wingers have been dehumanized. They are not entitled to have emotions anymore. Trauma, anger and sadness are reserved for marginalized people. For instance, the term 'white tears' refers to someone who is upset over something that could be threatening to their white privilege. In response to claims that the phrase is offensive, English and Africana Studies Professor Valerie Thomas says "I do want the people who are offended ... to pause for a moment and breathe with it, and see if it's really damaging them and hurting them" (196). But that could be said of virtually any slur. Thomas is telling people they can't really be offended. In other words, she's invalidating their feelings. So, according to social justice warriors, your feelings are valid... except if you're privileged in some way.

Ultimately, conservatives are weak people who pretend to be strong. Unlike liberals, who use emotion to attain a political goal, conservatives are genuinely scared of the issues they talk about. Liberals misinterpret conservative's fear. They wrongly assume their fear is hyperbole and label the conservatives as cruel and selfish. But it's their fear that stops them empathizing. Next time you see someone talking about the right to bear arms, about Mexican rapists entering the US illegally or for stronger policing, remember there's a scared, hurt child inside them. They don't talk about their anxiety, but it's there.

Mental Health Activism

With this politicisation of mental health has come an army of liberal mental health activists. Mental illness has become part of people's identities. One symbol of this is the semicolon tattoo. These tattoos were generally placed on a visible part of the body, such as the wrist. This tattoo was to symbolize that a person had experienced suicidal thoughts or self-harm. The semicolon was used to represent a life that could have ended but continued; similar to how a semicolon represents a sentence that could have ended with a full stop, but goes on (197,198). The concept of these tattoos was created by Project Semicolon, a suicide prevention charity. They were intended to raise awareness of mental illness, like with the AIDS red ribbon, or the yellow testicular Cancer wrist band. But the big difference is you can take off a ribbon or a wristband, but a tattoo is always there. Even in situations where you might not wish to discuss your mental illness. Having a permanent symbol for mental illness on their body shows how social justice warriors see their mental health as a part of who they are. This movement largely dissipated after Amy Bleuel, the founder of Project Semicolon, died of suicide in 2017 (199). But the tattoos are there forever.

As well, mental illness is celebrated as courageous in liberal-leaning publications. There are many articles that praise celebrities for talking about their mental health. Examples from the listicle website *Buzzfeed* include an article about actor Dax Shepard relapsing in his addiction to opiate medication. It espouses the benefits of making gratitude lists (200). Another article praises the singer Lady Gaga for "opening up" about her mental health struggles (complete with a trigger warning) (201). While mental health shouldn't be stigmatized, it shouldn't be celebrated either. Yet the barrage of articles praising celebrities for opening up is influencing young people to revel in their fragility. From these articles, mental health

101

sounds like something brave and special that happens to unique and talented people. And that having a mental illness means that you are an extraordinary person who is misunderstood by mainstream society.

Indeed, mental health has become romanticized. An article published in *The Atlantic* describes how the social media site Tumblr portrays the concept of "beautiful suffering". This is where people share photographs and articles celebrating Depression. For instance, black and white pictures of pretty young women with captions about suicide and sadness are a common finding (202). These celebratory articles must contribute to the romanticization of mental illness on social media. In other cases, mental health is portrayed as cutesy. If you search 'mental health' on a social media site, you'll see lots of pink and purple memes, along with pastel and brightly coloured drawings. Often, these include political slogans (such as a cute character saying "defund the police" or a cat saying "listen to trans kids"). This has little to do with real mental health. It gives the misleading impression that mental illness is fun and exciting. As well as a sign of personal strength and the virtue that social justice warriors perceive to come from being a minority.

From a mental health point of view, this is a problem. The people who have the most serious mental illnesses can't always advocate for themselves. The focus in mental health has moved more on to helping people with less serious mental health issues such as Anxiety, Depression and Stress. Meanwhile, social justice warriors overlook more serious mental illnesses such as personality disorders, Bipolar Disorder and Schizophrenia. Consequently, the needs of these people aren't focused on in the same way as those with milder mental illnesses. Also, these illnesses remain stigmatized.

Furthermore, the idea that mental health is only for oppressed people is inaccurate and damaging. Evidence shows that non-marginalized people can be more seriously affected by mental illness than other groups. In the USA, white men are more likely to die by suicide than any other demographic (203,204). But from the liberal media, you'd truly think that mental illness is just for oppressed people. By presenting mental illness in this way, it could make it more difficult for white men to get help. It might increase the stigma of mental illness by increasing the perception that mental illness is a weakness. It also means there are less resources devoted to white men's mental health than there is for other groups.

Safe Spaces and Trigger Warnings

Safe spaces and trigger warnings are used online, at colleges and other social justice warrior spaces to protect people from being traumatized or 'triggered'. Safe spaces are a metaphorical concept, where a place is declared to be free of discrimination. For instance, a university might declare itself to be a safe space for LGBT+ students. Or a certain event will be a safe space for sexual assault survivors. These aren't generally actual designated rooms or buildings (205), but they can be. For example, at Brown University, a designated safe space was set up for a debate on rape culture. Students set up the room so any audience members who were upset by the debate could go there to recuperate. This particular safe space was "equipped with cookies, colouring books, bubbles, Play-Doh, calming music, pillows, blankets and a video of frolicking puppies, as well as students and staff members trained to deal with trauma" (206). Terms such as 'psychological safety' are also thrown around in the social justice warrior movement.

These concepts are derived from the idea that certain views are harmful to a person's mental health, and so people should be prevented from hearing them. The problem is, when you designate somewhere as a safe space, it's hard for people to speak out. Also, safe for who? For instance, a student who is against gay marriage could be violating a college's safe space policy by voicing their opinion. They might not necessarily hate homosexual people, but they believe that marriage should be only for a man and a woman. This view isn't very common nowadays, and it could be upsetting for gay students to hear it. But at the same time, who is to say that the gay student is right, and the Christian student is wrong? We can't objectively say that one opinion is harmful, and another isn't. There's a difference between disagreeing with someone and being insulted by someone. But social justice warriors don't know that.

Trigger warnings (also known as 'content warnings' or abbreviated to TW or CW) are warnings given before showing a piece of material that could be upsetting. In some contexts, these might have an actual benefit. For instance, warning of rape or severe violence in a piece of literature, or for a lecture where images of seriously injured people are shown. But they are also being used to flag up oppression, such as colonialism, and cissexism. At Oberlin College, a trigger warning policy was developed. The policy encouraged academics to "Be aware of racism, classism, sexism, heterosexism, cissexism, ableism, and other issues of privilege and oppression. Realize that all forms of violence are traumatic, and that your students have lives before and outside your classroom, experiences you may not expect or understand". The policy also advised faculty to avoid including "triggering" content in the syllabus where possible. And to give trigger warnings when covering material that features oppression. For example, it states that the novel *Things Fall Apart* by Chinua Achebe "may trigger readers who have experienced racism, colonialism, religious persecution, violence, suicide, and more" (207).

The problem with trigger warnings in the classroom is that it frames the discussion in a particular way. For example, if a student is warned that a book being studied for a literature class contains sexist attitudes, they cannot judge for themselves as to whether the book is sexist. Especially if this is disputed. If a politics student is warned that an international relations lecture includes colonialism, that is a huge assumption. It is automatically assumed that colonialism is a bad thing. While most people agree that sexism and colonialism are bad, university is about exploring ideas. This includes looking at controversial perspectives. And it is about drawing your own opinions. By saying 'this is sexist', or 'this is colonialist', students are being told how to think about the topic. This goes against the aim of university. Also, when does a label apply? What if there is disagreement whether, say, a certain historical figure was racist, or if a certain war was colonialist? Do we class content about them as triggering, just in case?

In addition, trigger warnings aren't helpful for students with mental health issues. Greg Lukianoff and Jonathan Haidt point out that avoiding triggers isn't a treatment for PTSD, but a symptom (182). Indeed, many therapists use these triggers in their therapeutic practice. For example, a commonly used treatment for many mental illnesses is exposure therapy. In exposure therapy, people are exposed to scary or upsetting things, until they can tolerate them (208). The left's use of trigger warnings does the precise opposite of this. Furthermore, by presenting something has harmful, it becomes a self-fulfilling prophecy. Trauma debriefing is one example which proved this principle. Trauma debriefing was a type of talking therapy given immediately after a major traumatic event. Such as a natural disaster or a terrorist attack. It was intended to reduce the rates of PTSD in survivors of such events. However, multiple studies found that people given trauma debriefing were actually more likely to develop PTSD than those who didn't receive the therapy (6,209,210). It has been proposed that the therapy pre-empts PTSD. A person is told they have experienced trauma and will take time to recover. And so, they respond by feeling traumatized (211). It has never been studied, but something similar could occur with trigger warnings. Finally, if a person is constantly protected from things that might upset them, they will never develop the resilience to cope. The political commentator Van Jones compares confronting ideas you disagree with to lifting weights at the gym. If there were no weights in the gym, it would be easier, but you wouldn't get stronger (212). Although Van Jones was talking about university when he made these remarks, it's true for life in general. It's the challenge that strengthens us. But social justice warriors have not learned that it's possible to cope with difficult things.

Emotional Blackmail

A further manifestation of the social justice warrior's fixation with emotions and mental health is the rise of emotional blackmail. Emotional blackmail has become frighteningly common in left-wing spaces. Many social justice warriors make threats of suicide and self-harm in response to political events. They also do this when they feel invalidated.

Threatening Self-Harm

Threatening suicide has turned to the go-to response for many social justice warriors. However, social justice warriors encourage this by threatening suicide in response to political issues. You say something social justice warriors don't like; you are killing people. You are responsible for their suicide. It's basically a way of saying 'Agree with me or I'll kill myself'. An example of this from the UK, is where Owl Fisher, a trans-identified male and journalist, claimed that debating the validity of transgenderism was one of the reasons for high self-harm and suicide rates in trans-identified people (213).

Emotional blackmail is a very serious and alarming problem. It is well-known that suicide appears to spread. When a person kills themselves, there can be a cluster of similar suicides. This is described as suicide contagion (214). By using suicide as a threat, it could encourage others to take their own lives.

Cry Bullies

Interestingly, these people who will talk about how frightened and upset they are, are actually quite assertive. This manipulative behaviour has been termed 'cry-bullying'. A cry-bully is someone who is aggressive and rude to others. But they act like the victim when they are called out on their actions or when people retaliate (215). Often, when they are called out, they evoke their various minority identities as an explanation for their behaviour. For instance, they may cite unease over their sexuality, or their mental illness. At other times, they will completely overlook their own conduct and act as if any retaliation is completely unprovoked.

Fragile Minorities

Minority stress

Another more subtle form of emotional blackmail is claiming that certain ideas are causing 'minority stress'. Minority stress is a theory that the emotional difficulties associated with being a member of a marginalized group leads to poorer health. It's true that many minorities do experience worse health than the general population. For instance, in the UK, people who are not white have fewer life years without a serious health condition than white people (216). This disparity might be explained by discrimination. Experiencing discrimination might contribute to higher rates of mental illness, and engaging in harmful behaviours such as smoking, drug use and being obese. And these behaviours in term might explain the higher rates of long-term physical illnesses for ethnic minorities.

But the concept of minority stress is being used as a form of emotional blackmail to silence valid criticisms of identity politics. An example of this occurred in an article in *VICE* titled 'Biphobia Is Killing the 'B' in LGBTQ. Literally' (217). The article argues that people on the bisexual+ spectrum (defined as anyone who is attracted to "more than one gender") experience minority stress. This results in bisexuals having poorer health than either gay or straight people. The article cites studies showing higher rates of certain mental and physical health issues in bisexual people. But none of them actually show any reduced life expectancy for bisexual people. Furthermore, the article classes questioning the validity of bisexual+ orientations as biphobic. While bisexuality is real, as discussed in chapter three, there are reasons to doubt the existence of some sexual orientations. Particularly those where someone claims to be attracted to more than two genders, such as pansexuality. So, if you doubt that a person who has only ever been in heterosexual relationships is actually 'queer', you are killing that person. Or if you point out that you cannot be attracted to more than two genders because there are only two genders, you are killing bisexual people. Of course, this is an exaggeration to say the least.

The problem with any form of emotional blackmail is that it derails logical debates. If someone is talking about hurting themselves, it doesn't convince you of their argument. It merely stops people talking about the topic for a short while. Generally, we don't take very emotional people seriously. We assume their thoughts and feelings reflect their emotional state rather than reality. By saying 'we mustn't discuss this topic because it could make people suicidal', it implies that marginalized people are mentally unstable. It shows that marginalized people aren't capable of handling debates and discussions. If anything, it provides evidence that marginalized people are irrational or unstable.

Intergenerational Trauma

Another popular concept in the social justice warrior movement is intergenerational trauma. This is the idea that trauma can be passed down through the generations. It is said to occur through a combination of learned behaviours from older generations, and from epigenetics. Epigenetics are changes to the way a gene is expressed-the gene itself doesn't change, but it is 'turned on' or 'turned off'. These changes can occur in response to environmental factors, such as diet and smoking (218).

The theory of intergenerational trauma is that the genes change in response to traumatic events. These changes are passed on to a person's offspring. Therefore, a person can experience PTSD-type symptoms from trauma that they never experienced. For example, the great great grandchild of a slave might be traumatized by discussing slavery, even though they themselves have never been enslaved. The purported solution to this is to be aware of triggering people who may have ancestors who experienced trauma. For example, white people should consider the 'safety' of black people who experience intergenerational trauma (219). However, the scientific evidence for the existence of intergenerational trauma is weak. Many scientists say that the concept of intergenerational trauma is implausible. They argue that insignificant findings have been overblown to exaggerate the effect of trauma on RNA (220). Therefore, intergenerational trauma almost certainly doesn't exist. In addition, every family has experience trauma at some point in their history. If intergenerational trauma were real, wouldn't everyone have intergenerational trauma? Nonetheless, this insane theory is part of the reasoning behind using trigger warnings for oppression.

A related concept that people are traumatized by things that happen to other members of their marginalized people. For instance, that black people were traumatized by death of George Floyd. Even if they neither knew him nor witnessed the events first hand (221). His death was upsetting. But to say you were traumatized by something you weren't personally involved with sounds melodramatic. It is also unhelpful for those who were involved first hand.

Is telling people they are affected by trauma from earlier generations or to other people actually helpful? Because something bad has happened to your ancestors, you're damaged goods, who can't cope with as much as white people can? It's treating every ethnic minority as if they are mentally ill. Of course, most black people are not mentally ill- being black is not a sickness. Even if they were, treatment for mental illness focuses on resilience and learning to cope, not having the world adapt to you.

Call-out Culture: Mental Health and Kindness Matter, Except When They Don't.

Don't make the mistake of thinking this concern about mental health extends to anyone outside the social justice warrior movement. Nagle points out that vulnerability and humility are cornerstones of the liberal-left ideology. But at the same time, these people can be incredibly vicious (1). Tactics such as mass blocking on social media and public shaming are often employed by the social justice warrior movement. The movement also shows pleasure when bad things happen to people they disagree with. An example that Nagle recounts is the suicide of the academic Mark Fisher, who was a left-winger with a negative view of identity politics. His death was celebrated by social justice warriors, even though they purport to care about kindness and good mental health. Nagle also describes how the social justice warrior movement hold purges, where people are banished from the left. And they throw baseless accusations at other lefties to secure their own place in the social justice warrior movement. Which they did with Fisher. He was accused of transphobia, even though nobody could identify what Fisher had done or said that was transphobic. They'd rather argue with other left-wingers instead of going after actual bigots.

Another facet of the social justice warrior movement is call-out culture. Call-out culture is when a member of the public who has done something offensive or upsetting is 'called-out'. The reason their behaviour is discriminatory is pointed out on social media and the person is publicly shamed. The frightening thing is that the victims of call-out culture generally aren't trying to court publicity. They are ordinary people who find themselves the target of public scorn. Which is something that wouldn't have happened before the internet. suddenly becoming notorious across the world for something trivial is terrible for someone's mental health. It certainly isn't kind or tolerant. Or any of the other values social justice warriors purport to believe in.

'Permit Patty', a white woman whose real name is Alison Ettel, was one victim of call-out culture. Ettel was at work while a black girl and her mother were selling water outside her office. Ettel went out of her office and asked the girl if she had a permit, which she did not. She then appeared to phone the police to report the girl for "illegally selling water". Ettel says she was only pretending to call the police, and her issue was that the girl was noisy and distracting her from her work (222). A video of this went viral. The child's mother even implied that the police might have killed her daughter. As a result of the outcry, Ettel was forced to resign from her job. A similar case was that of 'BBQ Becky'. Environmental scientist Jennifer Schulte, who was also a white woman, phoned the police to a group of black men. They were having a barbeque in a park, where it was illegal to do so (223). This was in Oakland, California, which has a history of wildfires (224). Something which Schulte's job would have almost certainly made her aware of. Like with Ettel, a video of her calling the police went viral.

Perhaps Ettel's actions were disproportionate, and she could have resolved the situation differently. However, in Schulte's case, she had a good reason to be concerned. If the fire had gotten out of control, it could have done considerable harm to both the environment and to local people in the area. Nobody ever thinks their barbeque will be the one to cause the big fire. Until it is. She had already spoken with them and they refused to stop barbequing. It's possible that there was an element of racism in her actions. But at the same time, they were breaking the law and it's hard to believe that a person can be shamed for doing what most people would regard as their civic duty. In any case, did either of them deserve the level of vitriol they received? They are now infamous across the world for their relatively trivial actions. Furthermore, misogyny is a factor in call-out culture. There have been many examples of women being called out for racism, but far fewer examples of men. Does that mean men are less racist? Or is it that women are an easier target and are they being held to a higher standard than men? Also, for a group of people who claim to be so caring, they can be incredibly vicious. Does the mental health and wellbeing of these women not matter? What must it have done to them? Their lives are ruined. What happened to them was greatly disproportionate to what they did.

Overall, social justice warriors have been taught to be weak and fragile. That has become a huge part of their politics Furthermore, they confuse their political ideology with mental illness. Which benefits nobody. The social justice warrior movement's remedies for mental illness aren't much help either. They are based on ideology rather than scientific evidence. It's time to depoliticize mental health. Meanwhile, the left must stop fetishizing weakness and learn how to fight again.

6. Speech, Language and Violence in The Social Justice Warrior Movement

A further major idea in the social justice warrior movement is that words create many forms of oppression. In some cases, this use of language is even regarded as a form of violence. This chapter will examine the way the social justice warrior movement polices speech and language. It will also look at how the movement conflates speech with violence. This chapter will look at why this is. It will also assess the implications of the social justice warrior's views for free speech.

The focus on speech and language in defeating oppression originates from postmodernism. A big part of postmodernism is looking at the way that language is used to construct the social world. Jacques Derrida, another postmodernist philosopher, introduced the idea that language can be violent. He claimed that writing itself is especially violent as it is ethnocentric. Ethnocentric means to treat western culture as superior to other cultures. Furthermore, he says that language is used to create social hierarchies (225). Another argument Derrida makes is that language creates The Other. The Other refers to oppressed people. They are called The Other because they are considered different to the rest of society. Words and spoken expressions create The Other by forming certain associations. For instance, by saying the phrase 'it was a dark day for all of us', a person is re-enforcing racism, by linking the concept of darkness- like dark skin- with negativity. That means that when a person says something that could be construed as offensive, the very utterance causes inequality. However, it is difficult to prove if everyday figures of speech or other uses of language actually do promote inequalities. Language matters. But the idea that language is the cause of oppression is a hugely over-simplistic explanation for a very complex problem. While it's difficult to establish how much or how little power language has, there are more concrete ways of achieving a more equitable society than policing speech. Thus, it's unlikely that language is as powerful in constructing inequalities as Derrida claims.

The Language Police

Weak solutions have always been a problem with liberalism. Controlling language is their current focus. It has been part of identity politics for a long time. Many readers will recall the age of political correctness in the 1980s and 1990s. Admittedly, some examples of political correctness were urban myths, such as the Winterval controversy in the UK. In the late 1990s, many newspapers claimed that Birmingham City Council had banned the word Christmas. Instead they made people call it Winterval. But this isn't true. Actually, the term Winterval was created by the council for promotional materials for various events in the city during winter. This included celebrations for Halloween, Guy Fawkes' Night and Christmas. It wasn't replacing Christmas. It was a brand name for all the various winter festivals (226). So, you can't always believe everything you see about political correctness.

Other things dismissed as 'political correctness' were actually quite offensive. It's right that some words are not used any more. They reflect outdated beliefs and attitudes. An example of this is the term 'Mongoloid' to describe people with Down Syndrome. It was based on the idea that other ethnic groups were less intelligent than white people. John Langdon Down, the man who discovered Down's Syndrome, observed that some residents of a psychiatric institute for people with intellectual disabilities had features that were commonly found in people from east Asia. Especially epicanthic folds on the eyes. Epicanthic folds are small pieces of skin that cover the inner corner of the eye, giving it an almond shape (227). He theorized that a form of reverse evolution had took place, leading to white parents giving birth to Mongolian children (228). At the time, this idea was accepted. However, we now understand that the concept of Mongolism is not only racist and ableist, but also scientifically incorrect. It has now been proven that Down Syndrome is caused by a duplication of the trisomy 21 gene. It has nothing to do with race. Nor is there any evidence that people from East Asia are less intelligent than white people, or any other ethnic group. Also, the country of Mongolia and the term Mongolian are still used in everyday speech. Therefore, it is right that the term Mongolism is no longer used in a medical context. Indeed, there's no denying that words can be offensive.

At the same time, words change. Words can come to mean something completely different. Even in the social justice warrior world, the meanings of some words change. One example is the word 'queer'. For many years, queer meant strange. If you're from the UK, you might remember reading the Enid Blyton books as a child, where queer was often used in this context. Phrases such as "he looked rather queer" or "she was acting queerly" were frequently used. And for many years, using the word queer to describe someone who was gay was regarded as homophobic. The gay community then reclaimed the word. Now, social justice warriors embrace the term and proudly describe themselves as queer.

This is true of many other words too. For instance, 'idiot' used to be a diagnostic term. The term has not been used in a medical context for many years (the phrase was initially superseded by profound mental retardation. Then, profound learning disability in the UK. Now, the term profound intellectual disability is preferred). Today, we use idiot as a mild insult for someone acting ridiculously. Many people probably aren't aware that idiot used to be a medical term. The same is true of many other common insults including moron, cretin, imbecile, stupid and crazy. All of these were once used as medical terms.

But social justice warriors say that we mustn't use idiot as an insult. An article published in *Everyday Feminism* argues that these everyday insults were ableist (229). It's right not to use idiot as a medical diagnosis. But like with queer, the meaning of idiot has changed. As well, we have to be realistic about our priorities. There are better ways to help marginalized people. If we stopped calling people idiots, would life get any better for people with intellectual disabilities? Probably not. What would improve life is better public services for people with intellectual disability. Things like better social care provision, special education, anti-discrimination laws, and a stronger social security system. Providing all of those is an achievable goal.

It's not just disability-related words that are being classed as offensive. Many phrases are now being deemed racist too. Twitter banned common computer terms such as 'blacklist', 'grandfathered' and 'dummy variable' from internal documents, as they could be offensive to black people (230). 'Hard worker' is another term that is now racist. On the *MSNBC* news channel, presenter Mellissa Harris-Perry told conservative pundit Alfonso Aguilar not to describe former Representative Paul Ryan as a hard worker. When Aguilar said this phrase, she interrupted him and said, "I just want to pause on one thing, because I don't disagree with you that I actually think Mr Ryan is a great choice for this role, but I want us to be super careful when we use the language 'hard worker.' Because I actually keep an image of folks working in cotton fields on my office wall, because it is a reminder about what hard work looks like" (231). The trouble is, so many words and phrases could be loosely linked with slavery. There are many kinds of hard work. It's extreme to say we shouldn't use the phrase 'hard worker' because the slaves worked hard.

Another case of a word being deemed offensive because it could be reminiscent of slavery is the word 'master'. Harvard University stopped referring to staff as masters for this reason. For example, the job title for the role of house master was changed to faculty dean (232). As well, there have been calls for the Master's golf tournament to be renamed for this reason (233). Furthermore, the phrase 'master bedroom' deemed racist because, according to *CNN*, it evokes the history of plantations and slavery. Even though the term wasn't used until 1926, after slavery had been abolished (234). But master isn't just a slavery-related word. Master has been used for many years and in many contexts, to mean the biggest, best or main one. For instance, we speak of the master copy (meaning the original copy), a master's degree, or mastering a skill. Moreover, it's not realistic to purge the English language of any word that is tenuously related to slavery.

Trying to find ways in which every word is tainted is not helpful for solving inequalities. Even if these words really were upsetting, aren't there bigger issues to fight? There are more offensive words than these everyday expressions. And there are people who are outright bigots. Also, fixating on everyday language can stop people taking more serious action. If someone thinks that all they need to do to fix racism is to stop saying 'master' or 'hard worker', are they going to be prepared to spend time fighting for more serious action? These tokenistic efforts require a lot of work with very little results. It would be better for people to focus on activism that could produce tangible outcomes. Such as attending demonstrations and writing to government representatives to influence policy.

New Social Justice Warrior Words

Social justice warriors are also fond of creating new words and expressions to replace words previously regarded as unoffensive. As I wrote in my previous book, there are many new social justice warrior words about gender and sex. Most of which are intended to replace the word 'woman'. Examples include 'menstruator', 'person with a cervix' and 'pregnant person' (73,235,236). These terms are intended to avoid upsetting transgender people. For instance, 'menstruator' is meant to avoid offending trans-identified females who menstruate. It's also intended to avoid making trans-identified males feel left out of womanhood. Even though they are offensive to women by reducing them to their reproductive organs and bodily functions. Creating new terminology to replace inoffensive words is done with other things too.

BIPOC is another new social justice warrior term. It stands for Black and Indigenous People of Colour, replacing the term People of Colour (PoC). It is intended to represent that black and indigenous people have special struggles separate from other people of colour. According to an article in the *New York Times*, this is more inclusive than PoC (237). Although, aren't black and Indigenous people already included in the term PoC? And by separating black and Indigenous people from other ethnic minorities, isn't this less inclusive? Oddly, BIPOC is used in Britain, where white people are indigenous. One case of this was an article published by the UK Collaborative on Development Research, which refers to "BIPOC communities in the UK" (238). It shows how woke terminology is used without much thought into what it means.

This new vocabulary has a special purpose in the social justice warrior movement. Writing in *Tablet* magazine, journalist Nicholas Clairmont argues that woke language is used to obfuscate woke ideas. Like with postmodernism, it is intended to prevent ordinary people from joining the woke elite. It limits wokeness to those who are well-educated. The average person can't understand what social justice warriors mean, so they can't join with the movement. But it lets arrogant social justice warriors dismiss people who don't understand their terminology as ignorant. As with postmodernism, it also hides that what social justice warriors say is actually nonsense (239).

As well, the social justice warrior's fixation with language is about holding power and control over others. Correcting someone is a way of making yourself feel superior to others. There's a concept of the language bully- a person who corrects other people's speech and grammar to feel superior to others (240). When someone stops you and tells you to use the 'correct' word, it can make you feel embarrassed and insecure. And that makes the person correcting you feel powerful. As well, we all hate being interrupted. It stops you in your flow. When social justice warriors do it, it's meant to be upsetting. It's a way of making it more difficult to communicate your thoughts. If the words aren't allowed anymore, you can't say what you think. This difficulty communicating leads to misunderstandings. And the social justice warriors would gladly exploit any misunderstandings to make you look bad. It also pushes the focus onto the words you use rather than the point you make. It's another way of making people look bad. When someone makes a fuss over correcting a phrase, people remember the 'bad' words the speaker said rather than the sentiment they were trying to express. It's a subtle way of undermining people when you don't have any solid arguments.

The X Factor

The way words are spelt can also be oppressive. There has been a trend for replacing letters in words with the letter X to make a word more inclusive. The most commonly used example of this is Latinx. Latinx is a gender-neutral form of Latino. Compared to other examples, this makes some sense. Spanish is a gendered language. Words that end in 'o' are in their male form, whereas words ending in 'a' are female. If you were talking about a Hispanic woman or a group of Hispanic women, they are Latinas. But if you were talking about a Hispanic man or a group comprising of Hispanic men or of both men and women, they would be described as Latinos. Latinx is an attempt to remove the gender from the word. Although this word is widely used by social justice warriors, a survey by the Pew Research Center found that only three percent of Latinos actually use Latinx (241). There is a similar trend with other letters and symbols. For instance, the academic discipline Chicano studies is increasingly written as Chican@ studies (71). As I wrote in my previous book, a similar thing has happened with the word womxn. This is supposedly more inclusive than woman because the X signifies the inclusion of trans-identified males and ethnic minority women (73,242).

However, this trend has spread to other words. Even when there wasn't a gendered element to them in the first place. Folks is said to be more inclusive than other ways of greeting a large group of people. It is gender neutral, unlike other greetings, such as 'guys', which arguably means men only. But now folks isn't inclusive enough. Instead, it should now be spelt as 'folx'. According to the website For Folx Sake, spelling folks with an x, "...signals to the reader that the writer means to include people of colour, queer people, and other marginalized groups that tend to be excluded or ignored" (243).

The website goes on to claim that because gender-critical feminists use the word 'folks', it is now exclusionary. How and why does it do that? Many people across the political spectrum use the word folks. It doesn't belong to anyone. Gender-critical feminists use almost every other word of the English language too. Are those words now tainted? And are the letters K and S now oppressive? By saying 'folks' is exclusionary, it makes it be so. By turning something benign into a problem, it is inventing new ways of accusing people of oppression. Now, if someone writes folks instead of folx, they're a covert bigot. In practice, folk means whoever you want it to be about. Many people refer to their family as their folks. As in 'I'm going to stay with my folks during the holidays'. Like many words, folks takes on different meanings in different contexts. If someone addresses an email to everyone at work and uses the word folks, they presumably mean everyone in the workplace, including ethnic minority and gay, lesbian and bisexual members of staff. How folks is spelt doesn't change that. Folks is no more inclusionary or exclusionary than folx.

More to the point, how will calling women as 'womxn', or spelling folks as 'folx' solve oppression? Society isn't divided because of how these words are spelt. And changing the spelling of a word won't make it more inclusive. It's a very tokenistic measure. A person could write about 'folx' and fail to include marginalized groups by only writing about white, heterosexual, non-disabled, male experiences. Conversely, a writer could go to great lengths to ensure issues relating to marginalized groups are covered, but not spell folks with an X. But which text is more inclusive?

Censorship

As speech supposedly can now be deeply harmful, censorship has become more commonplace.

No platforming at universities is happening more than ever. In the past, this was only done for speakers with very extreme views. But now, not explicitly supporting social justice warrior values is enough justification to no-platform someone. In the UK, feminist comedian Kate Smurfwait was no-platformed from performing her stand-up routine at Goldsmiths University. The reason for this was that she does not support the full decriminalization of sex work. The student union described her views as "whorephobic". But she wasn't even planning to discuss sex work (244). Right-wing speakers have also been banned from many universities. The Canadian psychologist Jordan Peterson had his visiting professorship at Cambridge University revoked because of his stance on transgenderism. Peterson disagrees with many elements of transgenderism, including using a transgender person's preferred pronouns (245).

As well, student unions have banned certain student societies because of their political beliefs. Pro-life societies have been banned or prevented from forming at multiple universities. These include Birmingham, Nottingham, Glasgow and Aberdeen (246). Birmingham University student's union said they banned the pro-life society because the pro-life movement is misogynistic. They also said the society's existence was threatening the safety of students (247). However, these bans were later overturned for legal reasons.

It's not just in the UK where censorship is an issue. In the USA, censorship is becoming a problem too. The former *Time* magazine editor Richard Stengel, who later worked as the State Department's undersecretary for public diplomacy and public affairs during the Obama presidency, argues that the US should have hate speech laws. He claims that the first amendment of the US constitution, which guarantees free speech, doesn't protect hate speech. Stengel says that burning the Qur'an or inciting violence both constitute hate speech (248). But the big issue with all forms of censorship, including hate speech laws is that one person's hate speech is another's fair point. Everyone thinks they are right and when they censor something, it's for the best.

It's also difficult to determine what constitutes discriminatory speech. What is racism? What is sexism? What is homophobia? What is ableism? These all sound like simple questions. But they're not easy to answer. Most people don't regard themselves as racist, sexist, homophobic or ableist. But people are. Furthermore, what is hate speech? Most definitions of hate speech are based on the view that speech can be harmful. But harmful to who? For example, is blasphemy hate speech? A Christian might argue that blasphemy is sinful. And so, hearing blasphemous words encourages others to be sinful, which could harm a person by leading them to an eternity in hell. Therefore, blasphemy could fall under the remit of hate speech. Of course, people who aren't followers of Christianity would disagree. Furthermore, hate speech laws could be used to suppress political opposition. Is criticizing the president hate speech? A sensitive president might say that criticizing them is damaging to the country because it makes it harder for them to do their job. Hence, criticizing the president could also be construed as hate speech. There are endless ways that something could be interpreted as hate speech. And left-wing hate speech laws could easily be turned against us.

The other big problem with censorship is: what is it that social justice warriors so desperately need to hide? When you challenge social justice warrior ideology, you'll often either get a defensive response such as 'I don't have to explain it to you' or 'why don't you Google it ?' Alternatively, you get blocked, no-platformed or censored. They don't like it when you question them. Often, they declare things aren't up for debate. Why are they so defensive? Social justice warriors argue that ordinary people aren't capable of understanding these concepts. Therefore, it's not worth discussing it with them. Or that explaining difficult things is 'triggering' for minorities, so they shouldn't be burdened with this task. The truth is that their ideology can't stand up to rigorous analysis. If what social justice warriors say gets questioned, their arguments fall apart because there is no actual logic or evidence to support it. When something genuinely isn't up for debate, there is simply nothing to debate. Any attempt to debate would immediately fall flat. There is no valid counterargument or controversy. And there is nothing that can show the position to be untrue. Things don't get beyond debate because people refuse to debate it. They get beyond debate because any counterarguments are discredited.

Also, by fighting censorship, we got to where we are now. We have an open democracy, where we a free to criticize our leaders, religion and all other institutions and views. The world we live in isn't perfect, but it's better than the past. For many years in England, it was illegal to criticize the sitting monarch. Technically, it's still illegal to call for the abolition of the monarchy. Although nobody has been prosecuted for this since 1879 (249). In more recent times, being gay used to be censored. There have been protests against allowing gay people on television in case it 'promotes' homosexuality. The UK had section 28, which prohibited discussions of homosexuality in schools (250). Homosexuality was censored in the media too. In 1989, the soap opera EastEnders featured the first gay kiss on British television. After this aired, the programme sparked outrage. There were questions in Parliament about the appropriateness of showing a gay couple on television (251). These examples show the dangers of limiting speech, as well as the benefits of free speech.

Cancel Culture

Another way of restricting free speech is via cancel culture. Cancel culture refers to the social justice warrior's propensity to 'cancel' public figures. A high-profile celebrity is 'cancelled' if they say something that social justice warriors disagree with. That person is blocked en masse on social media. Their products might also be boycotted, and other media engagements may be called off. Often, fairly innocuous things can get a person cancelled.

One high profile victim of cancel culture is JK Rowling, the author of the Harry Potter children's book series. Rowling was loved by the left for many years for her story of overcoming poverty with the help of the welfare state. But she is now regarded as evil because she doesn't agree with some aspects of the transgender rights movement. This means she is a wicked person who wants to hurt transgender people, and everything she has ever been associated with is now tainted (252). Former fans of the Harry Potter series report crying and feeling distraught over her views. Many people are now burning her books and Harry Potter DVDs in protest (253). More bizarrely, people are now claiming that Daniel Radcliffe, the actor who played Harry Potter in the film series, wrote the books (254). What makes this statement particularly outlandish is that Radcliffe was just eight years old when the first book was published. This inability to tolerate dissenting views results from black and white thinking: 'you're either with us or against us'. The journalist James Kirkup describes this as the Twitterization of society (255). In this case, Rowling is 'against us', regardless of her progressive views.

The problem with cancel culture isn't limited to free speech. It stops people from thinking critically. Social justice warriors can't imagine why someone doesn't think the same way that they do. So, it comes as a huge shock when people disagree with them. It leads to the social warriors being unable to put things into context. They find disagreement truly devastating. They have never learned to accept dissenting opinions. Which is why they have such a simplistic view of the world.

The root of this obsession with limiting speech is the idea that speech can be harmful- something that the next section will explore.

'Violence'

Do you remember the saying 'sticks and stones may break my bones, but words will never hurt me'? The social justice warriors think the opposite of that. Physical violence against people they don't like is fine. But there are numerous other types of 'violence' that are non-physical. These include various forms of language. Although, like many social justice warrior terms, these concepts are poorly defined, and so it is difficult to explain them. Some examples of metaphorical violence include:

- Administrative violence: Where the legal system creates inequalities. An example of this is not allowing people to change their sex to gender-neutral or to the opposite gender on government documents (256).

- Structural violence: where social structures create inequality, such as the unequal distribution of physical resources and power (257).

- Cultural violence: where culture is used to justify structural violence. For example, using religion to justify racism and sexism (258).

- Discursive violence: attacking or dismissing someone's experience of oppression or other form of victimization (259).

Not using someone's preferred gender pronouns is also violence. After an article was published in *Scientific American* that proposed the abolition of gender pronouns (260), a group of activists responded that this would be a form of violence against nonbinary people (261). In other words, not explicitly recognizing that nonbinary people are special and must be called different pronouns from the rest of us is violent.

Another common form of metaphorical violence is the idea that something is threatening the 'right to exist'. For example, Chelsea Manning, (the transgender whistle blower who used to be known as Bradley Manning) says that not allowing a trans-identified person to choose their own gender in legal documents is denying their 'right to exist' (262). This is melodramatic to say the least. Nobody is stopping transgender people from existing. It's not as if there is a plan to wipe out transgender people.

Describing supposed discrimination as 'genocide' is also prevalent within the social justice warrior movement. For instance, a potential pre-natal test for Autism has been described as genocide (263). As has encouraging obese people to lose weight (264). Neither of these things are genocide. In the case of the Autism test, an unborn baby is not a person. And Autism is a disability, not an ethnic group. We don't describe prenatal diagnosis of other disabilities as genocide. And as for obesity, losing weight wouldn't kill someone. On the contrary, it would help them to live longer. Obese people aren't an ethnic group either.

So why is speech considered violent? Amongst social justice warriors, there's a belief that emotional harm is the same as physical harm. An example of this thinking was in the psychologist Lisa Barrett's *New York Times* op-ed. She argues that speech can be violence because it can cause physical harm to the body. Barrett claims that hearing hurtful things on a regular basis induces chronic stress. This stress causes many major physical health issues, including inflammation, brain cell death and reduced life expectancy. Therefore, restricting freedom of speech is permissible to prevent this stress (265).

Barrett cites several studies, none of which directly prove what she asserts. She cites two animal studies in her article. One paper is on the effect of stress on rat's brains, and another on life expectancy of baboons. She also cites an article on adverse family experiences and levels of inflammation in teenagers. None of these relate to the premise of the article. The only study she cites that directly relates to the topic is a study on the effect of verbal abuse on young adult's brains (266).

These studies weaken Barrett's argument considerably. For instance, the study on baboons looked at the impact of difficult life circumstances in youth on the baboon's life expectancy (267). Some of these circumstances were physical issues, such as there being a drought in the first year of the baboon's life. Others were things that might contribute to such problems. For instance, being part of a dense group, which increases competition for food. Others were major emotional upheavals, such as the death of the baboon's mother or having a sibling born in close proximity to their own birth. The study doesn't distinguish between these types of circumstances. So, it could be that the baboons died sooner because of issues arising from poor physical health in early life, rather than emotional stress.

Secondly, stress is a relative term. For example, maternal loss was the highest correlated factor with early death. Losing a parent is a major upheaval. For a human child, losing a parent would have a devastating impact on them. They have lost the person they rely on for their material needs, and the emotional support the parent provides. It would affect them for their whole life. The same might be true for the baboons. On the other hand, an adult seeing an offensive post on social media isn't being subject to anything nearly as traumatic. The two things are not comparable. Also, the early mortality in the baboons could be explained by other reasons. For instance, couldn't the mother have had a genetic disorder or other genetic predisposition to illness that she passed to her offspring? If she died young because she was born with a genetic illness, her progeny might have died young for the same reason.

Furthermore, with both the baboons and humans, adults aren't children. A child can't cope with as much as an adult. Childhood experiences influence a person for their whole life and affect their ability to cope with stress and how they see the world. A bad childhood often leads to a bad adulthood. Thus, the trauma the young baboons experienced is not the same as an adult hearing something offensive. Nonetheless, Barrett's theories have been widely adopted as justification for restricting freedom of expression.

Paradoxically, physical attacks are fine by social justice warriors. Consequently, there have been many violent protests and cases of people being physically attacked for their political views. In the UK, Tara Wolf, a trans-identified male, punched Maria MacLachlan, a 60-year-old gender critical feminist. MacLachlan was speaking about the dangers of transgenderism at Speaker's Corner in Hyde Park in London when she was punched (268). In the USA, a Democrat supporter attacked a 15-year old Republican campaigner in New Hampshire in 2020 (269). Another person attacked a man wearing a Make America Great Again-style "Make Fifty Great Again" cap on his birthday (270). Indeed, in the past decade, there have been a string of riots, including in Minnesota after George Floyd's death (271). These riots spread to 30 other cities (272). There were further riots in Kenosha, Wisconsin, after the shooting of Jacob Blake (273). None of these attacks could be justified. None of the people were directly harming others.

In some cases, protesters feel they have a duty to act violently towards someone they disagree with. Recall Marcuse's work from the introduction, where he said that peaceful protest was complicit with oppression (38). In other words, that people have a duty to protest violently. That's the rationale for violent protests. This view is taken by Antifa and other left-wing groups who engage in violent protest (274). Even if you accept the premise that certain views are harmful, two wrongs don't make a right.

As well, according to historian and gay rights activist Sarah Schulman, a trend has emerged for people to perceive conflict as abusive. This results in one party overstating the harm done by the conflict and this exaggeration is used to justify violence (275). As this chapter has shown, the left constantly accuses people of violence or killing those they don't agree with. This is an example of overstatement of harm. And in turn, that makes physical violence feel justified. Lukianoff and Haidt make a similar point that equating words with violence has made physical violence against the perpetrators of metaphorical forms of violence more acceptable (182).

The other problem with turning violence into a metaphorical concept is that if you accuse everyone of violence, people automatically switch off when genuine harm is occurring. If we hear someone talking of genocide, we don't know if they actually mean genocide (people being killed on a large scale because of their ethnicity) or if they mean something much less serious. Also, sticks and stones do break bones. People are being seriously hurt in violent attacks that are vastly disproportionate to anything they have done or said.

Cultural Appropriation

A further form of metaphorical violence is cultural appropriation. Cultural appropriation is the idea that things such as music and clothing can be stolen from other cultures. A prominent example of this was when socialite Kylie Jenner wore her hair in cornrows. This was regarded as cultural appropriation from the African American community (276). Food is another area where people are often accused of cultural appropriation. In the USA, Oberlin College's cafeteria was accused of cultural appropriation for serving 'inauthentic' food from other cultures (277). This resulted in protests from the student body (278). According to social justice warriors, using creations from other cultures is only acceptable if the culture in question gives permission and is credited. Also, a dominant culture can't be stolen from (279,280). So, an

Indian person wearing jeans isn't the same as a white person wearing a sari. The trouble with cultural appropriation is, who owns a culture? You can't exactly ask a culture if something is okay. Also, cultures borrow from each other all the time. So, it's hard to say where an idea really originates from.

Micro-Aggressions

Micro-aggressions are another form of metaphorical violence. The term 'micro-aggression' was coined in the 1970s by Chester M. Peirce, a professor of psychiatry. This phrase originally described subtle racist behaviours (281). The term has since been expanded to other minority groups, such as lesbian and gay people and the disabled. Micro-aggressions are generally quite trivial. Examples of micro-aggressions include mispronouncing the name of someone with a non-English name (282), asking 'where are you from?', interrupting people when speaking, confusing people's names and referring to a person as 'crazy' (283). The supposed solution to micro-aggressions is to call them out, by publicly pointing out when someone has committed one (284). However, evidence shows that most minorities aren't offended by micro-aggressions (285). It seems micro-aggressions are too micro for even the people they affect to care about.

Admittedly, some of these micro-aggressions are rude. For instance, touching a black person's hair out of curiosity. Touching someone's hair who you aren't close with or for no other good reason is insensitive. It's understandable that black people are upset when people

138

do this. However, other types of micro-aggression, such as mispronouncing a person's name, are simple mistakes. People generally try their best to not make mistakes. Nobody likes getting people's names mixed up or saying a name wrong. But nobody is perfect; we all make mistakes. If people are afraid of making a mistake around you, it will frighten them away. They will become afraid of talking to you because they think they might upset you.

Indeed, the problem with the concept of metaphorical violence as a whole is that it encourages a negative view of the world. Does someone making a speech or writing an article really want people to die? Probably not. But that's what social justice warriors think. Also, the concepts of micro-aggressions and cultural appropriation makes minorities paranoid by turning innocent comments and actions into covert discrimination. As Lukianoff and Haidt say, it's an example of what therapists describe as dichotomous thinking- one of the thought errors that CBT aims to fix. It's the kind of way a person with Depression or Anxiety might think. They often assume that a throwaway comment means something darker than the speaker intended (182). The idea of metaphorical violence teaches marginalized people that the world is quietly set against them and that small everyday actions represent a deep hatred of them. It tells people that they must think the worst of everyone. For instance, if someone compliments a person by saying they are very articulate, they could take the praise. Or they could assume it's a veiled insult in reference to their race, sex, disability, sexuality or gender identity, and be hurt by it. Marginalized groups are learning that everybody who doesn't explicitly support them hates them and wishes they were dead. They are being encouraged to perceive opposition to their cause as violence. And they react as if they were being physically threatened. This makes it difficult to discuss things in a calm and civil manner.

As a consequence, for other people, it creates a sense of 'walking on eggshells' around minorities. You are afraid of speaking in case you upset them with a well-meaning remark or a small mistake. It can feel as if you can't do right for doing wrong. This anxiety makes social interactions with oppressed people feel uncomfortable. It leads to people avoiding socializing with those from marginalized communities in case they unintentionally cause offense.

Overall, speech isn't violence. The only violence is physical violence. Yet social justice warrior craziness mixes up the two. If anything, they treat hurtful language as being worse than physical injuries. Also, the social justice warrior movement overstates the role of language in creating oppression. Language can be used to hurt, but the world isn't a piece of literature, where metaphors and other figures of speech convey some form of symbolism. Words don't need to wound.

7. Capitalism and the Social Justice Warriors

The left has traditionally been anti-capitalist. But not anymore. This chapter will explore the relationship between capitalism and the social justice warrior movement. It will examine how the social justice warrior movement results from the left's embrace of capitalism. And how this relationship is damaging the left.

Despite what they often claim, social justice warriors are liberals, not socialists. One of the key features of liberal ideology (as opposed to socialism) is supporting capitalism. It doesn't matter if only 10 people owned all the wealth in the world. Just as long as they're not all straight, white, nondisabled, thin, cisgender men! On the other hand, socialists understand that capitalism is deeply problematic. Class inequality is a core component of capitalism. There is always someone at the bottom. The capitalist system can't exist without this. To socialists, this is unacceptable. But the social justice warrior movement does not question capitalism.

Woke Companies

Big business is the epitome of capitalism. So why is big business supporting woke causes that are ostensibly antithetical to their views?

The Influence of Woke Companies on Politics

Many large companies donate to organizations that promote woke causes. Google, Facebook, Apple, Amazon, Walmart, Ubisoft, Etsy, Spanx, Coca Cola and Peloton are some of the many companies who have donated to organizations allied to Black Lives Matter (286). Why do they do this? The answer is that companies that donate to left-wing causes can use this to excerpt control over an organization. This becomes a 'don't bite the hand that feeds situation', where the organization relies on such funding. Hence, they can't criticize a company or the wider capitalist system because they would lose the funding from the companies.

You can see this when you look at who donates to the Democrats and Democrat candidates. Some people who donated to Joe Biden's campaign in the Democratic primary include Eric Schmidt from Google and Aileen Roberts, the wife of Brian Roberts from Comcast. Biden also received many large donations from people whose wealth comes from hedge funds, finance and property. These include Judy Dimon, the wife of Jamie Dimon, from JPMorgan Chase (287). As a result, Biden and the Democrats are in the position that they can't do anything to upset these people if they were to win, because they would lose their financial support in the future. It also ensures that candidates sympathetic to big business win.

You can see how this influences the Democrat's policies. For example, when campaigning in the 2016 election, Hillary Clinton famously said:

"If we broke up the big banks tomorrow... would that end racism? ... Would that end sexism? Would that end discrimination against the LGBT community? Would that make people feel more welcoming to immigrants overnight?" (288)

This is a prime example of the Democrats pandering to big business. It also demonstrates how identity politics has displaced concerns over capitalism. The position of the social justice warriors is to leave big business as it is and focus on identity groups instead. Identity politics doesn't threaten big business. So big business accepts it. It's a tiny crumb toward social progress that they will tolerate if it prevents bigger social change that threatens these companies. By getting the Democrats to move their attention away from them and toward various other issues, the banks can continue operating without scrutiny. It quietens any talk of extra regulations or taxation and turns everyone's focus to more nebulous concerns. Regulating or breaking up the banks is a concrete policy idea. Solving discrimination isn't. What policies could Clinton have introduced that would have ended racism, sexism or discrimination against the LGBT community? These are social attitudes. And you can't legislate people into changing their attitudes.

This is a matter that will only get worse. After Trump's election win, the Democrats looked to its billionaire donors to steer them to victory in 2020. They held conferences and retreats looking at how to win the support of wealthy people (289). Which is why the Democrats are focusing on identity politics over economics and other policy areas. Biden has promised some modest tax rises for the wealthiest Americans and some new subsidies for college education and healthcare (290). These are good. But they will only have a miniscule impact on social inequalities.

Sadly, money is a big part of American politics. Campaigns are expensive. Hillary Clinton spent nearly $1.2 billion on her 2016 election campaign, while Trump spent almost $650 million (291). And a total of $14 billion was spent on campaigning in the 2020 election (this includes Congressional races and spending by Political Action Committees) (292). It's not easy to raise this kind of money. Which is why both the Republicans and Democrats rely on wealthy donors and candidates. That means they can't impose heavy restrictions on businesses or make other policies that might displease them. Unfortunately, the US government can't regulate campaign donations because of the 2010 Citizen's United ruling. In this case, the Supreme Court ruled that campaign donations were protected as free speech under the first amendment of the constitution. Therefore, they couldn't be restricted. Since that ruling, parties and candidates can raise unlimited amounts of money. This gives wealthy donors and organizations significant influence over political parties (293).

Woke Marketing

Woke advertising has become another facet of the social justice warrior movement. Companies are increasingly using identity politics issues in their promotional material. For example, Nike made an advert featuring the mixed-race American football player Colin Kaepernick. Kaepernick is notable for starting the trend of kneeling during the national anthem as a protest against racism. The advert featured many representations of diversity, such as disabled people and people from various ethnicities. Throughout the advert, Kaepernick talked about the importance of dreaming big. Kaepernick went on to launched Nike's 'True to 7' shoes that sold out within minutes of going on sale (seven is his jersey number) (294). This example shows that woke marketing sells. Would these shoes have sold so well if they weren't linked to the Black Lives Matter movement? Probably not.

It's not just racial issues that companies use in their marketing either. Gillette has made two high-profile advertisements with strong transgender themes. The first was a television advertisement showing a trans-identified female (a woman who lives as a man) being taught to shave by his father (295). Another online advertising campaign for Gillette Venus featured Jazz Jennings, a trans-identified male who is famous for transitioning as a toddler. This was a social media campaign called 'My Skin, My Way'. In this campaign, Jennings talks about how shaving her body hair validates her gender identity (296).

Sometimes, these companies make a direct connection between buying a certain product and social justice causes. A common example of this is purchasing products for self-care. Naturally, the woke companies have run with this concept and use it to sell their products. One instance of this was when CNN Underscored ran a feature on beauty products for self-care during the Coronavirus pandemic. The article opens with a section on the benefits of self-care for mental health (297). CNN Underscored is a marketing website that is owned by CNN. They receive revenue from purchases made from clicking links from the site (298). So, they are making money out of the current mental health fad. By framing beauty products as beneficial for mental health, they are turning these items from a luxury to an essential. Ordinarily, in a time when people are struggling financially, a woman might cut her spending on cosmetics so she can spend it on things she needs. But by making her feel that she needs to use these products for the good of her mental health, she is less likely to stop buying them.

Many companies also now support gay rights. When gay pride started, being gay was much more deeply stigmatized than it is today. Few people were openly gay. To hide their sexuality, many people married opposite sex partners. Now, gay pride has become big business. For example, a *Huffington Post* article was written encouraging people to spend money with a range of companies that have issued public statements of support for the LGBT community. These companies include Starbucks and Doritos (299). This isn't about genuine concern with gay rights, but with piggy-backing their products to a socially progressive cause. Which these companies have only started doing in the past few years, since homosexuality became socially acceptable. It's interesting how they never cared when homosexuality was stigmatized and supporting gay rights was truly radical.

Why do these companies use social issues to market their products? Couldn't it be simple kindness? No. As always, it's about the money. Companies spend a lot of time and money getting us to think positively about their brands and products. To sell their products, consumers need to associate their products with goodness. Woke advertising helps do that by saying 'look, we care about this cause'. Secondly, it's attention-grabbing. If we see a company featuring an advert with something we don't normally see or hear, such as a transgender person or a severely disabled person, we remember it. If it's something really attention grabbing, like Nike's Kaepernick advert, we might share it on social media or talk to friends and family about it. Third, it cancels out bad press. A company can be an environmental disaster, but hey, they support Black Lives Matter! They might make very unhealthy products, but it's fine to eat them because they are pro-feminism!

But surely, consumers are bright enough to see that this wokeness is a cynical marketing ploy? Not necessarily. Much of how we think about brands happens at a sub-conscious level. So, we might not think 'I will buy these Nike trainers because they ran an advert supporting Black Lives Matter'. But on a level we are not aware of, we think of Nike as being synonymous with goodness, and that gets us to buy their products.

If anything, buying these products exacerbates social inequalities. Nike use sweatshops to manufacture their products. Workers in their factories in Vietnam work for 48 hours a week and are paid less than a dollar an hour (300). They also work in poor conditions, including extreme heat. Sometimes the workers get so hot that they collapse at their machines (301). As well, Nike practices tax evasion. They syphon their profits to offshore tax havens and exploit various other mechanisms (302). As a company, Nike do not actually care much about social inequalities. Nor do many other large multi-national companies. In addition, buying things you don't need is bad for the environment. Consumer goods and services are responsible for 60% of global carbon emissions. There are carbon emissions for sourcing and transporting raw materials. As well as for making these products and transportation (303,304). There's nothing progressive about consumerism. The problem is that buying products where woke marketing is used to promote them will not help resolve social inequalities. All it helps is the company's profits.

Social Media, Social Justice Warriors and Capitalism

A further way in which capitalism impacts on the social justice warrior movement is through social media. In recent years, many ideas that are popular with social justice warriors have been formed on social media. Sites such as Tumblr, Twitter and Instagram have huge social justice warrior communities. As well, social media companies themselves are sympathetic to liberal causes. For instance, after the death of George Floyd, Twitter's own Twitter account @Twitter changed its bio (a short biography at the top of an account page) to #BlackTransLivesMatter and #BlackLivesMatter. It's clear what side of the culture wars they're on. But a bigger issue is that social media is not merely a platform for ideas. They pick and choose what we see. Companies make algorithms that show us the type of content they think we'd find appealing. They can ban and demonetize accounts of controversial people and remove offensive posts. These companies can use their platform to influence their users.

We've already explored why many large companies support woke causes. But why do social media companies in particular support social justice warrior causes? The answer is that the target market for social media is young, middle-class people. Politically, young people tend to be more left leaning than older people. This isn't a generational trend- it has gone on for many decades (305,306). The reason companies target this demographic is because of advertising. This is the main source of revenue for these companies (307,308). Young people are important to advertisers. As younger customers are more impressionable than older customers, they are always a target for advertisers. In addition, companies want to cultivate brand loyalty and create a life-long customer (309). Which is why young people matter so much to marketers. Advertisers also want to target people who are wealthy enough to buy their products, or will be soon, which is why university students and young graduates are often targeted. As well, people with a college degree are more likely to vote for the Democrats (310). As people with a degree tend to earn more than those who don't have a degree, this demographic is also targeted. Young, degree educated people bring advertisers to social media. So, it's in the company's interest to show they care about the causes that are important to their customers.

At the same time, if customers started using the platform to express anti-capitalist sentiments, and started voting for anti-capitalist candidates in elections, these companies would be in big trouble. Social media is big business. Facebook (who also owns WhatsApp, an app for sending text-like messages to friends and Instagram, an app for sharing images) is estimated to be worth over $700 billion (311). Reddit is worth $1.8 billion (312). And in 2019, Twitter's net income was $1.47 billion (308). But if these companies expressed right-wing sentiments, they could drive many of their customers away. So, how does a company look left-wing without actually being left-wing? The answer: they champion identity politics. That way customers feel that they are using a company that's aligned with their values, even when it isn't. Also, these companies have liberal tendencies. Their job applications include questions on social attitudes. People with the 'wrong' attitudes are not selected for jobs (7). This ensures all employees support the company's social views. This matters because these employees are responsible for moderating content and creating algorithms.

To keep customers on side, social media companies ban users and pages that question the dominant narrative. This is why Reddit banned pages such as El Chapo Trap House (a far-left discussion group), Gender Critical (a radical feminist group, who rejected transgenderism) and The Donald (a pro-Trump board) (313,314). Furthermore, Facebook banned a number of anti-capitalist groups, including It's Going Down and Crimethinc (315). If that doesn't prove that social media censors ideas they don't like, then nothing can.

So why does social media ban right-wingers? After all, they tend to be pro-business. A naïve interpretation is that big tech is doing this out of political sympathy with the Democrats and the left. That might be true to some extent. Especially when it comes to certain social issues. And some individual employees might be acting in this way for that reason. But there are other factors. The biggest reason is that this type of content is unpopular with customers and advertisers, which in turn hits their revenue. As we saw earlier in this chapter, companies spend a lot of effort making customers feel good about themselves. As these companies don't want their brands associated with 'bad' things, they won't advertise on platforms which allow this. Some companies are already boycotting certain social media sites over the content they host. Including Starbucks, Coca Cola and Honda, who are currently refusing to advertise on Facebook (316). The tech companies must pander to big business if they want their money.

As well, social media censors Trump supporters in particular as Trump, the billionaire conservative and (soon to be former) president in his 70s doesn't fit well with social media's target market. Nor do his middle-aged children. They want fun, young, attention-grabbing users. They want to be cool. Not to be the kind of site your dad or your grandad would use. And the Trump family is not a good fit for that image. So, letting conservatives on social media platforms is likely to attract users who aren't in the advertiser's preferred demographic. Another factor in social media's hatred of Trump supporters is that he is anti-free trade. If Trump had put tariffs on China during his presidency, this could have hit social media companies hard. Even if they don't currently have any operations in China, it could have jeopardized future expansion opportunities. Social media companies value freedom of movement too, which is a branch of free trade. Technology companies, including Google and Facebook, have lobbied the government to relax immigration restrictions (317). And if you look at the demographics of the technology industry, that's not surprising. In 2018, 70% of workers in Silicon Valley were born outside the USA (318). Trump's limits on immigration meant that these companies were deprived of a source of cheap labour. For that reason, they don't want him or other politicians who support restrictions on immigration to win elections. Or for anti-immigration sentiments to become more widely spread.

Furthermore, most people who use social media don't actually think that deeply into what they're doing or why they're doing it. Most people use social media for relaxation. They don't want to be seeing some deep, complex content that requires a lot of thought. They just want to see a simple, feel-good message that floats along with everything else in their feed. Even though such messages often over-simplify complex issues. This turns complicated topics into a simple case of good fighting evil. For instance, the controversy over transgenderism is framed like so: transgender people are trapped in the wrong body. Good people think that society should treat them as their chosen gender. Bad people make them live as their birth sex. These bad people are making transgender people so unhappy that it drives them to suicide. There is no reason why a person would disagree with transgenderism other than bigotry. Any dissenting voices must be silenced, in case transgender people are upset. A person presenting a contrasting view might be banned, blocked or told they are a bigot. Meanwhile, the average social media user can feel good for fighting transphobic bigots by supporting a company that is in favour of transgender rights. This way of presenting information is problematic. There is no attempt to understand the nuances of the issue. In the case of transgenderism, the fact that it is not scientifically possible to be born as the wrong sex is glossed over.

Furthermore, social media companies are concerned about 'bad guys' because they drive away customers and advertisers. These 'bad guys' include legitimate bad actors (such as spammers and people trying to harm others, who make it difficult to use the site). However, they are also concerned about various people with unpopular or 'hateful' beliefs. For instance, right-wingers, gender critical feminists and others who say controversial things. These are damaging to a social media platform's young, liberal user base. So, these controversial people have to go.

Therefore, it is in the social media company's interests to promote ideas that are favourable to their company, palatable to advertisers and satisfying to their users. To achieve that, views that don't fit those criteria are hidden away. Identity politics is a perfect fit for social media. It makes them look caring, but it doesn't question capitalism, which would put these businesses under threat. And social media plays a huge role in influencing people. Which is why identity politics has become so popular with social media users.

Left-wing Media

A further manifestation of capitalism's hold over the left is the way that left-wing media has embraced identity politics. Like social media, the left-wing media more generally has also become woke. A typical example of a top story on a website like *VICE* or *Bustle* could be '50 examples of white privilege' (319) or 'I'm nonbinary. This is why pronouns matter' (320). These sites rarely feature coverage of more serious issues, such as war or global poverty. There is also very little coverage of politics in terms of what's going on in Westminster, Capitol Hill or any other type of government. Issues around class are also ignored. The only subjects which are covered are those that are of interest to young, affluent, socially liberal professionals who frequent these websites.

On rare occasions, these sites and magazines do experiment with supporting socialist ideas. The strangest case of this was *Teen Vogue's* article espousing the benefits of Marxism (321). The author of this piece doesn't have a very strong understanding of Marxism. In a socialist society, *Teen Vogue* magazine wouldn't exist. The main point of *Vogue* and its sister publications is to promote consumption of cosmetics and clothing that a person doesn't need. It is the antithesis of Marxism. Indeed, if capitalism were under any serious threat, this magazine would be constantly saying how unfair socialism is for failing to reward hard work. Along with various other pro-capitalist sentiments.

The Wokeness Industry

Wokeness is big business in itself. There is a huge market for products and services that claim to help an oppressor overcome the propensity to discriminate. Or to help the oppressed cope with the toll of their victim status. One huge part of the wokeness industry is diversity training. Diversity training is a big money spinner. The industry is estimated to be worth $8 billion (322). Yet there is little evidence that these courses actually promote diversity. On the contrary, diversity training has been found to reinforce negative stereotypes about ethnic minorities and built resentment toward low-income white people (285). Ultimately, it aggravates racial tensions rather than relieving them.

An infamous example of someone who's made a lot of money from wokeness is Robin DiAngelo. DiAngelo is a diversity trainer and author. Her book, *White Fragility*, argues that every white person is complicit in racism, whether they are aware of it or not. For white people to atone for racism, they must be willing to study it and challenge it. However, many white people are unwilling to do this. When a white person refuses to engage with discussions on racism, it is because of their white fragility. She says that white people learn early in life not to discuss race, which is the underlying cause of white fragility. This fragility can be overcome by continual discussions of race and by listening to the experiences of ethnic minorities. But surely, social justice warriors have already overcome their white fragility? That's where you're wrong. In fact, according to DiAngelo, the worst racists are what she calls "progressive whites". These are people who perceive themselves to be less prejudiced than the rest of society. So, they don't recognize that they have a problem. Which makes them resistant to learning about racism. She also adds that statements like "race doesn't matter" play into racist attitudes (104).

The other key argument of *White Fragility* is that while few people are openly racist, most white people are implicitly racist. One example of implicit racism is describing a predominantly black neighbourhood is dangerous, because white people inherently perceive black people as a threat. There are many other subtle ways white people are racist. For instance, according to DiAngelo, "Claiming that the past was socially better than the present is also a hallmark of white supremacy", because there was more racism in the past. Therefore, a white person saying the past was better is endorsing historical racism. Of course, this isn't correct. Many people have fond memories of the past for a variety of reasons that are unrelated to racism. We might look back at the simplicity of an earlier time. Or the excitement of youth. Or recall lost loved ones. It doesn't necessarily mean that people are reminiscing about the racism of the past.

What's particularly interesting about DiAngelo is that she herself is a white woman. Yes, really! Why does she feel she is the arbiter of what is and isn't racist? She even says in her book that it is not the job of non-white people to explain racism. This begs the question: what makes it her job? She has simply decided she is more enlightened than other white people. Surely there must be many people from ethnic minority backgrounds who would be happy to give diversity training. But for some reason, she -a white woman- thinks she is best placed to do it. Also, DiAngelo makes a hefty profit from her training. She charges $40,000 to speak at a half-day event and she is thought to have made at least $2 million from book sales (323). She has the perfect business model. The idea that only a lifelong commitment to discussing race can solve the problems caused by whiteness is handy for DiAngelo. It means you must keep paying her to talk to you if you want to make any progress. So too must the idea that we must constantly focus on race. After all, if you don't see race, you don't see racial diversity training as a valuable investment for your company.

Another popular idea promoted by diversity trainers is the Implicit Association Test (IAT). These tests display pictures of black people and white people, and various positive words and negative words. The test taker must press a certain letter on their keyboard when they see certain words or certain pictures. These tests purport to measure bias by measuring the response time between positive and negative words and photographs of black and white people's faces. These tests are widely available online. However, there is no evidence that the Implicit Association Test is actually useful in detecting prejudice. On the contrary, a study by a group of researchers from multiple elite universities found that the correlation between scores on the Implicit Association Test and racial prejudice was very weak (324). So, the test is useless. This undermines the claim that diversity training reduces unconscious bias. But if unconscious bias is not the reason for inequality, what is? Sadly, outright discrimination is still a big problem. There are white people who are openly prejudiced against other ethnic groups. There are people who refuse to make adjustments for the disabled. And there are people who would turn down a woman's job application because of her sex. So, much of the inequality attributed to 'unconscious bias' is simply frank discrimination.

Woke Feminism

The influence of capitalism on the left can also be seen in the rise of woke feminism. Woke feminism, or liberal feminism is a branch of feminism where you just say, 'I'm a feminist' and that's all the engagement with women's issues you have to do. You don't need to make any other kind of commitment, compromise or sacrifice to fight for women's equality. No pissing off men or challenging the status quo. You can just carry on as normal. Except that everything you do will be feminist. Wearing that skimpy, revealing top, shaving your body hair and caking your face in make-up are all feminist activities. Somehow, these are great for advancing women's equality. You don't need to look or think about actual issues facing women. It's all about pleasing men with hair, make-up, clothes and sex. Here are some examples:

Cosmetics

Woke feminism champions consumerism. Particularly when it comes to cosmetics. Cosmetics have played a major part in women's subjugation. The cosmetics industry posits that a woman's role in life is to look beautiful for men. Women are form. Men are function. Women are style. Men are substance. Looking pretty is all very well and good. But when there's a job that needs doing, you want something that's functional. Which is why women aren't taken seriously. They are seen as little ornaments for men to look at to take them away from their hard days at work. Men don't need to look good. They don't need to spend the morning putting make-up on. They have real work to do! Which is why women wear make-up and men don't.

The 'right' to wear make-up has become a huge area which woke feminists campaign on. They have constructed a view that their right is under threat from so-called make-up shaming. Make-up shaming is any kind of criticism of a woman for wearing make-up (325). This includes radical feminist critiques or comments that women wear make-up to please men. Or simply saying that a particular woman is wearing too much make-up or that she looks better without make-up on. Given that only a small number of women don't wear make-up, make-up certainly isn't under threat. Only 10% of women aged 18-29 years old, 11% of women aged 30-59 and seven percent of women over 60 say they never wear make-up (326). But woke feminists feel so threatened by this small group of women. In 2015, the #PowerOfMakeup hashtag was started on social media to protest make-up shaming. Women would post pictures with make-up only on one side of their faces (327). The idea was to show how much better women look with make-up on than without it. But this reinforces the point about make-up being purely about appearances. It proves that make-up isn't about self-confidence or some other non appearance-related quality that woke feminists believe it to be.

The beauty industry has played a big part in presenting make-up as empowering. A survey ran by make-up company Sally Hansen and the polling company IPSOS was produced to show that women wear make-up because it is "empowering" (328). Words like "feel empowered" or "more confident" actually imply women do wear make-up and other cosmetics for other people. If you only cared about yourself, why would it matter what your face or nails looked like? There is no such thing as feeling that you look good for yourself. You can't see your face without a mirror. Only other people can see you. To feel as if you look good is doing it for other people. Indeed, women would be better off if they didn't wear make-up. Make-up is expensive, time-consuming, and can be harmful to skin health. There is no real good reason for a person to wear it. Especially every day.

However, proper feminists have known about the dangers of the beauty industry for a long time. In 1991, Naomi Wolf wrote *The Beauty Myth*, which outlines the role of beauty in the patriarchy (329). The book describes how women are pressured to focus on their appearance over other qualities and how this limits women's progress. Woke feminists have not heeded that book's lessons. If anything, they have fallen for the idea that the most important thing a woman can be is pretty. The way that woke feminists fixate on 'make-up shaming', has been part of teaching women not to question the role of capitalism in the patriarchy.

Indeed, the true winners of a campaign to promote make-up as a feminist issue is the cosmetics industry, which is predominantly owned by men. The beauty industry is estimated to be worth $445 billion (330). Although there are a myriad of cosmetic brands and products, the beauty industry is controlled by seven companies who own most of these brands: Johnson and Johnson, Procter and Gamble, L'Oreal, Estée Lauder, Unilever, Shiseido and COTY (331). And who controls these companies? Men. Proctor and Gamble's CEO is David Taylor (332). L'Oreal's CEO is Jean-Paul Agon (333). The CEO of Johnson and Johnson is Alex Gorsky (334). The CEO of Estée Lauder is Fabrizio Freda (335). Unilever's CEO is Alan Jope (336). And Shiseido's CEO is Masahiko Uotani (337). All of these are men. Only COTY has a female CEO, Sue Nabi (338). And if you look at the corporate structure of these companies, you'll see that nearly all the people at the top are men too. So, the real winners of woke feminism's obsession with beauty and make-up is these male CEOs, who are profiting from women's insecurities.

Celebrating make-up is neither anti-capitalist nor pro-woman. By discouraging women from questioning why they wear make-up, the beauty industry is keeping itself in business. The industry has spent many years teaching women that their natural appearance is unacceptable. That's not going to change any time soon. But it is very sad that the social warriors have fallen for the beauty industry's tricks and have turned the use of cosmetics into part of their politics.

Prostitution

While the cosmetics industry is an issue, the laissez-faire nature of liberal feminism shows its much darker side when it comes to prostitution. Social justice warriors support the legalization of prostitution. Being a SWERF (Sex Worker Exclusionary Radical Feminist) or a whorephobe, is one of the worst things a modern-day feminist can be. Social justice warriors claim that prostitution is empowering. And that not making it legal is limiting women's autonomy and control of their bodies (339). But is this really the case?

There are numerous good reasons for prostitution being illegal. Firstly, prostitution is the most dangerous career a woman could do. She is at constant risk of being seriously injured, contracting STIs, and being raped. Prostitutes are 13 times more likely to have HIV/AIDS than the general public. And nearly one in 10 people with HIV/AIDS in the world is a sex worker (340). Furthermore, sex workers have a much higher rate of mental illnesses than the general population (341). You could argue that all jobs have risks. And that's true. But no job carries as much risk as prostitution. To compare, logging has the highest work-related mortality rate for any occupation in the USA. In 2015, the Bureau for Labor Statistics calculated that the mortality rate for loggers was 132.7 per 100,000 (342). However, a study of prostitutes in Colorado Springs found that their mortality rate was 459 per 100,000 (343). Prostitutes are more than three times as likely to die from work-related injuries or illnesses than loggers. That means that prostitution is more dangerous than any legally recognized job. Such dangers would be unacceptable in any other line of work. It is hard to argue that sex work is like any other job when there is such a high chance of being killed or seriously injured.

As well, sex work is not empowering for women. Sex work has the biggest gender pay gap of any industry; women often receive less than 10% of the proceeds, while the rest goes to the pimp (344). Furthermore, most people who go into prostitution don't do so out of choice. Many start in childhood. Around 40% of adult prostitutes are former child sex trafficking victims (345). And the average child sex trafficking victim is 13 to 14 years of age when they are first prostituted out (346). Human trafficking is a huge issue too. Think about this: if prostitution was such a fine career to go into, why would people be trafficked into it? Of course, not many people would voluntarily choose to be a prostitute. Not only is sex work very dangerous, it is also exploitative. It couldn't be less empowering.

The other favourite woke feminist argument is that decriminalization would protect prostitutes. Writing in *Harper's Bazaar*, journalist Jennifer Wright claims that by legalizing prostitution, it would make it more open. She contends that legalization would enable the government to regulate prostitution, thus making it safer (347). This can't work. In most industries, workplaces must ensure health and safety measures are followed carefully. For instance, protective clothing is worn, equipment must be used and stored safely, and regular training is given on safety procedures. As well, a person can claim compensation if they are injured at work. How would this work in prostitution? The private nature of the job makes it difficult to regulate. Nobody can check that safety procedures are being followed while a sex worker is with a customer. And it's unlikely there'd be any way to claim compensation for an injury or disease contracted from sex work. After all, who would you claim from? And how could a sex worker prove that they contracted an STI from a client? Which removes the impetus for anyone to comply with health and safety legislation. Therefore, legalization does not protect prostitutes.

Prostitution commodifies a woman's body. Thus, to be pro-prostitution is to be pro-capitalism. Which is why social justice warriors support it. Andrea Dworkin, the feminist author, makes the excellent point that left-wingers only cherish the free market when women's bodies are being profited from (348). And pro-prostitution liberals don't know the realities of what they are advocating for. They buy into the patriarchal fantasy that it's somehow liberating for women to be able to sell their bodies. They turn a blind eye to the dangers of prostitution. This shows how woke feminism is unconcerned with women. If anything, it fully accepts the patriarchy.

Overall, capitalism has distorted the left- it has become hyper-capitalist. Business is using identity politics to displace concerns about capitalism. And the average social justice warrior is totally blind to it. Furthermore, business interests have infiltrated the left more broadly. So now, it doesn't matter who is elected: there will be a pro-capitalist government. In addition, the social justice warrior has no interest in politicians questioning capitalism. Instead, they simply go along with the woke feel-good messages that big multi-national corporations put out about social progress. Because of this, the left is losing its essence.

8. The Social Justice Warrior Movement and Reality

The left used to be on the side of science, rationality and evidence. It was the right who peddled bizarre conspiracy theories and other anti-scientific beliefs, such as Young Earth Creationism, and climate change denial. The social justice warrior movement has changed all that. Now, it's the left who are against science and other forms of empirical evidence. This chapter will examine how the social justice warrior movement distorts reality to fit its own ends. It will look at examples of times when the social justice warrior movement has come to put ideology over evidence.

Postmodernism and Reality

A greatly problematic facet of postmodernism is the emphasis on modes of knowledge. To help understand the social justice warrior's views on reality, it's important to look at postmodern epistemology. Epistemology is a branch of philosophy which examines where knowledge comes from. Postmodern epistemology emphasizes knowledge production by minorities. The claim that postmodern scholars make is that knowledge is produced by privileged people. They argue that focusing on the lived experience of minorities helps redress this balance (349). This is well-meaning, but problematic. Pluckrose (41) describes how the experience of minorities is placed above empirical evidence. One particular point she makes is that everything is seen through the frame of identity.

She gives an example from her own work on the Shakespeare play *Othello*. While speaking at a conference, she argued that racism as it is today did not develop until the trans-Atlantic slave trade begun. Another academic told her that this perspective was hurtful for African American people. It is as if something could not be both true and upsetting. More troublingly, she describes movements against science and medicine on the basis that these fields are dominated by white males. In postmodernism, the truth can't hurt. If something is hurtful or doesn't promote social equality, it must not be true.

As well, postmodernism argues that ignoring oppressed people's knowledge is a form of oppression. There are several ways in which a person can harm minorities through epistemology (49). First, there's epistemic oppression. This is where knowledge produced by marginalized groups is excluded from mainstream knowledge (350). Then, there's epistemic violence. Which is where marginalized knowledge is suppressed by the dominant culture (351). Confusingly, there's also epistemic exploitation. Which is where members of a marginalized community have to share their knowledge with non-marginalized people. Apparently, this is exploitative because it's exhausting for minorities. It also constitutes unpaid labour (352). Although, how can you get knowledge from marginalized people without asking them? It seems that anything you do regarding the knowledge from marginalized groups is oppressive (49).

Furthermore, in postmodern academia, there is the 'research justice' movement. This movement encourages academics to cite fewer works written by western men when writing books and papers. Instead, they should cite work by women and from other marginalized groups. While this isn't a bad thing in itself, this movement promotes citing forms of 'research' that have little scientific basis. This includes cultural traditions and accounts of personal experiences (49).

A related concept is decolonizing curriculums. Decolonizing curriculums is based on the idea that academic curriculums are imperialist, both in the content they teach and in their pedagogy. Measures to decolonize curriculums include removing works by white authors from syllabuses and replacing them with authors from other ethnic groups (353) or reforming teaching methods (354). It's right to include more diverse perspectives in a subject, such as teaching both western and eastern philosophy in a philosophy course. But it's wrong to assume that western means bad. It's also difficult to see how teaching and knowledge are imperialist. Given that education is the aim of university, what could realistically be changed to make teaching less imperialist?

Pluckrose and Lindsay go on to say that postmodernism is unconcerned how useful these knowledges are in uncovering reality. A marginalized community's knowledge might be objectively untrue. But that doesn't matter in postmodernism. Indeed, oppressed people are afforded a special position in the fight against oppressive social structures. Derrida argues that oppressed people have the unique capability to overcome the oppression created by facts and knowledge (355). This explains why minorities are held so highly within the social justice warrior movement. This strange view of reality explains some of the more bizarre aspects of the movement.

Re-writing History

One example of the social justice warrior movement's flexibility with the truth is the way they see history. Social justice warriors fail to understand historical contexts. Someone might have had a view which was uncontroversial in 1820, that is outrageous in 2020. In the same way that the views and attitudes we have in 2020 might be outrageous in 2220. Things change. And People change. The journalist Helen Lewis points out that Barack Obama was against gay marriage when he first became president. He changed his mind later in his presidency (322). Does that mean Obama was a bad president? Is he homophobic? Of course not. In fact, he is now heralded as a gay rights hero for being the first president to support gay marriage. It shows that we should only judge people by the standards of their time.

But social warriors can't cope with this. So, they try to re-write history in a way that is more favourable to their ideology. One example of this is the statue felling trend in the summer of 2020. Many statues of slave traders, colonialists and other unpleasant figures were pulled down by anti-racism protestors. We don't want to celebrate these people. But by removing the statues, it is a way of pretending that this chapter of history never happened. Furthermore, Brendan O'Neill, the editor of *Spiked!* magazine, argues that the assumption that ethnic minorities are devastated by historic symbols is patronizing and paternalistic. It is as if they are too delicate to see things that remind them of their history. He points out that the same is never assumed of white people. Statues of people who oppressed white people (such as those who oppressed the Irish) are not controversial (356). Could it be that white people are actually upset by the statues? After all, these statues are a reminder of a shameful chapter in history, that white people ought to be reminded of frequently. By hiding the statues away, we can pretend that it never happened.

Postmodern scholars also deny historical evidence. An occasion where this occurred was with two Oxford dons who studied witches. English literature scholar Dianne Purkiss criticized historian Keith Thomas's work on witches. Thomas's research shows that most women who were accused of witchcraft were elderly, unmarried and impoverished. But according to Purkiss, by saying this, Thomas is reinforcing the idea that women are weak. Tellingly, Purkiss has never provided any evidence that disproves what Thomas says. But because what Thomas said was not supporting women's empowerment, in Purkiss's eyes, it must be untrue (41,42). Historians are supposed to research what happened in the past. Not ignore evidence and forge a narrative that fits their ideological position or a personal agenda. Furthermore, it's not beneficial to pretend that unpleasant events did not occur in the past. By looking at the darkness of the past, we can learn from history. The persecution of witches reflects prejudices that still occur today- ageism, sexism and classism. And women accused of witchcraft were part of multiple oppressed groups. We don't accuse people of being witches today. But these groups still face discrimination. If we overlooked this and falsely claimed that women accused of witchcraft weren't oppressed, we miss out on understanding oppression today.

Furthermore, social justice warriors pretend that history was more diverse than it really was. An infamous example is Mary Secole. Secole was a Jamaican black businesswoman who lived in the UK in the 19th century. She ran a chain of hotels, including one in the Crimea, which she opened during the Crimean War. The hotel provided accommodation for officers, including those recovering from injuries. She also sold refreshments to spectators at the battlefield. Odd as it may sound today, battles were a tourist attraction in the 19th century (357). However, thanks to major historical revisionism, she is now said to be a nurse. But not just any nurse. She is a nurse whose heroism rivals that of her more famous counterpart, Florence Nightingale. The story goes that because of her race, she never received the recognition she deserved. Because of this, many buildings in the UK are named after her and she is regularly hailed as one of the greatest black Britons (358).

However, Secole never was a nurse. Indeed, she never called herself a nurse or worked in a hospital. She occasionally referred to herself figuratively as a "doctress, nurse and mother" to her patrons, and she sold herbal remedies at her hotel. Additionally, her own autobiography focuses on her hotel and restaurant business. She did donate remedies and food to the hospital which Florence Nightingale worked at. But it's a stretch to describe this as nursing (357). She did try to apply to be a nurse in the Crimean war, but her informal application was rejected. This appears racist. But bear in mind that she had no qualifications or experience of working in healthcare (359).

Now, it could be argued that Secole was a hero for going to a warzone. But there were many nurses who served in the Crimea. And many other conflicts for that matter. They have been forgotten by history. The reason that Nightingale is so widely celebrated is that she wasn't just a nurse. What made Nightingale special was that she was a campaigner who brought about major changes in nursing care. Nightingale pioneered the use of statistics to reduce hospital mortality rates. Her work uncovered the role of unhygienic conditions in death rates (360). Nightingale's contribution to nursing had a huge impact on the profession. In contrast, it appears that Secole has been transformed into a black nursing hero with the goal of creating a black role model, rather than because of any actual contribution to the field of nursing.

But according to social justice warriors, if you disagree with Secole being celebrated as a black Florence Nightingale, you are racist. The politics website *Operation Black Vote* ran an article entitled 'Mary Seacole and her wretched detractors'. The article implies that the reason people are doubtful of Mary Seacole's heroism is because she was black. The article also claims that Secole's critics have been refuted by a former nursing professor, Elizabeth Anionwu (361). Anionwu appears to be the driver behind the celebrations of Seacole. She almost certainly means well, but that doesn't mean she's right. But accusing people who question the myth of Mary Seacole is a prime example of how the social justice warrior movement works. If you don't like the truth, accuse the people telling the truth of discrimination. Qualms about capitalism aside, there's nothing wrong with remembering Secole as a writer and businesswoman. She was a remarkable woman. Especially for her time, where there were very few women in business. Even today, there are few black businesswomen who run a multinational business, as Seacole did. But she was not a nursing hero.

Ignoring Science

Social justice warriors don't just ignore historical evidence. They also disregard scientific evidence on many topics where it contradicts their ideology.

Science as a White Value

Another claim the social justice warriors make is that science is a white value. As whiteness is bad, that means science is automatically bad too. The Decolonizing Science movement contends that science is inherently white. An infamous video of a student seminar in South Africa which discussed the Decolonizing Science movement revealed the way this movement thinks. A student proclaimed science was inaccurate because it was a "product of western modernity". Another student said that science was flawed because it failed to explain witchcraft (362). It is alarming that a group of university students hold these views. They are surely clever enough to know that witchcraft doesn't exist. Or that science isn't automatically wrong because many discoveries come from the west.

It's not just the Decolonizing Science movement who say science is part of whiteness. The Smithsonian Institution made a chart about 'white values', which was widely distributed on social media. These values include an emphasis on time, rationality and using quantitative methods of science. The chart is based on a list made by Judith Katz. Like DiAngelo, she too is a white woman who worked as a corporate diversity consultant (363).

The concept of white values is flawed. Science is not a white value because scientific ideas and scientists come from many cultures. Many mathematical concepts originate from the Indian subcontinent. These include the concept of zero, the decimal system and negative numbers (364). So quantitative methods are not a white value. In addition, many medical discoveries originate from ancient Egypt. These include basic surgical procedures such as stitching wounds. They also knew how to set broken bones (365). It's right to make sure science education doesn't focus only on western cultures. And science from non-western cultures should be supported. But it's not correct to dismiss science as a white value.

As well, Katz. can't show how these are white values. She has a very stereotypical view of white people. These so-called white values are simply the opposite of what social justice warriors believe. They are against the scientific method and individualism. They have a preference for qualitative methods. And they support gender equality. These have nothing to do with whiteness. Indeed, many cultures do not have these views. White values are a simple way of lumping together everything social justice warriors consider 'bad' as having one unified cause.

Time

If there's one thing that few people dispute the existence of, it's time. But according to social justice warriors, the concept of the time on the clock is racist. Diversity training is teaching that timekeeping is difficult for black people. An article printed in the *New York Times* describes a diversity training session delivered for school staff. The article explains how "[Diversity trainer, Marcus] Moore expounded that white culture is obsessed with "mechanical time" — clock time — and punishes students for lateness. This, he said, is but one example of how whiteness undercuts black kids. 'The problems come when we say this way of being is the way to be.' In school and on into the working world, he lectured, tremendous harm is done by the pervasive rule that black children and adults must 'bend to whiteness, in substance, style and format'" (366). Clemson University's diversity training program made a similar point. A slideshow used in the training featured a scenario where a lecturer had scheduled a meeting with two groups of foreign students and lecturers. One group arrives early, and the others are late. According to the training, the lecturer who organized the meeting should not reprimand the late group. Instead they should "recognize cultural differences that may impact the meeting and adjust accordingly." (367).

From a practical standpoint, ignoring the time on the clock doesn't work well in the world we live in. Time is finite. For example, a student comes 15 minutes late to a lesson at school. They have missed a good chunk of the session and disrupted the rest of the class. How could this be done in a way that didn't rely on the clock? As well, while an insistence on punctuality might cause difficulties for some people, other marginalized people rely heavily on time. Many disabled people depend on structure. For example, people with Autism may become anxious about their routine being disrupted. And many chronic illnesses cause fatigue or pain, so a person may not be in a position to be flexible. 15 minutes stood waiting for someone could mean an event takes extra time and energy that a chronically ill person simply might not have. Other people need to eat or take medication at certain times, such as those with Type 1 Diabetes. It's not just people with disabilities who rely on the clock. A parent might need to be out of work or a meeting by a certain time to pick children up from school or their childcare provider. This is more likely to affect women, who bear the brunt of childcare responsibilities. Realistically, we can't just decide that time doesn't matter.

More importantly, isn't it racist to assume that black people find timekeeping difficult? It implies that black people are less capable than white people of managing everyday tasks. Indeed, the whole concept of white values gives this impression. Writing in *The Intelligencer*, journalist Jonathan Chait explains that white values are seen as virtues. By saying that white people value rationality, hard work, planning, education and co-operation, are diversity trainers saying that ethnic minorities are irrational, lazy, impulsive, uneducated and argumentative? This is a rather unflattering portrait of ethnic minorities. And is it that the likes of DiAngelo, Katz and other diversity trainers are actually racist? Chait also highlights worrying parallels between how white nationalists see non-white people, and how anti-racist trainers see ethnic minorities. Both consider ethnic minorities less able than white people (368). It plays into the idea that white people are superior to other ethnic groups.

The clock is a social construct, and it has arguably been a big driving force in industrialization. But that doesn't mean black people aren't capable of using it. Blackness isn't a disability. Black people are no less able to keep time than any person of any other ethnicity. In any case, unless there is a radical change in society, the clock isn't going away.

Medicine

Medicine is another area of science where social justice warriors put ideology ahead of evidence.

COVID Political Correctness

Another case where social justice warriors have put their beliefs over facts is during the Coronavirus (COVID-19) pandemic. COVID-19 started in a Chinese wet market. Wet markets are where live animals are sold and slaughtered for meat. They are predominantly found in Asia. These markets are notorious for poor hygiene practices, with blood-stained floors, along with an array of domestic and wild animals kept together (369). It's not surprising that these markets are breeding grounds for new viruses. Coronavirus is not the first virus to originate from a wet market either. Wet markets were the origin of many other viruses, including SARS and H1N1 (bird flu) (370). This has led to many people calling to ban them, including the USA's top infectious disease expert, Dr. Anthony Fauci (371).

But social justice warriors disagree. An article in *The Conversation* by anthropologists Christos Lynteris and Lyle Fearnley opposes closing wet markets. It argues that wet markets should stay open because these markets are a major part of Chinese society (372). The authors claim that calls to ban wet markets are motivated by safety concerns, but by Sinophobia (hatred of Chinese people) and ethnocentrism. They argue that people hate the Chinese in particular because of their economic success and how "capitalism is adapting to China". Thus, a moral panic around the wet markets has been created. The authors also state that markets should remain open as they serve as an "early warning system" for zoonotic disease. Oddly, the article cites a paper which describes how wet markets led to zoonotic illness, undermining Lynteris and Fearnley's point. The article concludes by saying "…a permanent shut down or abolition of 'wet markets' would have an immense and unpredictable impact on everyday life and well-being in China." The Coronavirus pandemic has also had an immense and unpredictable impact on everyday life and well-being in China. And on the rest of the world for that matter. Many things that were a major part of life across the world have been lost. Things like seeing family and friends in the flesh going to a bar or restaurant or out to school or work.

Furthermore, there's little dispute that these markets spread disease. We know eating unsanitary food can make people sick. The way social justice warriors have argued for keeping wet markets open is typical of the movement's thinking. They explain things with theory rather than evidence. Instead of using theory to understand reality, they are bending reality to fit with their theory. In this case, to fit in with the idea of China being a virtuous victim. The way social justice warriors see it is this: the Chinese are defying capitalism with their little markets where consumers buy directly from farmers. The nasty western health bodies are persecuting the Chinese by saying their markets make people sick. Obviously, the scientific evidence must be wrong, and these markets are fine.

As well, it's incorrect to say that ethnocentrism is the root of the criticism of wet markets. Other countries have experienced food-related diseases. The UK has had to implement many safety measures after the BSE (Bovine

Spongiform Encephalopathy, or 'Mad Cow Disease') outbreak in the 1980s and 1990s. BSE causes brain degeneration in cows. It was transmitted from feeding the cows ground-up bones and meat from cows with the disease (373). 4.4 million BSE-infected cattle were slaughtered. In 1989, it wasn't known that BSE could harm humans, but the British government banned beef offal from being sold as a precaution. However, in 1995, it was proven that eating beef from cattle who were infected with BSE could cause variant Creutzfeldt-Jakob Disease (vCJD) in humans. Like BSE, vCJD causes serious neurological issues and typically kills the affected person within a year (374). After this, certain cuts of beef were no longer allowed to be sold. This ban lasted between 1997 and 1999. But even after these safety measures were implemented, many other countries were reluctant to trust British beef. Indeed, China only started accepting British beef imports in 2018 (375). The safety restrictions undoubtably harmed British farming. But it was necessary to protect people. It shows that any country can have problems with food safety. Therefore, it's not Sinophobia or ethnocentrism that's driving the calls to ban wet markets.

Furthermore, Lynteris and Fearnley argue that a ban would drive markets underground. This might be true. But if consumers knew how unsafe these markets were, would they still buy meat from them? Nobody wants to eat food that makes them sick. Also, China doesn't have to do away with wet markets altogether. They could change the way they run. Most countries have farmer's markets. Which are markets where fresh meat and other produce is sold. But the animals are slaughtered beforehand, so it's much cleaner. Why couldn't China have this system? If this isn't feasible, the markets could have a separate abattoir section where animals are slaughtered. This would keep dead animals separate from live animals.

When it comes to wet markets, safety must be placed above tradition. Too many people have died of Coronavirus and from other pandemics. Which is why it's time to ban wet markets where animals are slaughtered and stored alongside live animals.

The Sad Case of 'DJ' and Anna Stubblefield

Social justice warriors also apply their insane logic to the treatment of disabilities too. Look at the story of 'DJ' and Anna Stubblefield. DJ (who is known by his initials to protect his privacy) is a man with Cerebral Palsy and profound intellectual disability. According to a psychologist's assessment, his mental ability is similar to that of an 18-month old toddler (376). He cannot speak and shows little understanding of the world around him. Anna Stubblefield was a disability studies professor at Rutgers's University. DJ's brother was a student in her class. Stubblefield taught her class about a technique called facilitated communication, which is purported to help non-verbal people to communicate.

What exactly is facilitated communication? It depends who you ask. But basically, a disabled person who can't speak is 'helped' to type out their thoughts. In most cases, the facilitator holds the person's hand or arm and guides it to the letters they think the person wishes to press on a keyboard. In other cases, the facilitator holds the letter board or keyboard. Its proponents say that nonverbal people have poor co-ordination, thus they require physical assistance to type (377). But scientific evidence shows the facilitator is actually communicating (378). Any perception that the disabled person is attempting to press or point to a letter is because of the psychomotor effect, similar to an Ouija board. In other words, the disabled person is being used like a puppet by the facilitator. This isn't like other forms of alternative communication. In most forms of alternative communication, the aim is for the person to communicate independently to the best of their ability. Once the person understands how to use the method of communication, nobody intervenes. So, we know they are communicating their own thoughts.

The 1993 *PBS* documentary 'Prisoners of Silence' provides a very good explanation for why facilitated communication doesn't work. The documentary features a number of demonstrations of how the facilitator is controlling the communication. For instance, it shows a case where the facilitator was working with someone who used a head pointer. The facilitator showed the person a board with words on. The non-verbal person appeared to point to a word. However, the film shows that the pointer stayed still. The facilitator had moved the board gradually, so the pointer was level with the position of the word on the board. In another instance, a facilitator and the disabled person were shown pictures of items and asked to name them. Unbeknown to the facilitator, the pictures they were shown were different to the picture the disabled person was seeing. When the facilitator was shown a different object to the nonverbal person, the facilitator named the item they saw. This proved it was the facilitator who was communicating (379). A further inconsistency was that children who used facilitated communication displayed writing skills that were far ahead of their age. Children as young as five would be able to write complex sentences, in paragraphs with no spelling mistakes. This too suggested that the adult facilitator was the one doing the writing. As well, the documentary points out there are many communication technologies for virtually any disability. These technologies respond to the slightest movements. This is even truer today. For instance, there is now eye gaze recognition software. A person can simply look at a computer to control it. This enables people to look at letters onscreen to spell out what they want to say (380). Few people who have the mental ability to communicate can't find some way of communicating. Therefore, it's hard to understand why facilitated communication persists in this day and age. But it does.

Anyhow, DJ's brother asked Stubblefield if the technique could be used to help DJ. She agreed to work with him. Like with many cases of people using facilitated communication, DJ appeared to possess great intellect. With Stubblefield's help, he was able to study college-level material. He was even able to write peer-reviewed academic papers and book chapters (376,381). His family were amazed by his progress. Stubblefield became an ardent supporter of facilitated communication. She wrote a paper claiming that scientific opposition to facilitated communication was hate speech. In this paper, Stubblefield argues that researchers had made the ableist assumption that profoundly disabled people lacked the intellectual capacity to communicate (382). Her view ignores empirical evidence that proves facilitated communication does not work. But that never stopped Stubblefield.

But one day, everything changed. While they were at a conference, DJ told Stubblefield that he loved her. And that he wanted to have sex with her. Stubblefield initially resisted DJ's advances, but then she started a sexual relationship with him. After they had sex on multiple occasions, DJ and Stubblefield decided to make the relationship public. With Stubblefield facilitating, DJ told his family that they were in love and were going to be a couple. At this point, his family were furious. They realized that Stubblefield was taking advantage of DJ. They phoned the police and reported her for rape. In court, Stubblefield admitted to having sex with DJ, but denied that it was rape. The court rejected this and she was found guilty (376). However, her conviction was later overturned and she is currently awaiting a retrial (383).

What made this case especially shocking was that Stubblefield's colleagues and other disability activists supported her. Rosemary Crossley, who pioneered facilitated communication in the 1980s testified in Stubblefield's defence. Many less prominent academics supported her too. This included going to the court hearing and donating money to Stubblefield's legal fees (384). In addition, many disabilities studies scholars claimed that Stubblefield was convicted because of ableist assumptions that a man with Cerebral Palsy was incapable of consenting to sex (385).

Even if facilitated communication did work, and DJ had the capacity to consent to sex, Stubblefield had not acted ethically. Stubblefield had considerable power over DJ for several reasons. Firstly, DJ was dependent on Stubblefield for help to communicate and other types of care. She describes changing his incontinence pad in a section of an edited book (386). She also helped with his academic work. As well, DJ was much younger than Stubblefield. He had little education, and more importantly, he had no experience of romantic relationships. Stubblefield took advantage of him. He would be under pressure to remain in the relationship because of the power imbalance between them. She must have known that entering a romantic relationship with DJ was inappropriate. This case highlights how social justice warriors can be so easily blinded by their ideology. They care more about proving their point than the well-being of disabled people.

The Fat Acceptance Movement

Another prominent example of the social justice warrior movement ignoring science is the fat acceptance movement. The fat acceptance movement claims that being obese is in no way inferior to being a healthy weight. It goes beyond criticizing a person's appearance because of their weight or shaming them for putting on weight. The fat acceptance movement denies any scientific evidence that being overweight is unhealthy. However, the scientific consensus is that obesity contributes to many serious health issues. These issues include Type 2 Diabetes, Heart Disease, some types of Cancer and Osteoarthritis (387). Many of these diseases can be directly attributed to fat build-up in organs or increased pressure placed on the body by the excess weight.

The origins of the fat acceptance movement can be traced back to the 1960s (49). But the current movement began with the book *Health at Every Size*, by nutritionist Linda Bacon (388). The book argues that obesity is not unhealthy and people who are overweight are so because they are meant to be. She contends that people are predisposed to being overweight, and nothing they can do can produce lasting weight changes. But Bacon is incorrect. Obesity rates have risen steeply after the 1970s. Which was when more calorie-dense foods became readily available (389). If some people are just meant to be obese, why did so many people become obese in the past 50 years? If people were always destined to be obese, the rates would not have changed as dramatically as they have done.

The book also encourages readers to eat whatever they please. She claims that "Sensual pleasure is our biological reward for taking care of ourselves". Bacon isn't incorrect in saying that we find unhealthy foods pleasurable because our bodies perceive it to be beneficial. Humans have evolved to crave high-energy foods so that we can put on weight for famines or extreme winters. This instinct dates from millions of years ago, when sweet, fatty and salty foods were rarely available. Nowadays, there is very little chance that most people will ever have to go without food. So, the extra weight keeps building up and makes us overweight (390). Your body doesn't know that you can buy food all day, every day from the supermarket. Or go to a fast-food restaurant or have a takeaway delivered whenever you want. Therefore, Bacon is wrong to say that enjoying calorie-dense foods is a sign you are caring for your body.

Despite the medical consensus, social justice warriors are firm in their convictions that obesity isn't unhealthy. For instance, the comedian Sofie Hagen (remember her from chapter 3?) accused Cancer Research UK of fat shaming. The charity had produced a set of billboard advertisements with the word: OB_S_ _Y. Underneath that, it has the caption: "Guess what is the biggest preventable cause of cancer after smoking". On Twitter, she called for the billboards to be removed because "Society viewing fatness as a negative thing is a thing that kills more than the cancer that you MIGHT get due to MAYBE something to do with you POSSIBLY weighing MORE than a CERTAIN weight POSSIBLY MAYBE." After Cancer Research responded to Hagen, she replied that dieting was the worst thing a person could do to their body (391). But this isn't true. Cancer Research knows more about the risks of obesity than a comedian.

In addition, the fat acceptance movement has become intertwined with other social justice issues, including race and feminism. *Huffington Post* ran an article entitled 'The

BMI Is Racist and Useless. Here's How to Measure Health Instead' the Body Mass Index (BMI) system for identifying obesity, is racist and sexist. The article states that the original measurements used to devise the system were taken exclusively from white men. It also claims that BMI is intended to stigmatize southern European and African people. The article argues that these ethnic groups naturally carry more body weight with no ill effects (392). However, scientific evidence shows that having a high BMI carries health risks for both white and non-white people. For example, black people are two times more likely than white people to have Type 2 Diabetes (393). This suggests the BMI classification isn't inaccurate for black people. They are more likely to be obese, and also more likely to have obesity-related diseases.

That's not to say that obesity is easy to resolve. Obesity is a huge public health crisis. Many people struggle with their weight. As of 2018, over 70% of American adults are overweight. This includes the nearly 40% of adults who are obese (394). Because obesity affects so many people, it's easy to understand why the fat acceptance movement has become so popular. But what they say simply isn't true. Losing weight is easier said than done. And obese people don't deserve to be ridiculed or shamed. But that doesn't mean that obesity is healthy.

Horoscopes

As well as not believing scientific and historical evidence, social justice warriors also believe in scientifically debunked phenomenon. A good example of this is horoscopes. Horoscopes have enjoyed a major resurgence. In 2017, *The Cut* (a left-leaning site aimed at millennials) saw traffic to their horoscopes section increase by 150% (395). And it has become a big part of the social justice warrior movement too. *Everyday Feminism* runs an e-learning course named 'Astrology as Healing Work'. It offers to help participants to cope "in today's triggering political climate" by studying their star charts (396). The concept of queer astrology has also been developed, which fuses academic queer theory with astrology (397). Astrology has no basis in science. It does not work. But according to a piece published in *VICE*, this doesn't matter because biological sex isn't real either. The author says that "it seems sort of arbitrary to make a distinction between assigning set meaning to predictable planetary movements and assigning set meaning to various specific parts of the human anatomy". This still doesn't make any sense. Even if sex weren't real, why would that make astrology valid? It is alarming that this pseudoscience has caught on in this technological age where scientific information has never been so readily available. It shows a disregard for empirical evidence.

This doesn't bode well for the future. By rejecting empirical evidence that doesn't support a certain narrative, this weakens public trust in the left. It also validates scepticism in climate change and other areas of scientific controversy. If these people say that horoscopes work, how can we trust them when they say that carbon dioxide emissions are causing the Earth to heat up? Furthermore, anti-science beliefs put individuals at risk. For instance, alternative medicine endangers people.

Even harmless alternative therapies, such as homeopathy, can lead to poorer treatment outcomes. One study found that people who use complementary therapies while undergoing Cancer treatment are twice as likely to die compared to those who only use conventional medicine (398,399). Which demonstrates the harms of being anti-science.

As well, by constantly dubbing scientific phenomenon as 'ethnocentric' or 'racist', real issues with racism and ethnocentrism in science get overlooked. Science and medicine do fail to include ethnic minorities. And that's a problem. Look at the case of Olufemi Akinnola, a black man in the UK who died of Coronavirus. Before he died, his health had been declining. He called NHS 111, England, Scotland and Wales's telemedicine service. One of the questions he was asked is if his lips were blue. He responded that he was black, and he couldn't tell. The call taker marked this on the computer system as 'no' and told him he didn't need any further care. He later died of hypoxia (oxygen deprivation). His family suspect he wasn't referred for urgent care because he couldn't answer the blue lips question (400). This example proves that there are genuine issues with race and healthcare. The NHS 111 system hadn't considered how someone who wasn't white might display symptoms of hypoxia. And as a consequence, Akinnola died. This must be fixed. But ignoring science isn't the answer.

Frankly, social justice warriors are detached from reality. If reality is what you want it to be, then things like electoral success or practical implementation of policies don't matter. You can float along in your little bubble where you are always right, and you don't need to take any notice of anyone else. Of course, we can't change reality. Often, the truth hurts. Sometimes, history doesn't support our view of the world, or science disproves something we think ought to be true. But the biggest issue with the spread of postmodern epistemology into mainstream society is that it fosters a mistrust of scientists. It gives the appearance that scientists are part of a privileged group who simply invent ways of oppressing the ordinary person for their own benefit. Given the current Coronavirus pandemic, this is worrying. Is this mistrust of experts why people won't wear masks in public? Or why they refuse to social distance? More frighteningly, this could impact on the uptake of the Coronavirus vaccine. Coronavirus won't go away until there is herd immunity. And that won't happen if people don't get vaccinated. Which demonstrates the serious implications of the anti-science movement in the left.

9. The Consequences of Identity Politics

You've seen how crazy and hypocritical identity politics is. And you've seen how contradictory and nonsensical the social justice warrior's beliefs are. But what are the consequences of this lunacy? This chapter looks at the damage the social justice warrior movement has done to the left. It will explore how the social justice warrior movement carved out the way for right-wing politicians to win and enact regressive policies. As well, this chapter will examine how identity politics has ultimately hurt the very people it purports to serve.

Trump was Elected President

In 2016, Trump was elected as president of the USA. There have been many conservative presidents, so why was Trump any worse? Trump isn't just any conservative president. He was a uniquely bad president for several reasons. First, he was corrupt. He never divested or put his business in a blind trust- something which all previous presidents have done (401). His presidency and his business interests became enmeshed. Trump incorporated business trips with official presidential visits. For instance, he visited his golfing resort in Doonbeg, Ireland, while on official presidential business (402). He has also profited from the Trump Hotel in Washington D.C. Political journalists used to congregate at Willard InterContinental hotel. But during the Trump presidency, they went to Trump's hotel, because that was where all of Trump's key people were. That meant Trump was profiting from journalists buying food and drink from the bar (403). This is just one of many examples of how Trump has capitalized on his presidency. He cares only for himself and used the presidency for his personal benefit. He was also unqualified for the job, having never held a previous political or military position. He is the first president to have no prior political or military experience (404). This has led to him making many serious mistakes, such as his poor handling of the Coronavirus pandemic.

You might think that now Biden has been elected president, all of Trump's policies will go away. This is not the case. The Republicans still have control of two out of the three branches of government. The Republicans held the Senate after the 2020 election (405). They also control the supreme court. While in power, Trump appointed three new justices: Neil Gorsuch, Brett Kavanaugh and Amy Coney Barrett. These appointments have made a firm conservative majority in the supreme court. This is particularly concerning as there are no term limits for judges, so they may have influence for several presidencies to come. For this reason, Biden will have an uphill struggle to pass any significant legislation.

Also, Trump has changed the role of the presidency in other ways. He has set a new low for the standards of how a president should conduct themselves. Institutions such as the impartiality of the civil service and courts are based on norms rather than formal regulations. These norms may not return, now that Trump has set a precedent for partisan appointees (406). Furthermore, he has legitimized conspiracy theories and fostered mistrust in the electoral system. Trump may be gone. But Trumpism is here to stay for several more years.

The Damage Trump Did

Trump has enacted many deeply damaging policies while in office. First, Trump's social policy has been terrible. Trump cut Obamacare drastically, removing the individual mandate (407). The reforms to Obamacare have left many people without access to healthcare. Furthermore, he has not done enough to control the Coronavirus outbreak in the USA, leading to tens of thousands of needless deaths. In addition, Trump defunded Planned Parenthood, which has restricted low income women's access to abortion (408). Meanwhile, the wealthiest Americans saw a huge tax cut (409). As well, Trump has made many regressive environmental policies. He has withdrawn the USA from the Paris Accords (410) and the Clean Power Plan (411). Trump also has a disappointing record on human rights. At the start of his term, he signed an order to keep Guantanamo Bay open. It's funny how nobody talks about Guantanamo Bay anymore- torture is no longer on the liberal agenda (412). He has also started the federal death penalty again. The first prisoner to be executed in 17 years was killed in July 2020 (413). As well, Trump has withdrawn the USA from the UN Human Rights Council (414).

The Boy Who Cried Wolf

So how is any of this the social justice warriors' fault? The answer is that the social justice warriors paved the way for a Trump government through accusing people of wrongdoing for trivial reasons. This lets actual bad guys slip past. When everyone is bad, who is really bad? If every white person is guilty of racism and white supremacy, what makes Trump worse than any other white person? Or if all men are sexist, what makes Trump more sexist than any other man? When we are constantly hearing about micro-aggressions, and subtle racism and sexism, it gets hard to know if to take public accusations seriously anymore. But Trump is a bad man. He has acted despicably on many occasions. Here are some examples:

Although his business credentials were a major draw for voters, Trump often acted unethically when conducting business. The Trump Organization was accused of racial discrimination in the 1970s for not letting some of their apartments to black people. The Department of Justice brought a legal case against the company. Although Fred Trump, Donald Trump's father, was still in charge of the company, Donald Trump held a senior role. Indeed, Donald Trump's first significant media exposure was a *New York Times* article reporting on the case (415). After several years, the Trumps settled the case out of court (416).

But that wasn't the only time that Trump was racist at work. The book *Trumped*, written by Jack O'Donnell, a former Trump Organization employee, accused Trump of being racist. According to the book, which is about the collapse of Trump's casino business in the late 1980s and early 1990s, Trump described black people as "slow". He also said that he didn't like them counting his money. The book also alleges that he was sexist. According to O'Donnell, Trump kept 'assuring' him that the women in the company were no threat to him because of their sex. On one occasion, Trump said to O'Donnell "What are you worried about Ivana for? She's just a woman. She can't take the business" (417).

Trump has done many other unethical things too. In the 1980s he intimidated the few remaining rent-controlled tenants from an apartment block he wanted to demolish. He also let the block fall into disrepair and cut off their utilities. He imposed strict rules, including forcing tenants who had remodelled their apartments (which the previous landlord had allowed) to put them back to their original design. They were given just 12 days to complete this work (418). Later, the *You've Been Trumped!* documentary showed him using the same shady tactics. At his golf course in Scotland, he waged war on some nearby farmers. He felt their farms spoiled the view. Like with his rent-controlled tenants in New York, he tried to coerce the farmers into leaving by cutting off their water and intimidating them. He also tried to compulsory purchase these farms (419). Furthermore, while building the golf course, he destroyed some sand dunes that had been designated as a site of special scientific interest. These sand dunes were home to a unique ecosystem. And it is against the law to modify a site of special scientific interest without permission (420). But that didn't matter to Trump.

There was also the Trump University scandal. Between 2005 and 2010, Trump ran courses under this brand.

However, it wasn't a university in the sense that it didn't award degrees. Students were promised workshops taught by real estate experts. The courses were very expensive- the most expensive cost $35,000. High-pressure sales techniques were used to recruit students on the promise that they would recoup their costs through business success in the future. Former students report being pressured to pay for the courses using multiple credit cards and their retirement savings. No cooling-off period was given (421). But these courses did not deliver what they advertised. As a result, the organization was forced to pay $25 million in compensation to former students (422).

The Trump Foundation was also used for nefarious purposes. In 2019, Trump's charitable foundation was wound down after giving its funds to Trump's presidential campaign. As well, it was forced to pay $2 million to other charities. The charity had been misusing its donations prior to the election as well. The foundation had paid for various expenses in the Trump Organization, including artwork for Trump buildings and legal settlements (423). The Trump Foundation also donated money to political campaigns, including the election campaign for Florida Attorney General Pam Bondi. Bondi later was part of Trump's legal team during his impeachment hearings (424).

As well, Trump treated his family terribly. He was very unkind to his elder brother, Fred Trump Jr. Mary Trump- Donald Trump's niece and Fred Trump Jr.'s daughter- claims Donald was unsympathetic to Fred Jr.'s alcoholism and ridiculed him for his career as a pilot. He forced Fred to leave his job and work for the family business. And he frequently called Fred by his favourite insult- "a loser". Fred Jr. died of an alcohol-related disease at the age of 42 (425).

In addition, during divorce proceedings, Ivana Trump accused Trump of raping her. This was written in *The Lost Tycoon*; another book published in the early 1990s about Trump's failing casino business and divorce from Ivana Trump. The book described how Trump grabbed Ivana, pulled out locks of her hair and then forced himself upon her. When the book was published, Ivana Trump's legal team sent a disclaimer. It said that she didn't want the word rape to be interpreted in "a literal or criminal sense" (426). Tellingly, Ivana didn't dispute the books description of what happened.

As well as abusing his wife, Trump abused his children. He has made many deeply inappropriate sexual comments about his eldest daughter, Ivanka. This includes saying that he fancied her more than his wife, and that he'd date her if she wasn't his daughter (427). As well, he participated in a photoshoot where he and Ivanka posed in sexually suggestive positions. Including one picture where he was on her lap and kissing him, and another where they were in bed together. Ivanka was 15 years old when the pictures were taken (428). Trump still displays inappropriate behaviour toward his daughter. According to Omarosa Newman, a former Apprentice contestant who later worked in Trump's white House, Trump continued to lust after Ivanka even when she was married (429).

He also abused his eldest son, Donald Trump Jr. When he was a small child, Trump would often call Don Jr. "a loser". Every day, from the age of four, Trump told his son to never trust anyone. He would then ask, "do you trust me?", to which young Don Jr. would respond "of course I trust you". Trump would respond by calling him a loser (430). Don Jr. freely admits this happened in his book. He doesn't seem to perceive that there's anything wrong with this (431).

Even as an adult, Trump mistreated his son. According to Scott Melkin, a man who knew Don Jr. at college, Trump was physically abusive toward Don Jr. Melkin recounts one occasion, when Don Jr. was going to a baseball game and Trump had come to pick him up. Don Jr. opened his front door, wearing a Yankees jersey. As soon as he saw him, Trump hit Don Jr. so hard that he fell to the floor. He then told Don Jr. to put a suit on. Don Jr. has denied this happened (432). However, other sources show that Trump was unkind to his son. Newman describes how Trump bullied Don Jr. while they were filming The All-Stars Apprentice series. Trump frequently called Don Jr. "stupid" and humiliated him in front of the other staff and contestants if Trump didn't agree with what he said (429).

Donald Trump Jr. has been left mentally scarred by all of this. Melkin describes Don Jr. as a disturbed person. He was an alcoholic in college. Don Jr.s' alcoholism was so severe that he would frequently black out and wet himself.

Because of this, he was nicknamed "diaper Don" (433). Another unnamed fraternity brother described an occasion where Don Jr. broke down in tears at a party while talking about his father (434). Don Jr. denies all of this. Don Jr. continued to drink excessively after college. In 2001, he was arrested for public intoxication in New Orleans after the Mardi Gras festival (435). He eventually gave up alcohol in 2002 (436). Even though he has overcome his alcoholism, Don Jr. is still a messed-up person. Based on the many accounts of how Trump treated his son, it's likely that Trump is the root cause of Don Jr's myriad psychological issues. Interestingly, there are many parallels between the way Donald Trump treated Fred Trump Jr. and Don Jr. He ridiculed them both and was controlling. Both turned to alcoholism to escape their troubles too.

As well, during his affair and marriage to Marla Marples, Trump showed little regard for Ivana or his children. He engineered the infamous frontpage "Best Sex I Ever Had" headline. Trump phoned up the *New York Post* and demanded a frontpage story. When the editor refused, Trump asked what would get a front-page story, the editor said that sex would. Trump responded that Marla said that sex with him was the best she'd had. When the editor asked for verification, Trump shouted Marla to ask if the best sex she'd ever had was with him. Somebody responded "yes" (in retrospect, Jill Brooke, who wrote the article, says she isn't sure if it was Marla who answered) (437). This article was upsetting for the whole Trump family. Don Jr. was especially badly affected. At 12 years old, he and his peers were old enough to read and understand the article. He has repeatedly spoken about how distressing this article was and how it led to his peers bullying him (431,433,436,438).Trump acted very selfishly. He made his divorce much more difficult for his family than it needed to be. There was no need for him to create this story or demand it be printed on the front page of the paper. It was just for attention.

Furthermore, after divorcing Marples, Trump abandoned his fourth child, Tiffany Trump. He had little involvement in her upbringing (439). Even now, she is not included in the campaign as much as Trump's other children. She doesn't have a job at the Trump Organization either, although this might be her choice. In one speech, Trump said he was proud of Tiffany "to a lesser extent" than his other children (440). She clearly isn't as close with her father as Trump's other children are.

Trump didn't just treat his wives and children disrespectfully. He has treated many other women badly too. 26 women have publicly accused Trump of sexual misconduct (441). There was also the infamous "Grab 'em by the pussy" Access Hollywood hot mic tape. Trump said that as a famous man, he could do what he wanted to women, and all he had to do was "grab 'em by the pussy" (442). This further demonstrates his lack of respect for women. As well, while he ran the Miss Universe beauty pageant, Trump would go into the dressing room while the contestants were getting dressed to look at them (443).

Trump has also been disrespectful toward veterans. He criticized John McCain for being a prisoner of war in Vietnam. When talking about McCain's military service, Trump said "I like guys who didn't get caught" (444). As well, when he was asked to visit a military cemetery in France, he refused to do so and he described the men who died during World War I as "suckers" and "losers" (445).

Few people see these behaviours as acceptable, especially for the leader of the free world. Most of these incidents predate Trump's run for president, so his accusers are not politically motivated. How could the American people trust a man who is prepared to cheat and defraud so many people? Who treats his own family so badly? Who is openly racist? Who shows such little respect for women? Who is so disparaging about veterans? But if you bring up the way Trump has treated his wives and children online, soon enough somebody will be along to say something to the effect of that they are white, rich people, so they do not feel sorry for them. The social justice warrior movement is giving Trump a free pass for his misdeeds because his victims are not considered oppressed. Is it okay for a white man to abuse his white children? Or his white wife? Is it acceptable to sexually harass white women? The answer, according to the social justice warriors, appears to be 'yes'. As well, Trump made his money in a bad way. There's little dispute that the Trumps have lied, cheated and conned their way into much of their wealth. Trump is fundamentally a bad guy.

But those misdeeds weren't mentioned much by the social justice warriors during the election campaign. Instead, they focused on more trivial matters. For instance, Lindy West, a fat rights activist, wrote an article in *The Guardian* describing how Trump was fatphobic. She urged fat people to form a coalition to vote against him (446). He was also accused of fatphobia when he said that the Democrat National Convention hacker could have been a 400lb man (447). Trump himself is obese, but the fat activists ignore that. Like with other minority groupings, only left-wingers can be oppressed.

When they accused him of racism, they fixated on more dubious examples. Writing in *Vox*, German Lopez gives examples of Trump's purported racism. These include criticizing America's trade relations with Japan and China, calling COVID-19 "the Chinese virus", firing a well-educated black candidate off The Apprentice, not supporting footballers who take the knee during the national anthem and referring to himself as a "law and order candidate" (Lopez describes this as a "dog whistle" for racists) (448).

Compared to prior accusations, these are all very mild. As a result, Trump's social justice warrior crimes meant more serious issues were overlooked. And so, this wicked man became president of the world's most powerful and important country.

Trump 2024?

Trump lost the election. That means he's gone for good, right? Actually, that's not correct. Firstly, he could run again. Admittedly, he would be 78 years old, which voters might find off-putting. By this stage, his health might not be strong enough for him to run either. It's more likely that we might have a Donald Trump Jr., Ivanka Trump or Eric Trump presidency to look forward to. All of Trump's eldest children have expressed an interest in running for office (449,450). If you think that the Trump kids can't be president because Trump lost the election, remember that George Bush Sr. was a one-term president. Yet George Bush Jr. still became president.

Donald Trump Jr., his eldest son, seems most likely to run. He often got "46" chants at rallies (451) (as in, they want him to be the 46th president, although that position is now occupied by Biden). A poll of registered Republican's preferences for the 2024 nomination put him second to Mike Pence (452). Although Pence has said he doesn't want to be president. Ivanka came joint second to last in the same poll and Eric wasn't included. Worryingly, Don Jr. is the most like his father. He described his views in *Triggered* and *Liberal Privilege*. He is massively pro-gun and loves hunting. He doesn't believe in climate change either. And he is anti-abortion. As well, he is against socialized medicine and holds many other distasteful views (431,453).

If any of the Trump kids did become president, they'd be as bad as their father. They all have little experience in politics aside from working with their father during the campaign or as unpaid advisors. Furthermore, the Trump children are not good people. They have been involved in nefarious activities in the Trump organization, that were on the boarder of legality. It would require an entire book to describe all the misdeeds of the Trump kids (and I might well write that book in the future). However, here are some of the most serious examples. In 2012, both Ivanka and Don Jr. were almost arrested for inflating the sales figures for the Trump SoHo hotel-condos to lure people into investing. The prosecution was mysteriously dropped after the Trump family's lawyer paid a visit to Manhattan's district attorney. Incidentally, this lawyer was the biggest donor to the district attorney's re-election campaign fund (454). The Trump children were also implicated in the Trump Foundation scandal. They were required to take training on the responsibilities of being a charity director (455). Are these the type of people who you want being president of the USA? Do they seem like caring, selfless people? Could you trust them with taxpayer's money? Would they care for the wellbeing of the country?

Labour Lose Four elections

In the UK, the left is in crisis. Labour haven't won an election since 2005. The 2010 election was most likely lost because of the 2008 recession. And the controversy over the UK's membership of the European Union, as well as the continuing implications of the 2008 recession were most likely why they lost in 2015. But in the 2017 and 2019 elections, political correctness was almost certainly a factor in Labour's defeat to the Conservatives.

Like with Trump in the USA, the Conservatives have introduced many harmful policies. They have also led the country badly. The biggest failing of the Conservative government has been their management of the Coronavirus pandemic. They have used it as an opportunity to help their friends at the expense of the rest of us. They put the economy ahead of people's lives. As a result, the UK has the highest excess mortality rate in Europe (456). It also has the 12th highest mortality per 100,000 people in the world as of October 2020 (457).

Nepotism has also been a problem for the Conservative government. A prime example of this is Dido Harding. Harding is a Conservative party peer who is married to a Conservative MP. She was put in charge of the Coronavirus track and trace system. To be blunt, Harding is a useless woman who has messed up repeatedly in her professional life. In 2017, she was CEO at the telecom company TalkTalk, when it was hacked by a 15-year-old boy (458). She was forced to resign after the company was fined £400,000 by the Information Commission for having inadequate security (459). Shortly after, she became chair of NHS Improvement. This is in spite of having no prior experience in healthcare (460). It's difficult to work out what NHS Improvement actually does (based on what their website says, it mostly seems to be managers holding meetings) (461). But it hasn't helped her in the current role. Given how bad she is at what she does, her connections to the Conservative party must be the only reason for her getting the track and trace job. Indeed, the Good Law Project has found that the role was never advertised and there was no application process (462).

Unsurprisingly, the track and trace system has been a huge failure. The system was supposed to reduce the spread of Coronavirus by telling the contacts of those who tested positive to isolate. Few people have been contacted, but there are numerous reports of tracers sat at home with nothing to do (463). As well, 16,000 positive test results were lost. This happened because the system used a Microsoft Excel spreadsheet which couldn't fit any more information. They should have used database software instead (464). Furthermore, track and trace has been outsourced to private companies (460). Local councils would have been better placed to do it. They are familiar with the local area and have access to other information about the area's residents. But instead, it's become a money-making opportunity for Serco and other companies.

If Labour had won in 2017 or 2019, would we be in this mess? It's impossible to know for certain, but it is unlikely that Labour would have treated the pandemic as a money-making opportunity in the same way the Conservatives have.

Brexit

Britain's decision to leave the European Union in the 2016 referendum was also partly caused by the social justice warriors. Although there were many factors behind this, part of the problem was the left's failure to understand the working-class. This results from the long-standing snobbery of the British liberal elite. They failed to explain how the EU worked to the general public. As a

Doesn't mention attempted Overthrow of a democratic vote.

result, many people blamed the EU for unpopular laws which actually had nothing to do with the EU. But perhaps the biggest issue was that many Eastern European migrants were moving to the UK and were employed in low-paid jobs. They had a reputation for refusing to learn English and for increasing pressures on schools and the NHS. Admittedly, not all of this was accurate. Many returned to their home countries when they required medical treatment (465). There were also high birth rates amongst British women, which led to a shortage of school places (466). Along with an ageing society in the 2010s, which put much more pressure on the NHS (467). But working-class people, who rely most on the state and on low-paid jobs, had most reason to be angry about all this.

That's not to say that the EU is flawless. The biggest issue is the democratic deficit. It has elected MEPs (members of the European Parliament). But the president and the commissioners are all unelected (468). Its policy making process is also opaque and the EU did a poor job of communicating what it was doing to the public. But the EU had its upsides too. It was the biggest international trade block- bigger than the USA (469). They also introduced many workers rights and other protections that were beneficial to the average person. These include the working time directive, that limited how many hours a person could work for. As well as guaranteed holidays, and stricter health and safety regulations (470). Those are now at risk thanks to Brexit.

Moreover, the biggest visible benefits of the EU were for middle-class cosmopolitans. These included the Erasmus foreign exchange program for university students, ease of travel to other EU countries (which benefits those who can afford to go abroad regularly), and the opportunity to move abroad (which benefits highly qualified workers with transferable skills). There was some funding for poor neighbourhoods (471), but that wasn't well-publicized. Out-of-touch politicians and the social justice warrior movement never tried to correct any misconceptions. Or understand why working-class people were unhappy. Nor did they ever try and find solutions to the pressures on the NHS, schools and other public services. Instead, they treated all opposition to the EU as bigotry. This shows in the big class divide in the referendum vote. 59% of people in the AB social grouping (upper middle class) voted remain, compared to just 36% of the DE group (lower working class) (472).

Splitting the Left

The most serious problem with the social justice warrior movement is that it has split the left.

First, the movement has divided the left by turning society-wide problems into personal issues. For instance, a young woman feels confined by the expectations of her gender. In the past, she would have found herself in good company with other women who felt the same way. And those women would have dedicated themselves to smashing women's oppression. Nowadays, she might find herself being told that her feelings are unique to her and that the reason she feels this way is because she is nonbinary. The implicit message being that every other woman is perfectly fine with being hemmed into traditional gender roles. She will be encouraged to change her appearance, pronouns and perhaps her name to fit her 'true self'. She might even take hormones or undergo surgery to reflect her new gender identity. Instead of her joining a fight against the patriarchy with other women (a society wide problem), the young woman has come to fight for her personal liberation from the woman's gender role (an individual problem).

Furthermore, focusing on identity and privilege theory divides the working-class. Writing in *Spiked!* magazine, Paddy Hannam explains that the Black Lives Matter movement emphasizes people's differences rather than their shared struggles. By saying white people are innately racist, black people are unwilling to work alongside them politically (473). However, people are stronger when they work together for a unified cause. And in many cases, there is a large overlap between different identity group's aims. Yet by focusing on different identity issues, this weakens the cause by splitting everyone's time and energy. For example, we could have a large movement of low-income people fighting for a universal income. Or we could have black people fighting for slavery reparations, disabled people fighting for more social security benefits and women fighting for more family-related benefits. In all these cases, the issue they are fighting against is poverty. But when they are divided, everyone ends up fighting for something slightly different, and nobody succeeds. Social justice warriors don't recognize that. On the contrary, they argue that the left needs to keep infighting. An article in *Everyday Feminism*, (474) said that "infighting isn't a weakness- it's a key part of who we are". The left doesn't have to emulate the right. But if the left keeps in-fighting in the way they do now, they will keep losing.

To illustrate this point, imagine this. You are at one of those team-building exercises where you have to put a kit together. The first team to complete the task wins. One team argues constantly over the best way to put the parts together. Members keep sulking and storming off when others disagree with them. They keep complaining, knit picking and undermining each other. The other team calmly work well together. They compromise and focus on completing the task in hand. Which team do you think will win? Of course, it would be the second team. All the arguing about the best approach that the first team did has wasted time and energy, instead of actually completing the task. Members who could have helped have instead not contributed or even hampered progress. Now, which team is more like the political left, and which team is more like the right? The left is always arguing, instead of working on a unified goal. And, like with the team-building exercise, this makes the left lose.

This division loses support for left-wing parties. If you're not on board with all the bizarre stuff the social justice warriors say (and let's face it, most people aren't), you're not going to vote for them. If you're being kicked out of a left-wing party, or told you're not welcome in the left, you're not going to vote for a left-wing party either. Nor will you contribute to left-wing parties and causes in other ways, such as volunteering or making donations. Floating voters don't like division either. The infighting in the left is not about resolving conflict. It's about egos and being out of touch. But more than anything, it's about proving that you're right and everyone else is wrong.

Hurting Marginalized People

The biggest issue with the social justice warrior movement is that it harms the very people it's meant to help. It has adversely impacted on marginalized people in many ways.

Although they intend to help the oppressed, the social justice warrior movement actually takes opportunities away from marginalized people. The concept of marginalized people is expanding to include more people who aren't oppressed. Meanwhile, actual oppressed people are being cast aside. One circumstance where this occurs is with gender. Since I wrote my previous book, I encountered the case of Tom Pashby. Pashby is an activist in the UK's Green Party who identifies as nonbinary and uses they/them pronouns. Pashby appears to have been born male (there are many old articles and blog posts where they use male pronouns) (475). They also have a strongly male appearance, including short hair and a beard. Pashby's conduct is a prime example of privilege laundering. In 2020, they ran for deputy leader of the Green Party. They were hailed for being potentially the first nonbinary person to hold a leadership position in a British political party (476). Even though Pashby is a white man. And there's no shortage of those in British politics.

What makes Pashby's actions especially problematic is that the Green Party has a gender balancing rule. For leadership roles, the Green Party elects two people for the position. They can either have two leaders of different genders and one deputy leader, or one leader, and two deputy leaders of different genders. The party recognizes nonbinary genders as being separate from male and female (477). At the moment, the party has a male and female leader, so this election was only for one candidate. But had that not been the case, they would have been electing two people.

For example, if five candidates stood for a leadership position, this is how it would work:

First place-male

Second place-male

Third place-female

Fourth place-female

Fifth place-male

The first placed male and the first placed female would get the position. In this case, that's the candidate in third place. Now, let's imagine that the male in second place declared he was now nonbinary. Here's what the results would look like:

First place-male

Second place-nonbinary

Third place-female

Fourth place-female

Fifth place-male

In this situation, the person in second place would get the position because he is a different gender to the person in first place. This means the woman would lose out on a leadership position, because she has been displaced by a man who considers himself nonbinary. It would also mean that there are now two male deputy leaders, defeating the object of the policy. In fairness to Pashby, after the leadership election, they said they felt the rule was unfair on women and that it should be reformed (478).

Nonetheless, allowing men who identify as nonbinary to be classed as a separate gender is depriving women of the chance to have their voices represented in politics. It's difficult to understand what makes Pashby different from any other man. They refuse to discuss their gender identity or explain what makes them nonbinary. When asked in hustings about the definition of a woman, Pashby gave a vague answer about identity. They then said it shouldn't be debated (479). Pashby, like most politicians, is a white man. This isn't a bad thing, but there is nothing remarkable about having yet another white man in politics. They have no understanding of women's issues.

They will never give birth, breastfeed a child, menstruate or require cervical smear screening or breast cancer screening. They are not more vulnerable to attacks on account of their sex as a woman is. Their career will never be held back by low expectations because of their sex. And they are less likely to carry the burden of being the primary carer of their children. Which is why Pashby can't represent women in the Green Party.

Positive discrimination or affirmative action can also disadvantage marginalized people. According to Murray, positive discrimination for high-ranking roles in organizations benefits the socially privileged. Many candidates who are chosen by positive discrimination programs were already on the path to success. For instance, in UK politics, the Conservative Party's drive to increase ethnic diversity amongst its members of parliament has led to a black former Etonian becoming an MP, along with an MP whose uncle is vice president of Nigeria (7). These might make the party more representative in terms of ethnicity, but not in terms of social class.

Where the social justice warrior's obsession with identity falls flat is that the world isn't neatly split into bad oppressors and good oppressed people. When an oppressed person doesn't behave how social justice warriors want them to behave, they hate that. They viciously attack that person. Social justice warriors emphasize the lived experience of minorities. But in practice, lived experience matters only when it supports the social justice warriors' views. When oppressed people don't agree with the social justice warrior movement, privileged people know best. Oddly, they spend more time attacking oppressed people they disagree with than they do attacking anyone else. For instance, a white Black Lives Matter protestor physically attacked a black man who removed a Black Lives Matter sign from a fence (480).

Another example of this viciousness is the case of Tom Clements. Clements is a man with Autism who is critical of the neurodiversity movement. He argues that it overlooks severely Autistic people, such as his brother. He has written books and articles about his views and experiences, including one which was published in *The Guardian* (83,481). However, his lived experience as a man with Autism and the brother of a man with much more severe Autism apparently aren't valid. Because he disagrees, he is relentlessly attacked by the neurodiversity movement. One activist wrote to *The Guardian* telling them that the entire neurodiversity community was suffering because of the article (482). Many others expressed similar sentiments on social media. Neurodiversity overlooks that Clements is Autistic. Because he doesn't agree with them and points out holes in their logic, he mustn't be one of them.

Another example is the gay community's rejection of Peter Thiel. Thiel is the co-founder of PayPal and several other technology companies. He is an ardent right-winger who spoke at the Republican Convention in 2016. He also happens to be gay. After speaking at the convention, the gay rights magazine *Advocate* published an article entitled

'Peter Thiel Shows Us There's a Difference Between Gay Sex and Gay'. The article claims that even though Thiel has sex with other men, he is not gay. As he supports a political party who are unsympathetic to gay rights, he can't be gay (7,483). The article said:

"'Gay' does not simply mean sex with another man or even interest in another man physically... but rather 'gay,' as defined by the liberation movement, meant an open declaration of acceptance within a community of people who understood that their sexual orientation made them a part of distinct culture."

So, according to the author of this article, you can't be gay and be right-wing. Of course, he is wrong. Gay simply means attracted to the opposite sex. It has nothing to do with politics. But for social justice warriors, being gay is first and foremost a political movement: you cannot be right-wing and gay. This is yet another example of the social justice warrior movement's black and white thinking. You are either an oppressed left-winger or an oppressive right-winger. Excluding right-wing people from marginalized groups is not helpful for the oppressed. It shows that the social justice warrior movement is not truly concerned with improving conditions for marginalized people.

Has anything changed for the better since the social justice warrior movement began? Both the UK and USA are going backward. Meanwhile, a small but vocal group of social justice warriors have alienated many people and push their countries to the right. All that social justice warriors have succeeded at is losing popular support for left-wing policies and politicians, and ultimately, sparking a major pushback on left-wing values. The social justice warrior movement has had many serious and wide-reaching implications for all of us. It's time for it to finish.

10. Conclusion

The social justice warrior movement has denatured the left and caused it to mutate into a terrible behemoth. The left used to champion free speech and tolerance, empiricism, communalism and compassion. All of those qualities are the antithesis of the social justice warrior movement's values. So, what are the social justice warrior's values? Remember in the introduction, the book described how the way that Generation Me were brought up. It found their upbringing made them individualistic, narcistic and fragile. And these attributes have been defining characteristics of the social justice warrior movement.

Individualism has been an enormous influence on the movement. The biggest way this has manifested is through the movement's embrace of capitalism. Capitalism centres selfishness and competition. Under capitalism, there will always be wealth inequality. As far as social justice warriors are concerned, that's perfectly acceptable. As long as a person's identity doesn't stop them from potentially rising to the top. Furthermore, the social justice warrior's emphasis on identity represents the left's changing focus to equality of opportunity over equality of outcome. By focusing on equality between different social groups rather than economic inequalities, this is a tacit approval of capitalism. Which is why they focus on eliminating these identity related inequalities, rather than on class oppression. This isn't right. Why does anyone deserve to be poor? As a species, humans have enough resources, compassion, and intelligence to provide enough for everyone. Everyone deserves to have the things they need in life. Seeing the left abandon this goal is deeply disturbing. Social justice warriors are committing to a society with deep economic inequalities. A society where people go without what they need for a decent standard of living. Would it really be much better to live in a society where there are more middle-class people from ethnic minority backgrounds, or more wealthy disabled people, if there are still millions of others suffering?

Furthermore, the social justice warrior's individualism atomizes social issues. Both being oppressed and an oppressor are now personal problems for an individual to work on. Rather than society-wide problems. Diversity training is an example of how being an oppressor is turned into an individual fault rather than an issue with society. In other cases, such as nonbinary genders, being oppressed is made into an individual struggle. This individualization of social issues stops people joining together for broader social change. Many individuals fighting for themselves cannot fight as effectively as a large group of people who are pushing for the same cause.

As well, because of the social justice warrior's narcissism, the left has become 'all about me'. All about my lived experience. All about my identity. All about my struggles. And all about what I need. But the people who are best at talking about their lived experience are the well-educated and middle-class. Those are not necessarily the people who are most marginalized. The social justice warrior movement is not a fair representation of either the population as a whole, or of society's most oppres. people. As a consequence, the most oppressed in societ, are overlooked by left-wingers. This is because they cannot advocate for themselves as well as social justice warriors can.

Instead of representing the working-classes and other downtrodden people, pushy, middle-class people have taken over the left. They have made it about the issues that matter to them: identity, the only thing that divides them and the only inequality they perceive. Because this group don't experience material deprivation, they are not aware or understanding of it. They aren't negatively affected by capitalism. Or immigration. Or deregulation. Nor do they have much experience with the social security system. So, they don't see why those things matter to people.

The narcissism of the social justice warriors has also made the left very arrogant. There's a certain amount of arrogance to assuming that you and you alone know best. That you are right about being a gender that most people don't recognize. Or that your sexuality is different to everybody else's, even when you are only attracted to the opposite sex. Or that your self-diagnosed disability is equally as valid as a professionally diagnosed disorder. It also takes some arrogance to say that your professor is wrong to let students be exposed to controversial ideas. Or that you know best about what content people should look at on social media. Or that other people's opinions aren't worth listening to. Rejecting empirical historical and scientific evidence that contradicts your ideology is also very arrogant.

Nor do the narcissistic social justice warriors understand that meaning well isn't always helpful. Their projects to help others are more about making themselves feel good rather than actually helping others. They don't see that a well-intended idea such as segregation to help black people can end up going very badly. Or that restricting freedom of speech could backfire. They think only of what makes them happy, rather than how to make the world a better place.

Furthermore, the self-obsession of the social justice warrior's means they are not connected with the concerns of the ordinary people. They are focused on arcane matters such as whether the word 'stupid' is ableist or the importance of nonbinary pronouns. These things don't matter to the majority of people. Most people have more pressing concerns. Like putting food on the table, getting the healthcare they need, or their children's education. And social justice warriors rarely talk about those things.

This disconnection from the rest of the world is a symptom of a middle-class insular left. A left who have little understanding of life for most people. In the social justice warrior movement, people live in the filter bubble; you are with people who agree with you all the time- mad ideas fly with nobody to question them. People keep bringing up even stranger ideas, that nobody disputes. As a result, their views get progressively more bizarre. The flawed logic that underlie these ideas (that reality is constructed to benefit the most advantaged in society) continues to go unchallenged. This too pushes voters away, who aren't prepared to vote for lunatics who spout outlandish ideas.

This narcissism is also why the social justice warriors treat wokeness as a competition. It's as if you score woke points by forging the most oppressed identity. This competition has little to do with any actual struggle. Their progressiveness and activism are purely for show. Instead, it's about forging an appearance of virtuousness and bravery. Which is why their activism is limited to superficial actions, such as purchasing 'ethical' products or posting about a cause on social media. They are not truly dedicated to left-wing causes. All they care about is making themselves look like good people.

The fragility of the social justice warriors has also been harmful. This fragility means the left don't have the strength and resilience to tackle the tough issues. Social justice warriors have learned that they are delicate, damaged little dears who need to be wrapped in cotton wool. As they have been raised to focus on mental health and self-esteem, they do not know how to cope with discomfort and defeat. They have spent their whole lives being protected from such things. Consequently, they have never matured into resilient adults.

This causes many serious issues. Firstly, social justice warriors can't cope with disagreement. That makes co-operation and compromise difficult. Few people agree all the time, so not coping with disagreement leads to in-fighting. As well, being too fragile to debate is off putting to potential supporters. Debates bring the opportunity to vince other people of your views. As well, once you understand why someone holds a certain view, it's easier to refute them and convert them to your way of thinking. Furthermore, sometimes, hearing other opinions presents an opportunity to refine your own views. It can help highlight weaknesses in your own viewpoint and enable you to consider solutions to those flaws. It can also help you to develop more nuanced positions on certain topics. But by shutting down debates, left-wingers are losing those opportunities. In addition, the insistence on shutting down debates and censoring words and ideas promotes intolerance and close-mindedness. Things which the left have traditionally stood against. The left is becoming as narrow-minded as the traditional conservatives.

In addition, social justice warriors are too fragile to endure the sacrifices that real progress requires. Social change requires sacrificing material comforts. Or questioning certain ideas that upset others. Or spending time and effort on a serious campaign. But the social justice warriors are not prepared to do that. They instead waste time on ineffective campaigns aimed only at other social justice warriors, such as making a hashtag trend on Twitter. These do not produce social change in the way that other forms of campaigning do.

Social justice warrior concepts themselves also foster a mistrust of others. Thanks to the focus on micro-aggressions and unconscious bias, social justice warriors live in a world where everyone is out of hurt them. To social justice warriors, the smallest remark or the most subtle facial expression, might symbolize a deep hatred of them. This too has created fissures in the left. Again, it's hard to work with someone who is trying to harm you. So, when people perceive those they disagree with have some deep prejudice against them, this makes co-operation difficult. It also contributes to infighting in the left.

A further manifestation of this fragility is the way that social justice warriors perceive that speech and ideas can represent violence. They are truly devastated by disagreement and small insults that most people can shake off. Their physical violence towards opponents happens because they are so hurt that they lose control of their feelings. They cannot keep their emotions in check or conduct themselves in a mature way. Which makes it more difficult for the public to take the left seriously.

Ultimately, social justice warriors live in an infantile fairy tale world where life is a struggle between good oppressed people and the evil oppressors. They perceive that like the hero in a children's story, it's their job to fight the bad people. They do this by silencing and attacking those they disagree with. As well as by physically and emotionally harming them. With the goal of ultimately defeating them. The social justice warriors do not need to listen to the evil opposition or consider the nuances of an argument. They are right. Everyone should listen to them. End of story. Of course, life is not like a children's book. Reality is complex. Things are rarely a simple matter of good and bad. And everyone is unique in some ways, and the same in other ways. A poor white man might have more in common with a poor black man than he does with a rich white man, even though the poor man and the rich man are the same race. Which is one of the reasons why identity politics fails. But social justice warriors are not equipped to deal with the messy realities of life.

There are many serious implications of this. We have seen that the social justice warriors have a number of fixations. And we have seen the results of these. We have seen how their obsession with identity has pushed aside the left's concern with class. Their narcissism has overshadowed the left's compassion for the most needy. Their obsession with mental illness has destroyed the left's spirit and resilience. Their focus on the idea that words hurt more than actions has destroyed the left's open-mindedness and empathy. Their support of capitalism has damaged the left's core tenants. And ultimately, the social justice warriors have done irrevocable damage to politics, to policy and to society.

The left has left behind the people it is supposed to be for: the working-classes. As a result, the working-classes are left without a voice. In the UK and the USA, there has been a growth in working-class people voting for the Conservative party and the Republican parties respectively. Those parties have repaid their new voters by ignoring them. Nothing has got better for the people of northern England who voted Conservative in 2019, or the people of states such as Pennsylvania or Wisconsin who voted for Trump in 2016. These places have been hit hard by Coronavirus too. They have elected leaders who have no understanding of ordinary life. Neither Trump nor Boris Johnson have had anything remotely close to a normal life. They have grown up institutionalized in a world where they don't even do day-to-day tasks such as grocery shopping or cleaning. How can they make decisions for the rest of us?

The social justice warrior's rejection of facts has also been a serious problem. Postmodernism has led to pseudoscience and rejection of basic scientific principles becoming a defining characteristic of left-wing politics. For voters, this makes left-wingers look insane (does anyone with a microgram of common sense truly think that biological sex isn't real or that astrology really works?). The adoption of the idea that reality doesn't exist also makes it harder to know what's true and what's not. This has made the electorate more receptive to fake news. At the moment, both the left and the right say outlandish things, and nobody knows who to believe. But the left makes far more ridiculous statements than the right. So, the right's fake news feels credible in comparison.

Worst of all, they've made Trump look like a reasonable person. Under normal circumstances, there's no way that Trump would have won the election. He wouldn't have even got through the primaries. But social justice warriors have made him appear to be a credible candidate. Compared to the lunacy the social justice warrior movement spouted, he was a grounded, logical person. Who would the average person vote for: a man who says you can become biologically female simply by identifying as such, or a man who says America is being screwed over by every other country in the world? One view is plain wrong. The second is an opinion a lot of people might not agree with, but it can't be shown to be objectively untrue in the way that the former's view can. Most people would choose the latter, simply because he sounds less crazy. Most years, the latter man wouldn't have even got a look in, but we've created a situation where crazy things now sound perfectly reasonable.

Furthermore, when it came to Trump, the social justice warriors had cried wolf so many times. The wolf arrived. Nobody listened. They'd heard it all before. Everyone had heard about how this Republican was a huge bigot, or how that man was the worst person ever and who'd destroy the world. So of course, the electorate switched off when left-wingers tried to point out that Trump was genuinely a very bad man. The left were also complacent. They were too out of touch to see how popular Trump was with certain demographics. And they assumed that because they hated Trump, so must everyone else.

In the long-term, as a consequence of right-wing parties being in power, progress towards a more egalitarian society is lost. Although there will be more left-wing governments in the future, it can take many years to reverse certain policies. Especially big reforms such as reintroducing a service that had been abolished or changing the structure of an organization. Often, there are legal issues and other bureaucracy to contend with, such as being required to consult stakeholders. The practical implementations can also take a long time, such as staff recruitment and finding buildings for a service to be delivered from. In addition, policies may need approval from the legislature (UK Parliament or Congress in the USA). This can be difficult to get, especially in the USA, where congress may be controlled by the opposition party. In the USA, there is also the chance that a law will be blocked by the supreme court. As the supreme court currently has a strong conservative majority, this will impede progress for many years to come. The longer right-wing parties are in power, the harder it is to reverse the damage. In the case of climate change and other forms of environmental degradation, there may not be much time left to enact changes and prevent further damage from occurring.

There are implications on an individual level too. For instance, the politicization of mental health is damaging for both left-wingers and right-wingers. Socio-political issues such as poverty can affect mental health. But mental health isn't a left-wing thing. If you're politically right-wing and struggling with your mental health, the politicization of mental health might make it harder to get help. If you and those around you perceive getting treatment for a mental illness to be a left-wing activity, it could put you off seeking treatment. It almost makes being mentally ill appear optional. We don't think of any other illness as being associated with a certain political position. So why are we doing it with mental health?

The social justice warrior movement is also damaging individual's critical thinking faculties. People are not exposed to as many new ideas and differing opinions because of the level of polarization and dogma of the left. This is especially problematic in universities. The traditional aim of university education- especially the humanities and social sciences- has been to teach critical thinking skills. They do this by exposing students to a wide array of views on a certain topic. But by censoring 'triggering' material, students are not learning to think critically. This is leading to a generation of left-wingers who have been trained to swallow dogma without much thought. This is reinforcing the issues with identity politics by stopping people from challenging the social justice warrior movement.

And without a big change, these issues will only get worse. The left will sink into an even darker, deeper hole. They will lose sight of the outside world and drift further into the identity politics void. The social justice warrior movement loses votes for left-wing parties. So, we can expect to see many more right-wing governments in both the UK and the USA. For the USA there's also the chance of many more Republican-led congresses, even with a Democrat president.

So, what are the solutions to this? We all must fight the social justice warrior movement. That's easier said than done, but here's some ideas: first, push for class to be represented in the left. Join organizations that are all about class-based politics and traditional socialism. If you're already part of left-wing groups, push for class-related causes to be represented. Make sure issues relating to class and capitalism are not forgotten about. Next, vote for politicians and parties who stand for socialism and the economic left. After that, speak up for those who can't speak for themselves. Explain the issues with listening to lived experience. Especially why working-class people don't have as loud a voice online as middle-class people do.

Also, talk to your left-wing friends and family about the problems with identity politics and the social justice warrior movement. Make them understand why it's an issue. Show them how it's leading to more serious issues being ignored and how it's stopping left-wingers from achieving electoral success. Point out that it's paving the way for conservatives to win. And tell them why they need to act. The more of us there are working on this issue, the better. Some people might be happy to go along with wokeness, even when they don't really agree with it. Show them that it doesn't have to be that way by telling them about left-wingers who are against the social justice warrior movement. Encourage them to resist the woke leviathan.

Another thing that you can do to help is to speak up for free speech. Explain why free speech matters to your friends and family. Tell people why even restricting 'hate speech' comes with many problems. Campaign and join campaign groups that stand up for free speech. Protest restrictions on free speech, including restrictions on social media. Also, consider boycotting social media companies that don't support free speech. Or use social media sites that support free expression, such as Parler and Spinster. If you're a university student or a lecturer, protest no-platforming of speakers and groups. Even for speakers and groups you disagree with. Remember that one day, it could be you being censored. As well, stand up for victims of censorship. If there's a legal case (which is happening more frequently in the UK), donate to their legal fees. Give verbal and emotional support to people you know who are being censored too.

If you're a parent, make sure you're not raising tomorrow's social justice warriors. Part of the reason we are in this mess is because of the fragile young generation. Admittedly, parenting is hard. But ask yourself: are you overprotective? Do you avoid enforcing boundaries? Do you step in and fight your child's battles for them? Do you help them with things they could manage for themselves? Are you treating your young adult son or daughter like a child? Beware that if you are, you could have the next generation's social justice warrior on your hands. Kids need to be exposed to difficult situations. Let them lose games. Let them get upset. Let them be okay with not being good at everything. People need challenges to make them stronger. Remember the old saying 'prepare the child for the road, not the road for the child.' If you raise them well, they will grow into strong, resilient adults.

If your older kids are heading off to university, try to stop them taking victim studies disciplines. There's nothing wrong with social sciences and humanities. But encourage them to take a broad subject where they're not as exposed to social justice warrior thinking. For example, if your child is interested in literature by black writers, encourage them to take literature rather than black studies. Most courses offer the chance for students to specialize in areas of interest, so a student can still study what they love. These broader disciplines offer other benefits too, including higher rates of employment and more opportunities for further study. And it should help stop them becoming sucked into the social justice warrior movement.

Finally, don't get caught in the wokeness trap. Don't use content warnings on blog posts, articles or lectures. And don't shy away from talking about tough topics in real life or online in case someone finds it triggering. Humans as a species can cope. We are resilient. We can live with being upset or angry for a short time. Also, don't take any notice of people who complain they're offended without good reason. And ignore woke demands. Resist pressure to use 'woke' spellings and words, such as 'folx' or 'people with uteruses' too. Admittedly, this is difficult. Social justice warriors are good at guilt-tripping people. They will present their wokeness as a small curtesy: "You just have to do this tiny thing to put me at ease". Nobody likes seeing other people upset or uncomfortable. And nobody wants to be offensive. Which is why it's all too easy to go along with wokeness. If you don't want a confrontation, you can conveniently 'forget' to comply with requests to do such things. Social justice warriors are good at making you think you are a bad person. So, you'll have to find the strength to ignore their emotional blackmail. But have faith and confidence in yourself. You are doing the right thing. These feel like tiny, insignificant actions. But these tiny actions add up and make a big difference.

If you know someone who's been taken in by identity politics, you can gently try and convert them. Are they too self-absorbed? Try getting them away from social media.

Encourage them to spend time in the real world. Do activities with them to take their mind off the online world. This will reduce their exposure to social justice warrior views and help them realize the world isn't all about them. Also, be patient with them. Don't argue outright with them. Instead, carefully disagree and pick the right moments to do it. There are no quick fixes and it would take a lot of time and patience. But don't lose hope.

If you've been swept up by the social justice warrior movement, here's some tips:

First, stop being narcistic. The world doesn't revolve around you. You are one of over seven billion people on this earth. Therefore, you and your 'lived experience' isn't that important. And there are worst things in the world than micro-aggressions or unconscious bias. Like torture, severe poverty and human trafficking. Also, remember that the middle-class, educated experience of oppression isn't the same as oppression for poorer people. In any case, your experience of oppression isn't necessarily representative. You don't speak for everyone; your lived experience is no more valid or important than someone else's lived experience. Instead, think of others. Think of the people who can't stand up for themselves. Understand that everyone has pain in their lives. Even white, cisgender, nondisabled heterosexual men. Be selfless and empathetic.

Next, stop being so out of touch. Sometimes reality doesn't fit with your ideology. Often, things are both true and upsetting. For instance, obesity is unhealthy. This isn't something that's been dreamed up by wicked white men as a way of keeping everyone else down. The diet industry or medicine industry argument doesn't work either. There's an even bigger processed food industry who make a lot of money out of getting people to overeat. This is just one of many examples of why you need to look at the evidence, not make evidence fit your worldview. Other times, things aren't quite as you imagine them to be. Take sex work for example. Sex work is bad for most people. And most data proves that. Not everyone is an empowered university-educated person whose Mum and Dad pay for everything. Many are truly reliant on horrible things like sex work to live. You can't twist reality to fit the way you feel the world ought to be.

Also, judge people for what they do and say, not who they are. Nobody is innately good or bad. There are good and bad people of all genders, sexualities, races and with and without disabilities. If someone is trying to do the right thing, embrace that, regardless of their identity. Remember too that everyone makes mistakes. Having a 'one strike and you're out' approach to people is not good. For example, someone said something you found offensive or didn't quite get it right when talking about a sensitive topic. That doesn't mean their life should be ruined or that they have no place in the left. Nor do they need to be publicly humiliated. Instead, consider this: do they show contrition? Have they made the mistake again since it was pointed out to them? If they have learned their lesson, forgive them.

Next, stop being offended all the time. Sometimes, being offended is a case of 'seek and ye shall find'. If you look for signs everyone is secretly out to get you, you'll find them, even when most people don't actually want to hurt you. It's bad for you. It's not healthy to think everyone wants to harm you. And it gives other people the feeling that they can't do right for doing wrong. Most people mean well, even when they make mistakes. Furthermore, being fragile is not an attribute to be proud of. Stop framing everything as a great trauma. You are stronger than you realize. Even if you do have a mental illness.

As well, learn that your feelings aren't always valid. You don't need to be guided by your emotions unquestionably. Sometimes feelings can be disproportionate to a situation. They can make you think things are worse than they really are. Questioning if your feelings are reasonable is not invalidation. It can be the right thing to do. To help with this, stop using self-help mental health groups and following mental health accounts on social media. They tell you what you want to hear, not what you need to hear. Good mental health matters. There are good groups and accounts out there who can help, like registered charities and medical organizations. But watch out for those that encourage you to wallow in your feelings. The same problem can occur in real life too. Think about if your friends are good for your mental health. Ask yourself: are your peers who encourage you to listen to your feelings really helping? That initial validation might feel good, but do you feel good the rest of the time? Maybe spend time with different people who can challenge your negative thoughts. Mental illness has become an enormous industry. A lot of people are making a lot of money out of your continued misery.

Finally, compromise with other left-wingers. When people disagree, it's not because they hate you. They simply have a different perspective. Do you hate the people you disagree with? Most people aren't closeted bigots. Sometimes, in life, you'll have to work with people who you disagree with. You'll have to get people who you hate to support your causes to win elections or to convince policymakers or others of your views. But that's life. We have to do it because if we don't, we won't achieve our goals, or for an election campaign, someone worse will swoop into power. Remember that the only person who thinks exactly as you do is you. You can't have your way all of the time. If co-operating with others to secure an electoral victory is too difficult, think about this: which is better? A party who supports 70% of what you believe in being elected? Or a party who supports 20% of what you believe in coming to power? Those are your choices.

Right now, it's time to be sensible. The world is in grave danger. We need to work together to protect it. It's time to use reason and logic, not emotions. It's time to think like a mature adult, not a self-involved adolescent. We need tough, fair-minded leadership to solve the world's problems. The left can provide that much better than the right can. But the social justice warrior movement does not have the answers.

References

1. Nagle A. Kill All Normies: Online Culture Wars from 4chan and Tumblr to Trump and the Alt-Right. Zero Books; 2017. 137 p.

2. Power G. What Is Identity Politics? [Internet]. The Week UK. 2019 [cited 2020 Oct 18]. Available from: //www.theweek.co.uk/104473/what-is-identity-politics

3. Hobsbawm E. Identity Politics and the Left. New Left Review. 1996;217:10.

4. Caldwell D. Social Justice Warrior [Internet]. Know Your Meme. 2015 [cited 2020 Aug 24]. Available from: https://knowyourmeme.com/memes/social-justice-warrior

5. Chua A. How America's Identity Politics Went from Inclusion to Division. The Guardian [Internet]. 2018 Mar 1 [cited 2020 Oct 1]; Available from: https://www.theguardian.com/society/2018/mar/0 1/how-americas-identity-politics-went-from-inclusion-to-division

6. Bell L. Trigger Warnings: Sex, Lies and Social Justice Utopia on Tumblr. Networking Knowledge: Journal of the MeCCSA Postgraduate Network [Internet]. 2013 Aug 8 [cited 2020 Feb 3];6(1). Available from: http://www.ojs.meccsa.org.uk/index.php/netknow/article/view/296

7. Murray D. The Madness of Crowds: Gender, Race and Identity. Bloomsbury Continuum; 2019. 341 p.

8. Sullivan A. Is Intersectionality a Religion? [Internet]. Intelligencer. 2017 [cited 2020 Jul 4]. Available from: https://nymag.com/intelligencer/2017/03/is-intersectionality-a-religion.html

9. Twenge JM. Generation Me: Why Today's Young Americans Are More Confident, Assertive, Entitled--And More Miserable Than Ever Before. Revised, Updated. New York: Atria Books; 2014. 377 p.

10. Brown A. What's Your Parenting Style? [Internet]. The Independent. 2017 [cited 2020 Aug 25]. Available from: http://www.independent.co.uk/life-style/health-and-families/helicopter-or-lawnmower-modern-parenting-styles-can-get-in-the-way-of-raising-well-balanced-children-a7850476.html

11. Dixon H. 'Helicopter Parents' Creating a Generation Incapable of Accepting Failure [Internet]. The Telegraph. 2013 [cited 2020 Aug 25]. Available from: https://www.telegraph.co.uk/education/10277505/Helicopter-parents-creating-a-generation-incapable-of-accepting-failure.html

12. Cain Miller C, Engel Bromwich J. Snowplough Parenting Is the Latest Worrying Trend for Overprotective Parents [Internet]. The Independent. 2019 [cited 2020 Aug 25]. Available

from: https://www.independent.co.uk/news/health/snow plough-parenting-helicopter-felicity-huffman-lori-loughlin-college-admissions-scam-a8828631.html

13. Kamenetz A. Are Helicopter Parents Ruining Summer Camp? [Internet]. NPR.org. 2017 [cited 2020 Aug 25]. Available from: https://www.npr.org/sections/ed/2017/07/24/5330 59271/are-helicopter-parents-ruining-summer-camp

14. Morin A. Researchers Say 3 Kinds of Parents Interfere with Their Adult Children's Careers [Internet]. Inc.com. 2018 [cited 2020 Aug 24]. Available from: https://www.inc.com/amy-morin/3-types-of-helicopter-parents-who-involve-themselves-in-their-adult-childs-career.html

15. Kidd SA, Eskenazi B, Wyrobek AJ. Effects of Male Age on Semen Quality and Fertility: A Review of the Literature. Fertility and Sterility. 2001 Feb 1;75(2):237–48.

16. Leridon H. Can Assisted Reproduction Technology Compensate for the Natural Decline in Fertility with Age? A Model Assessment. Human Reproduction. 2004 Jul 1;19(7):1548–53.

17. Loughran T. This Is How IVF Changed the World's Perception of Infertility [Internet]. The Independent. 2018 [cited 2020 Oct 19]. Available from: https://www.independent.co.uk/life-style/health-and-families/ivf-infertility-treatment-

how-change-louise-brown-motherhood-a8332241.html

18. Dunne C, Roberts J. Social Egg Freezing: A Viable Option for Fertility Preservation. British Columbia Medical Journal. 2016;58(10):573–7.

19. Petropanagos A, Cattapan A, Baylis F, Leader A. Social Egg Freezing: Risk, Benefits and Other Considerations. CMAJ. 2015 Jun 16;187(9):666–9.

20. Gibson FL, Ungerer JA, Tennant CC, Saunders DM. Parental Adjustment and Attitudes to Parenting After in Vitro Fertilization. Fertility and Sterility. 2000 Mar;73(3):565–74.

21. Paul M. Authoritarian Parenting, Permissive Parenting or Loving Parenting [Internet]. HuffPost. 2011 [cited 2020 Nov 27]. Available from: https://www.huffpost.com/entry/authoritarian-parenting-p_b_1148185

22. Blake A. The "Participation Trophy" Generation. Washington Post [Internet]. 2014 Aug 20 [cited 2020 Nov 27]; Available from: https://www.washingtonpost.com/news/the-fix/wp/2014/08/20/meet-the-participation-trophy-generation/

23. Sack D. Could Your Child Have Too Much Self-Esteem? [Internet]. HuffPost. 2012 [cited 2020 Feb 18]. Available from: https://www.huffingtonpost.com/david-sack-md/children-self-esteem_b_1822809.html

24. Leary MR. Sociometer Theory and the Pursuit of Relational Value: Getting to the Root of Self-Esteem. European Review of Social Psychology. 2005 Jan 1;16(1):75–111.

25. Zimmermann KA, Emspak J. Internet History Timeline: ARPANET to the World Wide Web [Internet]. livescience.com. 2017 [cited 2020 Oct 20]. Available from: https://www.livescience.com/20727-internet-history.html

26. Haimson OL, Dame-Griff A, Capello E, Richter Z. Tumblr was a Trans Technology: The Meaning, Importance, History, and Future of Trans Technologies. Feminist Media Studies. 2019 Oct 18;0(0):1–17.

27. Pariser E. The Filter Bubble: What the Internet Is Hiding from You. London: Penguin; 2012. 304 p.

28. Millar F. Some MPs Enjoyed a New Labour Education. Do They Know How Lucky They Were? [Internet]. The Guardian. 2020 [cited 2020 Oct 19]. Available from: http://www.theguardian.com/education/2020/feb/04/mp-new-labour-education-lucky-blair-brown

29. Vidler E, Clarke J. Creating Citizen-Consumers: New Labour and the Remaking of Public Services: Public Policy and Administration. 2005 Apr 1;20(2):19–37.

30. Capeheart L, Milovanovic D. Social Justice: Theories, Issues, and Movements. Rutgers University Press; 2007. 273 p.

31. Rawls J. A Theory of Justice. Reissue. Cambridge, Mass: Harvard University Press; 1971. 624 p.

32. Nozick R. Anarchy, State and Utopia. Wiley-Blackwell; 1974.

33. Mattix M. Should the B in Black Be Capitalized? [Internet]. The American Conservative. 2020 [cited 2020 Oct 3]. Available from: https://www.theamericanconservative.com/prufro ck/should-the-b-in-black-be-capitalized/

34. Appiah KA. The Case for Capitalizing the 'B' in Black [Internet]. The Atlantic. 2020 [cited 2020 Aug 28]. Available from: https://www.theatlantic.com/ideas/archive/2020/0 6/time-to-capitalize-blackand-white/613159/

35. Benavides L. Why Labeling Antonio Banderas A 'Person Of Color' Triggers Such A Backlash [Internet]. NPR.org. 2020 [cited 2020 Nov 7]. Available from: https://www.npr.org/2020/02/09/803809670/why-labeling-antonio-banderas-a-person-of-color-triggers-such-a-backlash

36. Kirkup J. Can You Go to Jail for 'Misgendering'? One British Journalist Is About to Find Out [Internet]. Spectator USA. 2019 [cited 2020 Mar 2]. Available from: https://spectator.us/misgendering-child-british-journalist/

37. Walton S. How the Frankfurt School Diagnosed the Ills of Western Civilisation [Internet]. Aeon. 2017 [cited 2020 Oct 19]. Available from:

https://aeon.co/essays/how-the-frankfurt-school-diagnosed-the-ills-of-western-civilisation

38. Marcuse H. Repressive Tolerance (full text) - Herbert Marcuse Official Website [Internet]. Herbert Marcuse Official Homepage. 1969 [cited 2020 Aug 2]. Available from: https://www.marcuse.org/herbert/publications/196 0s/1965-repressive-tolerance-fulltext.html

39. Laclau E, Mouffe C. Hegemony and Socialist Strategy: Towards a Radical Democratic Politics. Second. Verso; 1985. 225 p.

40. Lyotard J-F. The Postmodern Condition: A Report on Knowledge. Manchester: Manchester University Press; 1984. 144 p.

41. Pluckrose H. How French "Intellectuals" Ruined the West: Postmodernism and Its Impact, Explained [Internet]. Areo. 2017 [cited 2020 Feb 27]. Available from: https://areomagazine.com/2017/03/27/how-french-intellectuals-ruined-the-west-postmodernism-and-its-impact-explained/

42. Butler C. Postmodernism: A Very Short Introduction. Oxford: OUP Oxford; 2002. 152 p.

43. Baron-Cohen S. The Essential Difference. London: Penguin; 2004. 288 p.

44. Eliot L. Neurosexism: The Myth that Men and Women have Different Brains. Nature. 2019 Feb 27;566(7745):453–4.

45. League for the Fifth International. Marxism Versus Postmodernism [Internet]. League for the Fifth International. 1997 [cited 2020 Feb 13]. Available from: https://fifthinternational.org/content/marxism-versus-postmodernism?q=content/marxism-versus-postmodernism

46. Marx K. On Freedom of the Press [Internet]. Marx/Engels Internet Archive; 1842 [cited 2020 Jul 28]. Available from: https://marxists.catbull.com/archive/marx/works/1842/free-press/ch05.htm

47. Marx K, Engels F. Address of the Central Committee to the Communist League by Marx and Engels [Internet]. Marxists.org. 1850 [cited 2020 Feb 11]. Available from: https://www.marxists.org/archive/marx/works/1847/communist-league/1850-ad1.htm

48. Marx K. Economic & Philosophic Manuscripts of 1844 [Internet]. Marxists.org; 1844 [cited 2020 Aug 23]. Available from: https://www.marxists.org/archive/marx/works/1844/manuscripts/comm.htm

49. Pluckrose H, Lindsay J. Cynical Theories: How Activist Scholarship Made Everything about Race, Gender, and Identity—and Why This Harms Everybody. Durham: Pitchstone Publishing; 2020.

50. Paglia C. Junk Bonds and Corporate Raiders: Academe in the Hour of the Wolf. Halperin DM,

Winkler JJ, editors. Arion: A Journal of Humanities and the Classics. 1991;1(2):139–212.

51. Butler J. Gender Trouble. New York: Routledge; 1990. 272 p.

52. Sokal AD. Transgressing the Boundaries: Toward a Transformative Hermeneutics of Quantum Gravity. Social Texts. 1996;(46/47):217–52.

53. Sokal A, Bricmont J. Fashionable Nonsense: Postmodern Intellectuals' Abuse of Science. New York: St Martin's Press; 1999. 300 p.

54. Boghossian P, Lindsay J. The Conceptual Penis as a Social Construct: A Sokal-Style Hoax on Gender Studies [Internet]. Skeptic. 2017 [cited 2020 Feb 26]. Available from: https://www.skeptic.com/reading_room/conceptual-penis-social-contruct-sokal-style-hoax-on-gender-studies/

55. Tolliver S. What the 'Grievance Studies Affair' Says About Academia's Social Justice Warriors [Internet]. The Hill. 2020 [cited 2020 Aug 24]. Available from: https://thehill.com/opinion/education/490366-what-the-grievance-studies-affair-says-about-academias-social-justice

56. McIntosh P. White Privilege: Unpacking the Invisible Knapsack [Internet]. Racial Equality Tools. 1989 [cited 2020 Jul 10]. Available from: https://www.racialequitytools.org/resourcefiles/mcintosh.pdf

57. Ray W. Unpacking Peggy McIntosh's Knapsack [Internet]. Quillette. 2018 [cited 2020 Jul 11]. Available from: https://quillette.com/2018/08/29/unpacking-peggy-mcintoshs-knapsack/

58. Choonara E, Prasad Y. What's Wrong with Privilege Theory? [Internet]. International Socialism. 2014 [cited 2020 Jul 9]. Available from: https://isj.org.uk/whats-wrong-with-privilege-theory/

59. Dalmia S. The Right's Identity Politics Is More Dangerous Than the Left's [Internet]. Reason.com. 2019 [cited 2020 Jun 8]. Available from: https://reason.com/2019/03/17/why-the-rights-identity-politics-is-more/

60. Thandeka. Thandeka: Why Some Anti-Racist Programs Will Fail and Others Will Succeed [Internet]. Films for Action. 2015 [cited 2020 Jul 30]. Available from: https://www.filmsforaction.org/articles/why-antiracism-will-fail/

61. Crenshaw K. Demarginalizing the Intersection of Race and Sex: A Black Feminist Critique of Antidiscrimination Doctrine, Feminist Theory and Antiracist Politics. 1989;31.

62. hooks bell. Ain't I a Woman: Black Women and Feminism. Second. Routledge; 1981. 220 p.

63. Steinmetz K. She Coined the Term 'Intersectionality' Over 30 Years Ago. Here's What It Means to Her Today [Internet]. Time. 2020

[cited 2020 Jul 30]. Available from: https://time.com/5786710/kimberle-crenshaw-intersectionality/

64. BBC. BBC - Ethics - Abortion: Disability in the Foetus [Internet]. BBC Ethics Guide. 2014 [cited 2020 Nov 7]. Available from: http://www.bbc.co.uk/ethics/abortion/philosophical/disability.shtml

65. Hughes C. Reflections on Intersectionality [Internet]. Quillette. 2020 [cited 2020 Jul 6]. Available from: https://quillette.com/2020/01/14/reflections-on-intersectionality/

66. Henderson R. Thorstein Veblen's Theory of the Leisure Class—A Status Update [Internet]. Quillette. 2019 [cited 2020 Jun 8]. Available from: https://quillette.com/2019/11/16/thorstein-veblens-theory-of-the-leisure-class-a-status-update/

67. YouGov. The Economist/YouGov Poll [Internet]. 2020 Jun [cited 2020 Jun 21] p. 43–4. Available from: https://docs.cdn.yougov.com/vgqowgynze/econTabReport.pdf

68. Morgan RE, Oudekerk BA. Criminal Victimization, 2018 [Internet]. Bureau of Justice Statistics; 2018 p. 37. Report No.: NCJ 253043. Available from: https://www.bjs.gov/content/pub/pdf/cv18.pdf

69. Rubin D. Racism: Getting to the Truth | Coleman Hughes [Internet]. 2018 [cited 2020 Oct 7]. (Rubin Reports). Available from: https://www.youtube.com/watch?v=rdh8zPr_ZmI

70. @chipchromepml. dan and phil hate heterosexuals if u r cishet that is so embarrassing stay away from me Nauseated face [Internet]. Twitter. 2020 [cited 2020 Aug 10]. Available from: https://twitter.com/chipchromepml/status/1313848 252207308800

71. Bawer B. The Victims' Revolution: The Rise of Identity Studies and the Closing of the Liberal Mind. Broadside e-books; 2012. 405 p.

72. Bauman Z. Community: Seeking Safety in an Insecure World. Reprint edition. Cambridge: Polity; 2000. 166 p.

73. Roche K. 2+2=5: How the Transgender Craze Is Redefining Reality. Kindle Direct Publishing; 2020. 384 p.

74. McNamara B. Most Young People Don't Identify as Straight, Survey Says [Internet]. Teen Vogue. 2017 [cited 2020 Nov 4]. Available from: https://www.teenvogue.com/story/survey-says-young-people-dont-identify-as-straight

75. The Trevor Project on Twitter. Feelings can change ♥ If you're in crisis, reach out to us 24/7 at: 866.488.7386 or text/chat at: https://t.co/hxtScqt870 🔋 🎨 art by @IntrovertDoodle 🎨 #SuicidePrevention

#SuicidePreventionMonth
https://t.co/lCuvpH1OMq [Internet]. Twitter. 2020
[cited 2020 Oct 3]. Available from:
https://twitter.com/TrevorProject/status/13024590
11846070273

76. Lord E, Steber C. Here's What It Means to Identify
as Demisexual [Internet]. Bustle. 2020 [cited 2020
Jul 6]. Available from:
https://www.bustle.com/articles/155277-what-
does-demisexual-mean-here-are-6-signs-that-you-
may-identify-as-demisexual

77. Hagen S. I'm Pansexual and I've Only Slept with
Men - That Doesn't Make Me Any Less Queer
[Internet]. Metro. 2020 [cited 2020 Oct 4].
Available from:
https://metro.co.uk/2020/10/02/pansexual-only-
slept-with-men-not-less-queer-13320599/

78. Dennis RJ. Can Having Genital Preferences for
Dating Mean You're Anti-Trans? [Internet].
Everyday Feminism. 2017 [cited 2020 Mar 6].
Available from:
https://everydayfeminism.com/2017/04/cissexist-
say-never-date-trans/

79. Yardley M. The Cotton Ceiling [Internet]. Miranda
Yardley. 2014 [cited 2020 Mar 6]. Available from:
https://mirandayardley.com/en/the-cotton-ceiling/

80. Owens C. To End Fatphobia, We Need to
Dismantle Western Civilization, Says Philly
Therapist Sonalee Rashatwar [Internet].
https://www.inquirer.com. 2019 [cited 2020 Aug

25]. Available from: https://www.inquirer.com/news/sonalee-rashatwar-fat-positivity-body-acceptance-sexuality-therapy-20190703.html

81. Thomas SS. Why We Need to Talk About Kink-Shaming in Relationships [Internet]. Allure. 2018 [cited 2020 Aug 25]. Available from: https://www.allure.com/story/kink-shaming-guide-to-disclosing-kinks-fetishes

82. National Symposium on Neurodiversity at Syracuse University. What is Neurodiversity? [Internet]. National Symposium on Neurodiversity at Syracuse University. 2011 [cited 2020 Oct 7]. Available from: https://neurodiversitysymposium.wordpress.com/what-is-neurodiversity/

83. Clements T. What Is Autism? How the Term Became Too Broad to Have Meaning Any More. The Guardian [Internet]. 2019 Aug 26 [cited 2020 Feb 19]; Available from: https://www.theguardian.com/commentisfree/2019/aug/26/autism-neurodiversity-severe

84. Russo F. The Costs of Camouflaging Autism [Internet]. Spectrum | Autism Research News. 2018 [cited 2020 Aug 26]. Available from: https://www.spectrumnews.org/features/deep-dive/costs-camouflaging-autism/

85. Shekhar R. I Self-Diagnosed My Autism Because Nobody Else Would [Internet]. The Swaddle. 2020 [cited 2020 Jul 6]. Available from:

https://theswaddle.com/i-self-diagnosed-my-autism-because-nobody-else-would-heres-why-that-needs-to-change/

86.   Scuro J. Addressing Ableism: Philosophical Questions via Disability Studies. Lexington Books; 2017. 277 p.

87.   Learn from Autistics. Autism Interview #139 Part 2: Rakshita Shekhar on Self-Diagnosis and Privilege [Internet]. Learn from Autistics. 2020 [cited 2020 Aug 26]. Available from: https://www.learnfromautistics.com/autism-interview-139-part-2-rakshita-shekhar-on-self-diagnosis-and-privilege/

88.   Noor P, Conroy JO, Mahdawi A, Matei A, Wong JC, Rushe D, et al. What Were We Thinking? The Worst Trends of the Decade – Ranked! The Guardian [Internet]. 2019 Dec 23 [cited 2020 Jul 24]; Available from: https://www.theguardian.com/lifeandstyle/2019/dec/23/worst-trends-decade-ranked-2010s

89.   Fredericks B, Schwab N. Elizabeth Warren Admits to 'Mistakes' Regarding Native American Ancestry Claims. New York Post [Internet]. 2019 Aug 19 [cited 2020 Nov 28]; Available from: https://nypost.com/2019/08/19/elizabeth-warren-admits-to-mistakes-regarding-native-american-ancestry-claims/

90.   Sabur R. Cherokee Nation Condemns Elizabeth Warren's 'Inappropriate and Wrong' DNA Test to Prove Her Heritage. The Telegraph [Internet]. 2018

Oct 16 [cited 2020 Feb 12]; Available from: https://www.telegraph.co.uk/news/2018/10/16/che rokee-nation-condemns-elizabeth-warrens-inappropriate-wrong/

91. Akpan N. How White Supremacists Respond When Their DNA Says They're Not 'White' [Internet]. PBS NewsHour. 2017 [cited 2020 Aug 26]. Available from: https://www.pbs.org/newshour/science/white-supremacists-respond-genetics-say-theyre-not-white

92. Cillizza C. Elizabeth Warren's Native American Problem Just Got Even Worse [Internet]. CNN. 2019 [cited 2020 Feb 11]. Available from: https://www.cnn.com/2019/02/06/politics/elizabet h-warren-native-american/index.html

93. Karimi F. Rachel Dolezal, White Woman Who Portrayed Herself as Black, Accused of Welfare Fraud [Internet]. CNN. 2018 [cited 2020 Feb 11]. Available from: https://www.cnn.com/2018/05/25/us/rachel-dolezal-welfare-fraud-allegations/index.html

94. Spiked! The Rise of the Race-Faking Academic [Internet]. Spiked! 2020 [cited 2020 Oct 8]. Available from: https://www.spiked-online.com/2020/09/17/the-rise-of-the-race-faking-academic/

95. Google. Google on Twitter: 'As part of our ongoing commitment to racial equity, we're introducing an icon that makes it easier to identify and

#SupportBlackBusiness in the U.S., in partnership with @USBlackChambers → https://t.co/t5lbq4x1Hp Tag a Black-owned business you'd like to see add the icon 👇 https://t.co/br0cIaZlvn' / Twitter [Internet]. Twitter. 2020 [cited 2020 Aug 1]. Available from: https://twitter.com/Google/status/1288847740194050048

96. Fleishman C, Smith A. 'Coincidence Detector': The Google Chrome Extension White Supremacists Use to Track Jews [Internet]. Mic. 2016 [cited 2020 Aug 30]. Available from: https://www.mic.com/articles/145105/coincidence-detector-the-google-extension-white-supremacists-use-to-track-jews

97. Andrew S. An Oregon County Drops Its Mask Exemption for People of Color After Racist Response [Internet]. CNN. 2020 [cited 2020 Aug 30]. Available from: https://www.cnn.com/2020/06/24/us/oregon-county-people-of-color-mask-trnd/index.html

98. Kaur H. The Coronavirus Pandemic Is Hitting Black and Brown Americans Especially Hard on All Fronts [Internet]. CNN. 2020 [cited 2020 Aug 30]. Available from: https://www.cnn.com/2020/05/08/us/coronavirus-pandemic-race-impact-trnd/index.html

99. Desroches D. University of Connecticut Creates 'Scholars House' to Keep Black Men in School [Internet]. NPR.org. 2016 [cited 2020 Aug 30]. Available from:

https://www.npr.org/2016/03/06/468903152/unive
rsity-of-connecticut-creates-scholars-house-to-
keep-black-men-in-school

100. Gunter M. University Turns Frat into 'Safe Space
     for Black Students' [Internet]. Campus Reform.
     2018 [cited 2020 Jul 26]. Available from:
     https://www.campusreform.org/?ID=10679

101. Gray B. Beware the Race Reductionist [Internet].
     The Intercept. 2018 [cited 2020 Aug 24]. Available
     from: https://theintercept.com/2018/08/26/beware-
     the-race-reductionist/

102. Moylan B. If LGBT Rooms Make Gay Students
     Feel Safe, Let's Roll Out the Rainbow Carpet. The
     Guardian [Internet]. 2018 Jul 2 [cited 2020 Feb 28];
     Available   from:
     https://www.theguardian.com/commentisfree/201
     8/jul/02/lgbt-dorms-gay-students-safe-sheffield-
     university

103. Mogilevsky M. 5 Ways to Maintain Your Queer
     Identity in a Relationship People Read as Straight
     [Internet]. Everyday Feminism. 2016 [cited 2020
     Aug   26].   Available   from:
     https://everydayfeminism.com/2016/03/maintainin
     g-queer-id/

104. DiAngelo R. White Fragility: Why It's So Hard for
     White People to Talk About Racism. Boston:
     Beacon Press; 2018. 192 p.

105. Cozzarelli T. Class Reductionism Is Real, and It's
     Coming from the Jacobin Wing of the DSA
     [Internet]. Left Voice. 2020 [cited 2020 Aug 24].

Available from: http://www.leftvoice.org/class-reductionism-is-real-and-its-coming-from-the-jacobin-wing-of-the-dsa

106. Blakemore E. How the GI Bill's Promise Was Denied to a Million Black WWII Veterans [Internet]. HISTORY. 2019 [cited 2020 Aug 29]. Available from: https://www.history.com/news/gi-bill-black-wwii-veterans-benefits

107. Poverty USA. Poverty Facts [Internet]. Poverty USA. 2018 [cited 2020 Aug 5]. Available from: https://www.povertyusa.org/facts

108. Stewart N. When Caring for Your Child's Needs Becomes a Job All Its Own. The New York Times [Internet]. 2020 Jul 24 [cited 2020 Aug 10]; Available from: https://www.nytimes.com/2020/07/24/us/children-disabilities-parenting-poverty-assistance.html

109. Badgett MVL, Choi SK, Wilson BDM. A Study of Differences Between Sexual Orientation and Gender Identity Groups [Internet]. Los Angeles: Williams Institute; 2019 Oct p. 47. Available from: https://williamsinstitute.law.ucla.edu/wp-content/uploads/National-LGBT-Poverty-Oct-2019.pdf

110. Farley A. Perspective | Drug Prices Are Killing Diabetics. 'Walmart Insulin' Isn't the Solution. Washington Post [Internet]. 2019 Feb 19 [cited 2020 Jul 31]; Available from: https://www.washingtonpost.com/outlook/2019/0

2/19/drug-prices-are-killing-diabetics-walmart-insulin-isnt-solution/

111. UC Davis Center for Poverty Research. How Is Poverty Related to Access to Care and Preventive Healthcare? [Internet]. UC Davis Center for Poverty Research. 2015 [cited 2020 Aug 28]. Available from: https://poverty.ucdavis.edu/faq/how-poverty-related-access-care-and-preventive-healthcare

112. Elliott L. Poverty Causes Obesity. Low-Income Families Need to Be Better Off to Eat Well. The Guardian [Internet]. 2020 Aug 9 [cited 2020 Aug 29]; Available from: https://www.theguardian.com/business/2020/aug/09/poverty-causes-obesity-low-income-families-need-to-be-better-off-to-eat-well

113. Meyersohn N. Groceries Were Hard to Find for Millions. Now It's Getting Even Worse [Internet]. CNN. 2020 [cited 2020 Aug 29]. Available from: https://www.cnn.com/2020/06/09/business/food-deserts-coronavirus-grocery-stores/index.html

114. Chetty R, Stepner M, Abraham S, Lin S, Scuderi B, Turner N, et al. The Association Between Income and Life Expectancy in the United States, 2001-2014. JAMA. 2016 Apr 26;315(16):1750–66.

115. Mitchell JN. Breaking Poverty: Crime, Poverty Often Linked [Internet]. WHYY. 2018 [cited 2020 Aug 29]. Available from: https://whyy.org/articles/breaking-poverty-crime-poverty-often-linked/

116. Shure N. Second-Wave Feminism's Unfinished Business [Internet]. Jacobin. 2018 [cited 2020 Aug 29]. Available from: https://jacobinmag.com/2018/12/second-wave-feminism-care-work-wages

117. Akee R. Voting and Income [Internet]. Econofact. 2019 [cited 2020 Jul 30]. Available from: https://econofact.org/voting-and-income

118. Oser J, Hooghe M, Marien S. Is Online Participation Distinct from Offline Participation? A Latent Class Analysis of Participation Types and Their Stratification. Political Research Quarterly. 2013 Mar 1;66(1):91–101.

119. USAFacts. How Does Voter Turnout in the US Change by State, Age and Race? [Internet]. USAFacts. 2019 [cited 2020 Aug 2]. Available from: https://usafacts.org/articles/how-many-americans-vote-and-how-do-voting-rates-vary-state/

120. Tavernise S. Many in Milwaukee Neighborhood Didn't Vote — and Don't Regret It. The New York Times [Internet]. 2016 Nov 20 [cited 2020 Aug 2]; Available from: https://www.nytimes.com/2016/11/21/us/many-in-milwaukee-neighborhood-didnt-vote-and-dont-regret-it.html

121. Stansel A. Apoliticism Is Privilege [Internet]. The Daily Campus. 2019 [cited 2020 Aug 2]. Available from:

https://dailycampus.com/stories/2019/9/3/apolitici
smnbspisnbspprivilegenbsp

122. Shivaram AT Elizabeth Kneebone, and Ranjitha. Signs of Digital Distress: Mapping Broadband Availability and Subscription in American Neighborhoods [Internet]. Brookings. 2017 [cited 2020 Feb 21]. Available from: https://www.brookings.edu/research/signs-of-digital-distress-mapping-broadband-availability/

123. Anderson M, Kumar M. Digital Divide Persists Even as Lower-Income Americans Make Gains in Tech Adoption [Internet]. Pew Research Center. 2019 [cited 2020 Apr 3]. Available from: https://www.pewresearch.org/fact-tank/2019/05/07/digital-divide-persists-even-as-lower-income-americans-make-gains-in-tech-adoption/

124. Timsit A. 2020's Record Voter Turnout in the US Is Still Lower Than Many Other Countries [Internet]. Quartz. 2020 [cited 2020 Dec 1]. Available from: https://qz.com/1926959/2020-us-record-voter-turnout-is-still-lower-than-other-countries/

125. Wallace G. Voter Turnout at 20-Year Low in 2016 [Internet]. CNN. 2016 [cited 2020 Aug 29]. Available from: https://www.cnn.com/2016/11/11/politics/popular-vote-turnout-2016/index.html

126. Desilver D. U.S. Voter Turnout Trails Most Developed Countries [Internet]. Pew Research

Center. 2018 [cited 2020 Aug 29]. Available from: https://www.pewresearch.org/fact-tank/2018/05/21/u-s-voter-turnout-trails-most-developed-countries/

127. Regan MD. Why Is Voter Turnout so Low in the U.S.? [Internet]. PBS NewsHour. 2016 [cited 2020 Aug 29]. Available from: https://www.pbs.org/newshour/politics/voter-turnout-united-states

128. O'Neill B. What They Mean When They Talk About 'White People' [Internet]. Spiked! 2020 [cited 2020 Jul 7]. Available from: https://www.spiked-online.com/2020/07/07/what-they-mean-when-they-talk-about-white-people/

129. Parsons V. In These Trying Times, Lesbian Radical Feminist Julie Bindel Is Debating Whether 'Karen' Is a Slur. Yes, Really [Internet]. PinkNews. 2020 [cited 2020 Jun 24]. Available from: https://www.pinknews.co.uk/2020/04/06/karen-slur-meme-coronavirus-pandemic-julie-bindel-twitter-feminism-white-privilege-class/

130. Oxford Learner's Dictionary. Slur [Internet]. Oxford Learner's Dictionary. 2020 [cited 2020 Aug 30]. Available from: https://www.oxfordlearnersdictionaries.com/definition/english/slur_2

131. Tait A. Karen, Sharon, Becky, and Chad: How It Feels When Your Name Becomes a Meme [Internet]. New Statesman. 2018 [cited 2020 Oct 9]. Available from:

https://www.newstatesman.com/science-tech/internet/2018/01/karen-sharon-becky-and-chad-how-it-feels-when-your-name-becomes-meme

132. Soave R. Trump Won Because Leftist Political Correctness Inspired a Terrifying Backlash [Internet]. Reason.com. 2016 [cited 2020 Aug 14]. Available from: https://reason.com/2016/11/09/trump-won-because-leftist-political-corr/

133. O'Brien F, Schneeweiss Z. U.S. Ranked Worst for Workers' Rights Among Major Economies. Bloomberg.com [Internet]. 2020 Jun 18 [cited 2020 Aug 1]; Available from: https://www.bloomberg.com/news/articles/2020-06-18/u-s-ranked-worst-for-workers-rights-among-major-economies

134. Stone J. Why the US Urgently Needs Paid Sick Leave [Internet]. Forbes. 2020 [cited 2020 Aug 29]. Available from: https://www.forbes.com/sites/judystone/2020/03/10/why-the-us-urgently-needs-paid-sick-leave/

135. U.S. Department of Labor. Sick Leave [Internet]. U.S. Department of Labor. 2020 [cited 2020 Jul 31]. Available from: https://www.dol.gov/general/topic/workhours/sickleave

136. Bryant M. Maternity Leave: US Policy Is Worst on List of the World's Richest Countries [Internet]. The Guardian. 2020 [cited 2020 Jul 31]. Available

from: http://www.theguardian.com/us-news/2020/jan/27/maternity-leave-us-policy-worst-worlds-richest-countries

137. LaGrange K. Opinion: 10 Things Trump Has Done to Hurt Workers [Internet]. The Labor Tribune. 2020 [cited 2020 Jul 13]. Available from: https://labortribune.com/opinion-10-things-trump-has-done-to-workers/

138. Kullgren I. Trump Rolls Back Worker Safety Rules [Internet]. POLITICO. 2018 [cited 2020 Aug 29]. Available from: https://politi.co/2oD7A6h

139. Handrahan M. Voltage Entertainment Says Striking Writers Group 'Is Not a Union' [Internet]. GamesIndustry.biz. 2020 [cited 2020 Aug 1]. Available from: https://www.gamesindustry.biz/articles/2020-07-22-voltage-entertainment-says-striking-writers-group-is-not-a-union

140. Pyper D. Unfair Dismissal: Qualifying Service Rule [Internet]. London: House of Commons; 2018 Jul [cited 2020 Oct 9]. Report No.: CBP 4526. Available from: https://researchbriefings.files.parliament.uk/documents/CBP-8347/CBP-8347.pdf

141. Just A. 7 Employment Rights You Have Lost Under a Tory PM [Internet]. IER. 2017 [cited 2020 Oct 9]. Available from: https://www.ier.org.uk/news/7-employment-rights-you-have-lost-under-tory-pm/

142. Kimble M. Tiny Home Communities: Housing Solution or Gentrified Trailer Parks? The Guardian [Internet]. 2018 Jun 26 [cited 2020 Aug 2]; Available from: https://www.theguardian.com/cities/2018/jun/26/tiny-home-communities-housing-solution-or-gentrified-trailer-parks

143. US Department of Energy. Introduction to Mobile Homes Weatherization Installer/Technician Mobile Homes [Internet]. US Department of Energy; 2010. Available from: https://www.google.com/url?sa=t&rct=j&q=&esrc=s&source=web&cd=&ved=2ahUKEwiGvZzZqcHrAhXbaRUIHc4UCR0QFjAKegQIAxAB&url=https%3A%2F%2Fwww.energy.gov%2Fsites%2Fprod%2Ffiles%2F2016%2F06%2Ff32%2FSN%25201.%2520Introduction%2520to%2520Mobile%2520Homes.docx&usg=AOvVaw29uxnlj1KCFtDF5iMmmbc5

144. Levy E, Conlin F, Ho S. Moisture Problems in Manufactured Homes: Understanding Their Causes and Finding Solutions [Internet]. Manufactured Housing Research Alliance; 2000. Available from: https://www.huduser.gov/portal/publications/moisture.pdf

145. Robustelli T. After the Storm: Why Mobile Home Owners Continue to Suffer More from Tornado Damage [Internet]. Pacific Standard. 2019 [cited 2020 Aug 29]. Available from: https://psmag.com/social-justice/tornadoes-put-mobile-home-owners-at-severe-risk

146. Chávez A. Few in Congress Care About the Struggle to Pay Rent [Internet]. The Intercept. 2020 [cited 2020 Nov 8]. Available from: https://theintercept.com/2020/03/27/coronavirus-rent-suspension-evictions-bill-payments/

147. Robbins G. America's Public Housing Is a Mess – and the UK Is Copying Its Model [Internet]. The Guardian. 2012 [cited 2020 Aug 1]. Available from: http://www.theguardian.com/commentisfree/2012/apr/18/america-public-housing-uk-policy

148. Vale L. America's Public Housing Crisis May Worsen with Trump Budget [Internet]. The Conversation. 2017 [cited 2020 Aug 1]. Available from: http://theconversation.com/americas-public-housing-crisis-may-worsen-with-trump-budget-80654

149. BBC News. Housing Crisis Affects Estimated 8.4 Million in England - Research. BBC News [Internet]. 2019 Sep 22 [cited 2020 Oct 9]; Available from: https://www.bbc.co.uk/news/uk-49787913

150. BBC News. What Happened at Grenfell Tower? BBC News [Internet]. 2019 Oct 29 [cited 2020 Oct 9]; Available from: https://www.bbc.com/news/uk-40301289

151. BBC News. Grenfell Fire: Cladding Firm 'Confused' by Safety Rules. BBC News [Internet]. 2020 Sep 9 [cited 2020 Oct 9]; Available from: https://www.bbc.co.uk/news/uk-54088821

152. BBC News. Grenfell Tower Final Death Toll 71. BBC News [Internet]. 2017 Nov 16 [cited 2020 Oct 9]; Available from: https://www.bbc.com/news/uk-42008279

153. Elvin S. 2,000 Buildings Still Covered in Dangerous Cladding Three Years on from Grenfell [Internet]. Metro. 2020 [cited 2020 Nov 8]. Available from: https://metro.co.uk/2020/06/12/2000-buildings-still-have-grenfell-cladding-despite-promise-remove-month-12843420/

154. US Department of Agriculture. What Can SNAP Buy? [Internet]. Food and Nutrition Service. 2013 [cited 2020 Aug 2]. Available from: https://www.fns.usda.gov/snap/eligible-food-items

155. Baptiste N. Here's What Trump's Snap Cuts Will Really Do [Internet]. Mother Jones. 2019 [cited 2020 Feb 26]. Available from: https://www.motherjones.com/food/2019/12/heres-what-trumps-snap-cuts-will-really-do/

156. Polansek T. Trump Administration Moves to Remove 700,000 People from Food Stamps. Reuters [Internet]. 2019 Dec 4 [cited 2020 Jul 13]; Available from: https://www.reuters.com/article/us-usa-trump-foodstamps-idUSKBN1Y82C9

157. ORDP O. Understanding SSI - SSI Income [Internet]. Social Security Administration. 2020 [cited 2020 Aug 30]. Available from: https://www.ssa.gov/ssi/text-income-ussi.htm

158. SSA O. What Are the Statutory Resources Limits? [Internet]. Social Security Handbook. 2020 [cited 2020 Aug 30]. Available from: https://www.ssa.gov/OP_Home/handbook/handbook.21/handbook-2166.html

159. GOV.UK. National Introduction of Benefit Cap Begins [Internet]. GOV.UK. 2013 [cited 2020 Oct 9]. Available from: https://www.gov.uk/government/news/national-introduction-of-benefit-cap-begins

160. Citizen's Advice. How the Minimum Income Floor Works If You're Self-Employed [Internet]. Citizen's Advice. 2018 [cited 2020 Oct 9]. Available from: http://www.citizensadvice.org.uk/benefits/universal-credit/on-universal-credit/how-the-minimum-income-floor-works-if-youre-self-employed/

161. The Planetary Society. NASA's FY 2020 Budget [Internet]. The Planetary Society. 2020 [cited 2020 Aug 29]. Available from: https://www.planetary.org/space-policy/nasas-fy-2020-budget

162. Romano A. From Kaylor to Folklore: How Taylor Swift Became a Gay Icon [Internet]. Vox. 2020 [cited 2020 Aug 29]. Available from: https://www.vox.com/21337354/folklore-taylor-swift-kaylor-betty-gay-lesbian-subtext

163. Nguyen T. Student Activists Want Change — and They're Starting in the Classroom [Internet]. Vox. 2020 [cited 2020 Jul 31]. Available from:

https://www.vox.com/identities/2020/7/29/213451
14/students-diversify-curriculum-change-
antiracist

164. Nagle A. The Left Case against Open Borders
[Internet]. American Affairs Journal. 2018 [cited
2020 Jun 15]. Available from:
https://americanaffairsjournal.org/2018/11/the-
left-case-against-open-borders/

165. Miron J. Forget the Wall Already, It's Time for the
U.S. to Have Open Borders [Internet]. Cato
Institute. 2018 [cited 2020 Aug 30]. Available
from:
https://www.cato.org/publications/commentary/fo
rget-wall-already-its-time-us-have-open-borders

166. Firsing S. How Severe Is Africa's Brain Drain?
[Internet]. Quartz Africa. 2016 [cited 2020 Aug
31]. Available from:
https://qz.com/africa/599140/how-severe-is-
africas-brain-drain/

167. Tognotti C. 19 Sexist & Racist Halloween
Costumes You Should Stay the Hell Away From
[Internet]. Bustle. 2016 [cited 2020 Aug 30].
Available from:
https://www.bustle.com/articles/188057-19-sexist-
racist-halloween-costumes-you-should-stay-the-
hell-away-from

168. Gonzales R. For 7th Consecutive Year, Visa
Overstays Exceeded Illegal Border Crossings
[Internet]. NPR.org. 2019 [cited 2020 Feb 3].
Available from:

https://www.npr.org/2019/01/16/686056668/for-seventh-consecutive-year-visa-overstays-exceeded-illegal-border-crossings

169. Picard J. Illegal Immigrants Benefit the U.S. Economy [Internet]. The Hill. 2014 [cited 2020 Feb 3]. Available from: https://thehill.com/blogs/congress-blog/foreign-policy/203984-illegal-immigrants-benefit-the-us-economy

170. Underwood E. Unhealthy Work: Why Migrants Are Especially Vulnerable to Injury and Death on the Job [Internet]. Knowable Magazine. Annual Reviews; 2018 [cited 2020 Aug 30]. Available from: https://knowablemagazine.org/article/society/2018/unhealthy-work-why-migrants-are-especially-vulnerable-injury-and-death-job

171. Tondo L, Lamble L. Essex Lorry Deaths: How Dangerous Is the Journey to the UK? The Guardian [Internet]. 2019 Oct 23 [cited 2020 Feb 12]; Available from: https://www.theguardian.com/uk-news/2019/oct/23/essex-lorry-deaths-how-dangerous-is-the-journey-to-the-uk

172. The Scotsman. Morecambe Tide Faster Than a Man Can Run [Internet]. The Scotsman. 2004 [cited 2020 Feb 4]. Available from: https://www.scotsman.com/news/uk-news/morecambe-tide-faster-than-a-man-can-run-1-512819

173. Westmorland Gazette. Cockle Pickers Were Swimming the Wrong Direction [Internet]. The Westmorland Gazette. 2005 [cited 2020 Feb 12]. Available from: https://www.thewestmorlandgazette.co.uk/news/6 40835.cockle-pickers-were-swimming-the-wrong-direction/

174. BBC News. Cockle Jury Played Distress Call. BBC News [Internet]. 2005 Oct 21 [cited 2020 Feb 12]; Available from: http://news.bbc.co.uk/1/hi/england/lancashire/436 4586.stm

175. BBC News. Man Guilty of 21 Cockling Deaths. BBC News [Internet]. 2006 Mar 24 [cited 2020 Feb 12]; Available from: http://news.bbc.co.uk/1/hi/england/lancashire/483 2454.stm

176. Bedard P. Pelosi: 'What Is the Point' of Enforcing Immigration Laws? [Internet]. Washington Examiner. 2019 [cited 2020 Feb 3]. Available from: https://www.washingtonexaminer.com/washingto n-secrets/pelosi-what-is-the-point-of-enforcing-immigration-laws

177. Geiger AW, Davis L. A Growing Number of American Teenagers – Particularly Girls – Are Facing Depression [Internet]. Pew Research Center. 2019 [cited 2020 Oct 4]. Available from: https://www.pewresearch.org/fact-tank/2019/07/12/a-growing-number-of-american-teenagers-particularly-girls-are-facing-depression/

178. Gray P. Declining Student Resilience: A Serious Problem for Colleges [Internet]. Psychology Today. 2015 [cited 2020 Aug 27]. Available from: https://www.psychologytoday.com/blog/freedom-learn/201509/declining-student-resilience-serious-problem-colleges

179. Curran T, Hill AP. Perfectionism Is Increasing Over Time: A Meta-Analysis of Birth Cohort Differences from 1989 to 2016. Psychological Bulletin. 2019;145(4):410–29.

180. Perry P. Millennials Are at Higher Risk for Mental Health Issues. This May Be Why. [Internet]. Big Think. 2018 [cited 2020 Aug 24]. Available from: https://bigthink.com/philip-perry/millennials-are-at-higher-risk-for-mental-health-issues-this-may-be-why

181. Furedi F. Therapy Culture: Cultivating Vulnerability in an Uncertain Age. Routledge; 2004. 257 p.

182. Lukianoff G, Haidt J. The Coddling of the American Mind: How Good Intentions and Bad Ideas Are Setting Up a Generation for Failure. New York: Penguin Press; 2018. 352 p.

183. Spicer A. 'Self-Care': How a Radical Feminist Idea Was Stripped of Politics for the Mass Market [Internet]. The Guardian. 2019 [cited 2020 Aug 13]. Available from: http://www.theguardian.com/commentisfree/2019/aug/21/self-care-radical-feminist-idea-mass-market

184. Kraus R. Comfort Food in the Age of Self-Care: It's Complicated [Internet]. Mashable. 2019 [cited 2020 Nov 8]. Available from: https://mashable.com/article/comfort-food-self-care-emotional-eating/

185. Spark. What is Radical Kindness and Why We Should Do it [Internet]. Spark. 2020 [cited 2020 Nov 8]. Available from: https://thisisyourspark.com/2020/01/06/what-is-radical-kindness-and-why-we-should-do-it-2/

186. Borysenko K. Today in the knitting wars, the SJWs have decided to pursue a charity project in the name of "radical kindness." A few of us reached out to support them and celebrate it. Their response: Their kindness isn't radical enough to include everyone. You can't make this stuff up. [Internet]. Twitter. 2020 [cited 2020 Oct 6]. Available from: https://twitter.com/DrKarlynB/status/1229828500808486917

187. Flynn C. 5 Types of Subtly Toxic People to Cut Out of Your Life [Internet]. Bustle. 2016 [cited 2020 Oct 11]. Available from: https://www.bustle.com/articles/135835-5-types-of-subtly-toxic-people-to-cut-out-of-your-life

188. Kim S. 20+ Resources to Help You Process After the Election of Donald Trump [Internet]. Everyday Feminism. 2016 [cited 2020 Aug 27]. Available from: https://everydayfeminism.com/2016/11/resources-to-process-election/

189. Gockowski A. Schools Offer Counseling to Help Students Process Trump Win [Internet]. Campus Reform. 2016 [cited 2020 Oct 11]. Available from: https://www.campusreform.org/?ID=8369

190. tw:trump - Twitter Search / Twitter [Internet]. Twitter. 2020 [cited 2020 Oct 9]. Available from: https://twitter.com/search?q=tw%3atrump

191. Ries J. 7 Self-Care Tips If the News Cycle Is Pummeling You Right Now [Internet]. HuffPost UK. 2020 [cited 2020 Oct 9]. Available from: https://www.huffpost.com/entry/self-care-tips-news-covid_1_5f7c76f3c5b60c6bcc625bcf

192. Kanai R, Feilden T, Firth C, Rees G. Political Orientations Are Correlated with Brain Structure in Young Adults. Current Biology. 2011 Apr 26;21(8):677–80.

193. Oxley DR, Smith KB, Alford JR, Hibbing MV, Miller JL, Scalora M, et al. Political Attitudes Vary with Physiological Traits. Science. 2008 Sep 19;321(5896):1667–70.

194. Lite J. Political Science: What Being Neat or Messy Says about Political Leanings [Internet]. Scientific American. 2008 [cited 2020 Oct 24]. Available from: https://www.scientificamerican.com/article/organization-and-political-leanings/

195. Grohol JM. Conspiracy Theory Disorder: Understanding Why People Believe [Internet]. 2020 [cited 2020 Nov 8]. Available from:

https://psychcentral.com/blog/conspiracy-theory-disorder-understanding-why-people-believe

196. Donnella L. When The 'White Tears' Just Keep Coming [Internet]. NPR.org. 2018 [cited 2020 Oct 9]. Available from: https://www.npr.org/sections/codeswitch/2018/11/28/649537891/when-the-white-tears-just-keep-coming

197. Willard L. Semicolon Tattoo: Here's What It Means and Why It Matters. [Internet]. Upworthy. 2015 [cited 2020 Oct 5]. Available from: https://www.upworthy.com/have-you-seen-anyone-with-a-semicolon-tattoo-heres-what-its-about

198. Project Semicolon. One Million Project Semicolon Tattoos [Internet]. Project Semicolon. 2020 [cited 2020 Oct 5]. Available from: https://projectsemicolon.com/one-million-project-semicolon-tattoos/

199. Grohol JM. Project Semicolon Founder Amy Bleuel Dies at 31 [Internet]. PsychCentral. 2017 [cited 2020 Oct 5]. Available from: //psychcentral.com/blog/project-semicolon-founder-amy-bleuel-dies-at-31/

200. LaConte S. Dax Shepard Opened Up About Becoming Sober Again, And The Lesson He's Teaching His Daughters From It [Internet]. BuzzFeed. 2020 [cited 2020 Oct 10]. Available from: https://www.buzzfeed.com/stephenlaconte/dax-

shepard-relapse-kristen-bell-daughters-gratitude-lesson

201. Jokic N. Lady Gaga Opened Up About Her Mental Health And Why She Felt 'Exhausted And Used Up' [Internet]. BuzzFeed. 2020 [cited 2020 Oct 10]. Available from: https://www.buzzfeed.com/natashajokic1/lady-gaga-mental-health-chromatica

202. Bine A-S. Social Media Is Redefining 'Depression' [Internet]. The Atlantic. 2013 [cited 2020 Feb 27]. Available from: https://www.theatlantic.com/health/archive/2013/10/social-media-is-redefining-depression/280818/

203. Schumacher H. Why More Men than Women Die by Suicide [Internet]. BBC Future. 2019 [cited 2020 Mar 11]. Available from: https://www.bbc.com/future/article/20190313-why-more-men-kill-themselves-than-women

204. Chalk C. Validating Suicide in Response to Transgender Skepticism is Irresponsible [Internet]. The Federalist. 2020 [cited 2020 Mar 16]. Available from: https://thefederalist.com/2020/03/05/validating-suicide-in-response-to-transgender-skepticism-is-horrifically-irresponsible/

205. Crockett E. Safe Spaces, Explained [Internet]. Vox. 2016 [cited 2020 Oct 3]. Available from: https://www.vox.com/2016/7/5/11949258/safe-spaces-explained

206. Shulevitz J. Opinion | in College and Hiding from Scary Ideas. The New York Times [Internet]. 2015 Mar 21 [cited 2020 Oct 10]; Available from: https://www.nytimes.com/2015/03/22/opinion/sunday/judith-shulevitz-hiding-from-scary-ideas.html

207. Flaherty C. Are Trigger Warnings Inherently Anti-Education? [Internet]. Slate Magazine. 2014 [cited 2020 Nov 9]. Available from: https://slate.com/human-interest/2014/04/oberlin-college-tables-its-trigger-warning-policy-do-the-warnings-threaten-academic-freedom.html

208. American Psychological Association. What Is Exposure Therapy? [Internet]. https://www.apa.org. 2017 [cited 2020 Nov 18]. Available from: https://www.apa.org/ptsd-guideline/patients-and-families/exposure-therapy

209. Rose SC, Bisson J, Churchill R, Wessely S. Psychological Debriefing for Preventing Post Traumatic Stress Disorder (PTSD). Cochrane Database Syst Rev [Internet]. 2002 Apr 22 [cited 2020 Nov 9];2002(2). Available from: https://www.ncbi.nlm.nih.gov/pmc/articles/PMC7032695/

210. Bell V. Minds Traumatised by Disaster Heal Themselves Without Therapy [Internet]. The Guardian. 2013 [cited 2020 Nov 9]. Available from: http://www.theguardian.com/science/2013/may/12/natural-disasters-healing-psychology-worse

211. Devilly GJ, Gist R, Cotton P. Ready! Fire! Aim! The Status of Psychological Debriefing and Therapeutic Interventions: In the Work Place and after Disasters. Review of General Psychology. 2006 Dec;10(4):318–45.

212. Ciccotta T. Van Jones at University of Chicago: Safe Spaces Are a 'Terrible Idea' [Internet]. Breitbart. 2017 [cited 2020 Sep 2]. Available from: https://www.breitbart.com/tech/2017/02/25/van-jones-safe-spaces/

213. Fisher O. Channel 4 Needs to Understand That My Gender Identity Is Not up for Debate [Internet]. i News. 2018 [cited 2020 Mar 8]. Available from: https://inews.co.uk/opinion/comment/genderquake -channel-4-germaine-greer-trans-511131

214. Devitt P. 13 Reasons Why and Suicide Contagion [Internet]. Scientific American. 2017 [cited 2020 Mar 16]. Available from: https://www.scientificamerican.com/article/13-reasons-why-and-suicide-contagion1/

215. Burchill J. Meet the Cry-Bully: A Hideous Hybrid of Victim and Victor [Internet]. The Spectator. 2015 [cited 2020 Feb 13]. Available from: https://blogs.spectator.co.uk/2015/04/meet-the-cry-bully-a-hideous-hybrid-of-victim-and-victor/

216. Nazroo J. Ethnicity, Social Inequality and Health [Internet]. Socialist Health Association. 2017 [cited 2020 Nov 9]. Available from: https://www.sochealth.co.uk/2017/12/31/ethnicity -social-inequality-health-2/

217. Mukherjee S. Biphobia is Killing Bisexual People. Literally. [Internet]. VICE. 2020 [cited 2020 Oct 11]. Available from: https://www.vice.com/en/article/5dzxa3/bisexual-people-have-poor-mental-and-physical-health-due-to-biphobia

218. Center for Disease Control and Prevention. What is Epigenetics? [Internet]. Center for Disease Control and Prevention. 2020 [cited 2020 Nov 19]. Available from: https://www.cdc.gov/genomics/disease/epigenetics.htm

219. Zaman M. What Is Intergenerational Trauma? [Internet]. Refinery29. 2020 [cited 2020 Jul 28]. Available from: https://www.refinery29.com/en-us/2020/06/9848448/what-is-intergenerational-trauma

220. Carey B. Can We Really Inherit Trauma? The New York Times [Internet]. 2018 Dec 10 [cited 2020 Jul 29]; Available from: https://www.nytimes.com/2018/12/10/health/mind-epigenetics-genes.html

221. Cadet D. Dear White People, Your Black Colleagues Aren't Okay [Internet]. Refinery29. 2020 [cited 2020 Aug 2]. Available from: https://www.refinery29.com/en-us/2020/05/9841376/black-trauma-george-floyd-dear-white-people

222. Murdock S. White Woman Threatened to Call Cops on 8-Year-Old Girl Selling Water [Internet].

HuffPost UK. 2018 [cited 2020 Aug 15]. Available from: https://www.huffpost.com/entry/white-woman-sees-black-girl-selling-water-allegedly-calls-police_n_5b2e94a5e4b00295f15cf35f

223. Cleary T. Jennifer Schulte, 'BBQ Becky': 5 Fast Facts You Need to Know [Internet]. Heavy.com. 2018 [cited 2020 Aug 15]. Available from: https://heavy.com/news/2018/05/jennifer-schulte-bbq-becky/

224. City of Oakland. Wildfire Event [Internet]. City of Oakland. 2020 [cited 2020 Nov 19]. Available from: https://www.oaklandca.gov/resources/wildfire-event

225. Derrida J. Of Grammatology. Fortieth Anniversary edition. Johns Hopkins University Press; 1976. 561 p.

226. Arscott K. Winterval: The Unpalatable Making of a Modern Myth [Internet]. The Guardian. 2011 [cited 2020 Oct 1]. Available from: http://www.theguardian.com/commentisfree/2011/nov/08/winterval-modern-myth-christmas

227. Ward OC. John Langdon Down: The Man and the Message [Internet]. Down Syndrome Research and Practice. 1999 [cited 2020 Oct 1]. Available from: https://library.down-syndrome.org/en-gb/research-practice/06/1/john-langdon-down-man-message/

228. Shiel Jr. WC. Definition of Mongolism [Internet]. MedicineNet. 2018 [cited 2020 Sep 29]. Available from:

https://www.medicinenet.com/script/main/art.asp?
articlekey=4420

229. Cohen-Rottenberg R. 10 Questions About Why
Ableist Language Matters, Answered [Internet].
Everyday Feminism. 2014 [cited 2020 Oct 12].
Available   from:
https://everydayfeminism.com/2014/11/ableist-
language-matters/

230. Enck P. Twitter Will Drop 'Blacklist,' 'Whitelist,'
'Man Hours' From Its Code [Internet]. The
Federalist. 2020 [cited 2020 Oct 5]. Available
from: https://thefederalist.com/2020/07/06/twitter-
will-drop-blacklist-whitelist-man-hours-from-its-
code-and-docs/

231. Louder with Crowder. MSNBC Declares the Term
'Hard Worker' Racist. Yes, Really... [Internet].
Louder with Crowder. 2015 [cited 2020 Oct 2].
Available   from:
https://www.louderwithcrowder.com/msnbc-
declares-the-term-hard-worker-racist-yes-really

232. Coughlan S. Harvard Abolishes 'Master' in Titles.
BBC News [Internet]. 2016 Feb 25 [cited 2020 Oct
1];   Available   from:
https://www.bbc.com/news/education-35659685

233. Parker R. We've Lived with 'The Masters' Name
Long Enough [Internet]. Deadspin. 2020 [cited
2020   Oct   1].   Available   from:
https://deadspin.com/we-ve-lived-with-the-
masters-name-long-enough-1844121041

234. Andrew S, Kaur H. Everyday Words and Phrases That Have Racist Connotations [Internet]. CNN. 2020 [cited 2020 Oct 5]. Available from: https://www.cnn.com/2020/07/06/us/racism-words-phrases-slavery-trnd/index.html

235. Murphy M. Are We Women or Are We Menstruators? [Internet]. Feminist Current. 2016 [cited 2020 Mar 15]. Available from: https://www.feministcurrent.com/2016/09/07/are-we-women-or-are-we-menstruators/

236. Braidwood E. LGBTQ Campaigners Say Trans Men in Ireland 'Will be Denied Abortion Access' [Internet]. PinkNews. 2018 [cited 2020 Mar 5]. Available from: https://www.pinknews.co.uk/2018/05/31/transgender-activists-call-for-gender-neutral-language-in-irelands-abortion-law-2/

237. Garcia SE. BIPOC: What Does It Mean? [Internet]. The New York Times. 2020 [cited 2020 Oct 12]. Available from: https://www.nytimes.com/article/what-is-bipoc.html

238. Mburu S, Huxley N, Miles R, Scott L, Cross A, Tufet M. Race and Inequality in International Development Research: A UKCDR Perspective [Internet]. UKCDR. 2020 [cited 2020 Oct 12]. Available from: https://www.ukcdr.org.uk/race-and-inequality-in-international-development-research-a-ukcdr-perspective/

239. Clairmont N. The Language of Privilege [Internet]. Tablet Magazine. 2020 [cited 2020 Sep 30]. Available from: https://www.tabletmag.com/sections/arts-letters/articles/woke-language-privilege

240. Malady MJX. Are You a Language Bully? If So, Give It a Rest. [Internet]. Slate Magazine. 2013 [cited 2020 Sep 21]. Available from: https://slate.com/human-interest/2013/09/language-bullies-pedants-and-grammar-nerds-who-correct-people-all-the-time-cut-it-out.html

241. Noe-Bustamante L, Mora L, Lopez MH. Latinx Used by Just 3% of U.S. Hispanics. About One-in-Four Have Heard of It. [Internet]. Pew Research Center's Hispanic Trends Project. 2020 [cited 2020 Sep 27]. Available from: https://www.pewresearch.org/hispanic/2020/08/11/about-one-in-four-u-s-hispanics-have-heard-of-latinx-but-just-3-use-it/

242. Regan A. Should Women be Spelt Womxn? BBC News [Internet]. 2018 Oct 10 [cited 2020 Mar 5]; Available from: https://www.bbc.com/news/uk-45810709

243. For Folx Sake. What Does the Term 'Folx' Mean? [Internet]. For Folx Sake Podcast. 2019 [cited 2020 Sep 21]. Available from: https://forfolxsake.com/what-does-the-term-folx-mean/

244. McVeigh K. Goldsmiths Cancels Free Speech Show by Comedian Kate Smurthwaite. The Guardian [Internet]. 2015 Feb 2 [cited 2020 Feb 25]; Available from: https://www.theguardian.com/culture/2015/feb/02/goldsmiths-comedian-kate-smurthwaite-free-speech-show-feminist-campaigners

245. Horton H. Cambridge University Withdraws Visiting Fellowship of Academic Who Refuses to Refer to Transgender People by Chosen Pronouns. The Telegraph [Internet]. 2019 Mar 20 [cited 2020 Oct 12]; Available from: https://www.telegraph.co.uk/news/2019/03/20/cambridge-university-withdraws-visiting-fellowship-academic/

246. West E. Memes and Lawsuits: How Uni Pro-Life Societies Are Challenging Campus Bans [Internet]. UK. 2019 [cited 2020 Jul 2]. Available from: https://thetab.com/uk/2019/08/15/memes-and-lawsuits-how-uni-pro-life-societies-are-challenging-campus-bans-119389

247. Busby E. Pro-Life Student Society Approved Amid Freedom of Speech Row at University [Internet]. The Independent. 2019 [cited 2020 Sep 30]. Available from: https://www.independent.co.uk/news/education/education-news/pro-life-society-birmingham-university-abortion-free-speech-a8799641.html

248. Stengel R. Why America Needs a Hate Speech Law. Washington Post [Internet]. 2018 Oct 29 [cited 2020 Jul 12]; Available from:

https://www.washingtonpost.com/opinions/2019/1
0/29/why-america-needs-hate-speech-law/

249. Bowcott O. Calling for Abolition of Monarchy Is
Still Illegal, UK Justice Ministry Admits [Internet].
The Guardian. 2013 [cited 2020 Oct 12]. Available
from: http://www.theguardian.com/uk-
news/2013/dec/13/calling-abolition-monarchy-
illegal-uk-justice-ministry

250. Sommerlad J. This Is How Section 28 Affected the
Lives of LGBT+ People for 30 Years [Internet].
The Independent. 2018 [cited 2020 Oct 2].
Available   from:
https://www.independent.co.uk/news/uk/politics/s
ection-28-explained-lgbt-education-schools-
homosexuality-gay-queer-margaret-thatcher-
a8366741.html

251. Brooks L. Has Britain Finally Accepted
Homosexuality? [Internet]. The Guardian. 2003
[cited 2020 Oct 12]. Available from:
http://www.theguardian.com/world/2003/dec/12/g
ayrights.labour

252. Zanotti E. J.K. Rowling Smeared as Transphobe,
'Canceled' After Saying Biological Sex 'Is Real'
[Internet]. The Daily Wire. 2019 [cited 2020 Apr
15].   Available   from:
https://www.dailywire.com/news/j-k-rowling-
smeared-as-transphobe-canceled-after-saying-
biological-sex-is-real

253. Nolan E. J.K. Rowling Book Burning Videos Are
Spreading Like Wildfire Across Tiktok [Internet].

Newsweek. 2020 [cited 2020 Nov 9]. Available from: https://www.newsweek.com/jk-rowling-books-burned-tiktok-transgender-issues-1532330

254. James D. Harry Potter Fans Now Pretending That Daniel Radcliffe Wrote The Books [Internet]. We Got This Covered. 2020 [cited 2020 Nov 20]. Available from: http://wegotthiscovered.com/movies/harry-potter-fans-pretend-daniel-radcliffe-wrote-series/

255. Kirkup J. JK Rowling and the Road to Terfdom [Internet]. The Spectator. 2020 [cited 2020 Jun 9]. Available from: http://archive.is/hiUmT

256. Castricum S. Our Gender Is Not for Others to Decide. A Bill for Trans People to Self-Identify Is a Good Start. The Guardian [Internet]. 2019 Jun 20 [cited 2020 May 4]; Available from: https://www.theguardian.com/world/2019/jun/20/our-gender-is-not-for-others-to-decide-a-bill-for-trans-people-to-self-identify-is-a-good-start

257. Galtung J. Violence, Peace, and Peace Research. Journal of Peace Research. 1969 Sep 1;6(3):167–91.

258. Galtung J. Cultural Violence. Journal of Peace Studies. 1990;27(3):291–305.

259. Schiff J. Violence Requires Multiple Definitions [Internet]. The Oberlin Review. 2015 [cited 2020 Oct 6]. Available from: https://oberlinreview.org/8174/opinions/violence-requires-multiple-definitions/

260. Williams ACS and JA. Why We Should All Use They/Them Pronouns [Internet]. Scientific American Blog Network. 2019 [cited 2020 Mar 5]. Available from: https://blogs.scientificamerican.com/voices/why-we-should-all-use-they-them-pronouns/

261. Ahmed M, Hanna A, Keyes O, Stevens NL. Actually, We Should Not All Use They/Them Pronouns [Internet]. Scientific American Blog Network. 2019 [cited 2020 Mar 5]. Available from: https://blogs.scientificamerican.com/voices/actuall y-we-should-not-all-use-they-them-pronouns/

262. Manning CE. I Am a Transgender Woman and the Government Is Denying My Civil Rights [Internet]. The Guardian. 2014 [cited 2020 Sep 29]. Available from: http://www.theguardian.com/commentisfree/2014/ dec/08/chelsea-manning-transgender-rights

263. Evans M. The Autistic Genocide Clock. In: Kapp SK, editor. Autistic Community and the Neurodiversity Movement: Stories from the Frontline [Internet]. Singapore: Springer; 2020 [cited 2020 Sep 29]. p. 123–32. Available from: https://doi.org/10.1007/978-981-13-8437-0_9

264. Pluckrose H. Weight Loss Isn't Genocide: Fat Activism Risks Lives [Internet]. The Critic Magazine. 2019 [cited 2020 Sep 29]. Available from: https://thecritic.co.uk/issues/december-2019/big-fat-lies/

265. Barrett LF. When Is Speech Violence? The New York Times [Internet]. 2017 Jul 14 [cited 2020 Aug 13]; Available from: https://www.nytimes.com/2017/07/14/opinion/sunday/when-is-speech-violence.html

266. Teicher MH, Samson JA, Sheu Y-S, Polcari A, McGreenery CE. Hurtful Words: Association of Exposure to Peer Verbal Abuse with Elevated Psychiatric Symptom Scores and Corpus Callosum Abnormalities. AJP. 2010 Dec 1;167(12):1464–71.

267. Tung J, Archie EA, Altmann J, Alberts SC. Cumulative Early Life Adversity Predicts Longevity in Wild Baboons. Nature Communications. 2016 Apr 19;7(1):11181.

268. Burrows T. Radical Transgender Group Says it is FINE to Punch Women [Internet]. Mail Online. 2017 [cited 2020 Feb 15]. Available from: http://www.dailymail.co.uk/~/article-4914582/index.html

269. Singman B. New Hampshire Man Arrested After Allegedly Assaulting Pro-Trump Teen at Polling Site [Internet]. Fox News. Fox News; 2020 [cited 2020 Oct 12]. Available from: https://www.foxnews.com/politics/new-hampshire-man-arrested-after-allegedly-assaulting-pro-trump-teen-polling-site

270. Fox M. Man Sucker-Punched in the Face for Wearing MAGA-Style 'Make 50 Great Again' Hat [Internet]. pjmedia.com. 2020 [cited 2020 Sep 28]. Available from: https://pjmedia.com/news-and-

politics/megan-fox/2020/02/12/violent-left-man-sucker-punched-in-the-face-for-wearing-joke-maga-style-hat-n381475

271. The Week UK. Race Riots: What We Know About the Death of George Floyd [Internet]. The Week UK. 2020 [cited 2020 Oct 6]. Available from: //www.theweek.co.uk/107092/george-floyd-race-riots-what-we-know

272. Bucktin C. America Ablaze as Race Riots Spread with at Least 30 Cities Engulfed in Anger [Internet]. Express.co.uk. 2020 [cited 2020 Oct 12]. Available from: https://www.express.co.uk/news/world/1289417/George-Floyd-death-riots-america

273. Cavanagh N. Jacob Blake's Mom Says Son Would Hate the Protest 'Violence and Destruction' [Internet]. The Sun. 2020 [cited 2020 Oct 12]. Available from: https://www.thesun.co.uk/news/12503569/jacob-blake-mom-son-riots/

274. Ganim S, Welch C. Unmasking the Leftist Antifa Movement [Internet]. CNN. 2019 [cited 2020 Sep 5]. Available from: https://www.cnn.com/2017/08/18/us/unmasking-antifa-anti-fascists-hard-left/index.html

275. Schulman S. Conflict Is Not Abuse: Overstating Harm, Community Responsibility, and the Duty of Repair. Arsenal Pulp Press; 2016.

276. Johnson MZ. 7 Reasons Why White People Should Not Wear Black Hairstyles [Internet]. Everyday

Feminism. 2015 [cited 2020 Nov 9]. Available from: https://everydayfeminism.com/2015/07/white-people-black-hairstyles/

277. Tran CL. CDS Appropriates Asian Dishes, Students Say [Internet]. The Oberlin Review. 2015 [cited 2020 Jul 26]. Available from: https://oberlinreview.org/9055/news/cds-appropriates-asian-dishes-students-say/

278. Licea M, Italiano L. Students at Lena Dunham's College Offended by Lack of Fried Chicken [Internet]. New York Post. 2015 [cited 2020 Jul 26]. Available from: https://nypost.com/2015/12/18/pc-students-at-lena-dunhams-college-offended-by-lack-of-fried-chicken/

279. Johnson MZ. What's Wrong with Cultural Appropriation? These 9 Answers Reveal Its Harm [Internet]. Everyday Feminism. 2015 [cited 2020 Nov 20]. Available from: https://everydayfeminism.com/2015/06/cultural-appropriation-wrong/

280. The Week UK. What Is Cultural Appropriation and How Can You Spot It? [Internet]. The Week UK. 2020 [cited 2020 Nov 20]. Available from: //www.theweek.co.uk/cultural-appropriation

281. Sukhera J. Breaking Microaggressions Without Breaking Ourselves. Perspectives on Medical Education. 2019 Jun 1;8(3):129–30.

282. Dailymail.com. Is Mispronouncing a Student's Name a 'Micro-Aggression'? [Internet]. Mail Online. 2016 [cited 2020 Oct 9]. Available from: http://www.dailymail.co.uk/~/article-3805142/index.html

283. Ward M, Premack R. What Is a Microaggression? 14 Things People Think Are Fine to Say at Work — but Are Actually Racist, Sexist, or Offensive [Internet]. Business Insider. 2020 [cited 2020 Oct 10]. Available from: https://www.businessinsider.com/microaggression-unconscious-bias-at-work-2018-6

284. Rogers K. Anti-Racist Allies: How to Respond to Microaggressions [Internet]. CNN. 2020 [cited 2020 Oct 4]. Available from: https://www.cnn.com/2020/06/05/health/racial-microaggressions-examples-responses-wellness/index.html

285. al-Gharbi M. Diversity-Related Training: What Is It Good For? [Internet]. Heterodox Academy. 2020 [cited 2020 Sep 19]. Available from: https://heterodoxacademy.org/diversity-related-training-what-is-it-good-for/

286. Livingston M. These Are the Brands Giving Money to the Black Lives Matter Movement [Internet]. CNET. 2020 [cited 2020 Aug 31]. Available from: https://www.cnet.com/how-to/companies-donating-black-lives-matter/

287. Tindera M. Here Are the Billionaires Backing Joe Biden's Presidential Campaign, as of September

2019 [Internet]. Forbes. 2020 [cited 2020 Aug 12].
Available from:
https://www.forbes.com/sites/michelatindera/2019
/12/07/here-are-the-billionaires-backing-joe-
bidens-presidential-campaign/

288. Marcotte A, Tkacik M. Hillary Clinton Suggested
Breaking Up the Big Banks Won't End Racism and
Sexism. Is She Right? [Internet]. In These Times.
2016 [cited 2020 Aug 29]. Available from:
https://inthesetimes.com/article/break-up-banks-
end-racism-and-sexism

289. Sainato M. The Americans Dying Because They
Can't Afford Medical Care [Internet]. The
Guardian. 2020 [cited 2020 Aug 2]. Available
from: http://www.theguardian.com/us-
news/2020/jan/07/americans-healthcare-medical-
costs

290. Goodman JC. The Biden/Harris Economic Plan
[Internet]. Forbes. 2020 [cited 2020 Nov 21].
Available from:
https://www.forbes.com/sites/johngoodman/2020/
09/28/the-bidenharris-economic-plan/

291. Allison B, Rojanasakul M, Harris B, Sam C.
Tracking the 2016 Presidential Money Race.
Bloomberg.com [Internet]. 2016 Sep 12 [cited
2020 Aug 31]; Available from:
http://www.bloomberg.com/politics/graphics/2016
-presidential-campaign-fundraising/

292. Boatright R. Election Spending in 2020 Doubled to
$14 Billion − 3 Takeaways from a Campaign

Finance Expert [Internet]. The Conversation. 2020 [cited 2020 Nov 21]. Available from: http://theconversation.com/election-spending-in-2020-doubled-to-14-billion-3-takeaways-from-a-campaign-finance-expert-148700

293. Shribman DM. Citizens United Ruling Changed U.S. Politics, but Not in the Way People Expected [Internet]. Los Angeles Times. 2020 [cited 2020 Nov 10]. Available from: https://www.latimes.com/world-nation/story/2020-01-12/citizens-united-ruling-anniversary-how-it-changed-american-politics

294. Bote J. Colin Kaepernick Nike Shoe, with NFL Callout, Sells Out in Minutes [Internet]. USATtoday. 2019 [cited 2020 Aug 11]. Available from: https://www.usatoday.com/story/money/2019/12/26/colin-kaepernick-nike-shoe-nfl-callout-sells-out/2752312001/

295. Young S. Gillette Praised for Advert About a Transgender Man's First Shave [Internet]. The Independent. 2019 [cited 2020 Nov 10]. Available from: https://www.independent.co.uk/life-style/gillette-trans-advert-video-transgender-man-first-shave-father-video-watch-facebook-a8930981.html

296. Lubitz R. Jazz Jennings is Bringing Trans Representation to the Shaving Aisle [Internet]. Refinery29. 2019 [cited 2020 Mar 19]. Available from: https://www.refinery29.com/en-

us/2019/03/226907/jazz-jennings-transgender-gillette-venus-campaign

297. Edwards BT. Relaxing Beauty Products for Self-Care When You're Stuck at Home [Internet]. CNN Underscored. 2020 [cited 2020 Aug 31]. Available from: https://www.cnn.com/2020/03/20/cnn-underscored/beauty-products-for-self-care/index.html

298. CNN Underscored. About Us [Internet]. CNN Digital. 2020 [cited 2020 Aug 31]. Available from: https://www.cnn.com/cnn-underscored/about/

299. Nichols JM. This Holiday Season, Check Out These 21 Companies That Have Supported LGBT Rights [Internet]. HuffPost UK. 2015 [cited 2020 Aug 12]. Available from: https://www.huffpost.com/entry/21-companies-that-have-supported-lgbt-rights_n_5654bdece4b0879a5b0cbf7b

300. Huston WT. Nike Still Plagued by Accusations of Unsafe and Unfair Labor Practices [Internet]. Breitbart. 2019 [cited 2020 Nov 21]. Available from: https://www.breitbart.com/sports/2019/07/02/nike-still-plagued-accusations-unsafe-unfair-labor-practices/

301. Bain M. Nike Is Facing a New Wave of Anti-Sweatshop Protests [Internet]. Quartz. 2017 [cited 2020 Nov 21]. Available from: https://qz.com/1042298/nike-is-facing-a-new-wave-of-anti-sweatshop-protests/

302. Hopkins N, Bowers S. Revealed: How Nike Stays One Step Ahead of the Taxman [Internet]. The Guardian. 2017 [cited 2020 Nov 21]. Available from: https://www.theguardian.com/news/2017/nov/06/nike-tax-paradise-papers

303. Dockrill P. Consumers Have a Bigger Impact on The Environment Than Anything Else, Study Finds [Internet]. ScienceAlert. 2016 [cited 2020 Nov 21]. Available from: https://www.sciencealert.com/consumers-have-a-bigger-impact-on-the-environment-than-anything-else-study-finds

304. Ivanova D, Stadler K, Steen-Olsen K, Wood R, Vita G, Tukker A, et al. Environmental Impact Assessment of Household Consumption. Journal of Industrial Ecology. 2016;20(3):526–36.

305. Tilley J, Evans G. Ageing and Generational Effects on Vote Choice: Combining Cross-Sectional and Panel Data to Estimate APC Effects. Electoral Studies. 2014 Mar 1;33:19–27.

306. Tilley J. Do We Really Become More Conservative with Age? The Guardian [Internet]. 2015 Nov 3 [cited 2020 Feb 29]; Available from: https://www.theguardian.com/commentisfree/2015/nov/03/do-we-become-more-conservative-with-age-young-old-politics

307. Forbes. Twitter (TWTR) [Internet]. Forbes. 2020 [cited 2020 Sep 1]. Available from: https://www.forbes.com/companies/twitter/

308. Market Watch. Twitter Inc. [Internet]. Market Watch. 2020 [cited 2020 Sep 1]. Available from: https://www.marketwatch.com/investing/stock/twt r

309. Marketing Charts. Millennials and Brand Loyalty: A Complicated Affair [Internet]. Marketing Charts. 2014 [cited 2020 Jul 13]. Available from: https://www.marketingcharts.com/brand-related-41522

310. Andre M, Aufrichtig A, Beltran G, Bloch M, Buchanan L, Chavez A, et al. National Exit Polls: How Different Groups Voted. The New York Times [Internet]. 2020 Nov 3 [cited 2020 Nov 21]; Available from: https://www.nytimes.com/interactive/2020/11/03/ us/elections/exit-polls-president.html

311. Facebook Net Worth 2009-2020 | FB [Internet]. [cited 2020 Aug 11]. Available from: https://www.macrotrends.net/stocks/charts/FB/fac ebook/net-worth

312. Wagner K. Reddit Raised $200 Million in Funding and Is Now Valued at $1.8 Billion [Internet]. CNBC. 2017 [cited 2020 Aug 12]. Available from: https://www.cnbc.com/2017/07/31/reddit-worth-1-point-8-billion.html

313. Beeman A. Reddit Updates Hate Speech Policy, Bans Pro-Trump Subreddit Group [Internet]. Heavy.com. 2020 [cited 2020 Jul 2]. Available from: https://heavy.com/news/2020/06/reddit-banned-trump-group-hate-speech/

314. Milton J. Reddit Just Banned Its Viciously Transphobic 'Gender Critical' Page Amid Vigorous Crackdown on Hate Speech [Internet]. PinkNews. 2020 [cited 2020 Jul 2]. Available from: https://www.pinknews.co.uk/2020/06/29/reddit-bann-transphobia-gender-critical-page-hate-speech-donald-trump-steve-huffman/

315. Myers F. Facebook's Purge of Left-Wing Radicals [Internet]. Spiked! 2020 [cited 2020 Sep 1]. Available from: https://www.spiked-online.com/2020/08/31/facebooks-purge-of-left-wing-radicals/

316. Lyons K. Coca-Cola, Microsoft, Starbucks, Target, Unilever, Verizon: All the Companies Pulling Ads from Facebook [Internet]. The Verge. 2020 [cited 2020 Jul 29]. Available from: https://www.theverge.com/21307454/unilever-verizon-coca-cola-starbucks-microsoft-ads-facebook

317. Wagner K. Tech Giants Apple, Google and Facebook Are Fighting President Trump's Immigration Ban [Internet]. Vox. 2017 [cited 2020 Nov 11]. Available from: https://www.vox.com/2017/2/6/14519750/apple-google-facebook-trump-immigration

318. Binder J. Data: Foreign-Born Workers Overwhelmingly Outnumber Americans in Silicon Valley Jobs [Internet]. Breitbart. 2018 [cited 2020 Nov 11]. Available from: https://www.breitbart.com/politics/2018/01/18/dat

a-foreign-born-workers-overwhelmingly-outnumber-americans-in-silicon-valley-jobs/

319. Haidari N. What Are Some Examples of White Privilege? [Internet]. VICE. 2020 [cited 2020 Sep 1]. Available from: https://www.vice.com/en_uk/article/4ayw8j/white-privilege-examples

320. Lowrey S. A Guide to Non-Binary Pronouns and Why They Matter [Internet]. HuffPost. 2017 [cited 2020 Sep 1]. Available from: https://www.huffpost.com/entry/non-binary-pronouns-why-they-matter_b_5a03107be4b0230facb8419a

321. Corcione A. Everything You Should Know About Karl Marx [Internet]. Teen Vogue. 2018 [cited 2020 Jul 20]. Available from: https://www.teenvogue.com/story/who-is-karl-marx

322. Lewis H. How Capitalism Drives Cancel Culture. The Atlantic [Internet]. 2020 Jul 14 [cited 2020 Aug 12]; Available from: https://www.theatlantic.com/international/archive/2020/07/cancel-culture-and-problem-woke-capitalism/614086/

323. Fain Lehman C. The Wages of Woke: How Robin DiAngelo Got Rich Peddling 'White Fragility' [Internet]. Washington Free Beacon. 2020 [cited 2020 Sep 1]. Available from: https://freebeacon.com/culture/the-wages-of-woke-2/

324. Bartlett T. Can We Really Measure Implicit Bias? Maybe Not [Internet]. CHE. 2017 [cited 2020 Nov 11]. Available from: https://www.chronicle.com/article/can-we-really-measure-implicit-bias-maybe-not/

325. Lodge R. Why Is Makeup Shaming Not Taboo? [Internet]. Grazia. 2017 [cited 2020 Feb 20]. Available from: https://graziadaily.co.uk/beauty-hair/makeup/makeup-shaming-taboo/

326. Statista. Makeup: Frequency of Use by Age U.S. 2017 [Internet]. Statista. 2017 [cited 2020 Feb 20]. Available from: https://www.statista.com/statistics/713178/makeup-use-frequency-by-age/

327. Sanghani R. #PowerOfMakeup: Women Are Posting 'Half Makeup' Selfies Online [Internet]. The Telegraph. 2015 [cited 2020 Feb 20]. Available from: https://www.telegraph.co.uk/women/womens-life/11698179/PowerOfMakeup-Twitter-and-Instagram-selfies-fight-makeup-shaming.html

328. Borovic K. This Beauty Study Proves What Women Have Been Saying All Along About Makeup [Internet]. Bustle. 2017 [cited 2020 Feb 20]. Available from: https://www.bustle.com/p/women-wear-makeup-for-themselves-theres-a-study-to-prove-it-2953397

329. Wolf N. The Beauty Myth: How Images of Beauty are Used Against Women. Vintage Digital; 1991. 350 p.

330. Sorvino C. Why the $445 Billion Beauty Industry Is a Gold Mine for Self-Made Women [Internet]. Forbes. 2017 [cited 2020 Feb 21]. Available from: https://www.forbes.com/sites/chloesorvino/2017/0 5/18/self-made-women-wealth-beauty-gold-mine/

331. Willett M, Gould S. These 7 Companies Control Almost Every Single Beauty Product You Buy [Internet]. Insider. 2017 [cited 2020 Sep 1]. Available from: https://www.insider.com/companies-beauty-brands-connected-2017-5

332. Walton J. The Top 5 Individual Shareholders of P&G [Internet]. Investopedia. 2020 [cited 2020 Sep 1]. Available from: https://www.investopedia.com/articles/insights/08 1316/top-5-individual-shareholders-pg-pg.asp

333. L'Oréal Group. L'Oréal Group: Executive Committee [Internet]. L'Oréal. [cited 2020 Sep 1]. Available from: https://www.loreal.com/en/governance/executive-committee/

334. Alex Gorsky [Internet]. Johnson and Johnson Services. [cited 2020 Sep 1]. Available from: https://www.jnj.com/leadership/alex-gorsky

335. Estée Lauder Companies. Executive Leadership [Internet]. Estée Lauder Companies. [cited 2020 Sep 1]. Available from:

https://www.elcompanies.com/en/who-we-are/leadership/executive-leadership

336. Unilever Global Company. Alan Jope [Internet]. Unilever Global Company Website. [cited 2020 Sep 1]. Available from: https://www.unilever.com/about/who-we-are/our-leadership/alan-jope.html

337. Shiseido Co Ltd. Message from CEO [Internet]. Shiseido Co Ltd. [cited 2020 Sep 1]. Available from: https://corp.shiseido.com/en/company/top-message/

338. Reuters. COTY Changes CEO Again, Hires Former L'oreal Executive [Internet]. New York Post. 2020 [cited 2020 Sep 1]. Available from: https://nypost.com/2020/07/02/coty-hires-former-loreal-executive-sue-nabi-as-ceo/

339. Stossel J. Legalize Sex Work [Internet]. Reason.com. 2017 [cited 2020 Sep 1]. Available from: https://reason.com/2017/11/15/legalize-sex-work/

340. Avert. Sex workers, HIV and AIDS [Internet]. Avert. 2015 [cited 2020 Feb 24]. Available from: https://www.avert.org/professionals/hiv-social-issues/key-affected-populations/sex-workers

341. Vrangalova Z. Do Sex Workers Have More Mental Health Problems? [Internet]. Psychology Today. 2014 [cited 2020 Feb 24]. Available from: http://www.psychologytoday.com/blog/strictly-casual/201410/do-sex-workers-have-more-mental-health-problems

342. Bureau of Labor Statistics. Logging Workers Had Highest Rate of Fatal Work Injuries in 2015: The Economics Daily: U.S. Bureau of Labor Statistics [Internet]. Bureau of Labor Statistics. 2017 [cited 2020 Nov 12]. Available from: https://www.bls.gov/opub/ted/2017/logging-workers-had-highest-rate-of-fatal-work-injuries-in-2015.htm

343. Potterat JJ, Brewer DD, Muth SQ, Rothenberg RB, Woodhouse DE, Muth JB, et al. Mortality in a Long-term Open Cohort of Prostitute Women. Am J Epidemiol. 2004 Apr 15;159(8):778–85.

344. Skinner M. I Thought I Knew About Feminism – Then I Started Work in a Women's Prison. The Guardian [Internet]. 2019 Oct 17 [cited 2020 Feb 24]; Available from: https://www.theguardian.com/lifeandstyle/2019/oct/17/feminism-working-womens-prison-inmates-sex-work-marriage

345. Garfinkel R. A New Twist on World's Oldest Profession: Nab the Johns, Not the Prostitutes [Internet]. The Washington Times. 2017 [cited 2020 Aug 31]. Available from: https://www.washingtontimes.com/news/2017/mar/13/working-women-prostitution-law/

346. Adams W, Owens C, Small K. Effects of Federal Legislation on the Commercial Sexual Exploitation of Children [Internet]. US Department of Justice; 2010 Jul p. 12. (Juvenile Justice Bulletin). Available from: https://www.ncjrs.gov/pdffiles1/ojjdp/228631.pdf

347. Wright J. Why Prostitution Should Be Legal [Internet]. Harper's BAZAAR. 2018 [cited 2020 Sep 1]. Available from: https://www.harpersbazaar.com/culture/politics/a2 0067359/why-prostitution-should-be-legal/

348. MacKinnon CA, Dworkin A. In Harm's Way: The Pornography Civil Rights Hearings. Harvard University Press; 1997. 518 p.

349. Graham R. The Political and the Principled: A Different Take on Grievance Studies [Internet]. Medium. 2019 [cited 2020 Feb 27]. Available from: https://arcdigital.media/the-political-and-the-principled-a-different-take-on-grievance-studies-1984b0c3fb41

350. Dotson K. Conceptualizing Epistemic Oppression. Social Epistemology. 2014 Apr 3;28(2):115–38.

351. Dotson K. Tracking Epistemic Violence, Tracking Practices of Silencing. Hypatia. 2011;26(2):236–57.

352. Berenstain N. Epistemic Exploitation. Ergo, an Open Access Journal of Philosophy. 2016;3(22):569–90.

353. Muldoon J. Academics: It's Time to Get Behind Decolonising the Curriculum [Internet]. The Guardian. 2019 [cited 2020 Nov 10]. Available from: http://www.theguardian.com/education/2019/mar/20/academics-its-time-to-get-behind-decolonising-the-curriculum

354. Batty D. Only a Fifth of UK Universities Say They Are 'Decolonising' Curriculum. The Guardian [Internet]. 2020 Jun 11 [cited 2020 Dec 12]; Available from: https://www.theguardian.com/us-news/2020/jun/11/only-fifth-of-uk-universities-have-said-they-will-decolonise-curriculum

355. Derrida J. Writing and Difference. Second. London: Routledge; 2001. 446 p.

356. O'Neill B. Why Rhodes Must Stay [Internet]. Spiked! 2020 [cited 2020 Jun 20]. Available from: https://www.spiked-online.com/2020/06/18/why-rhodes-must-stay/

357. Dingwell R. Black History and the Myth of Mary Seacole [Internet]. 2016 [cited 2020 Oct 13]. Available from: https://www.socialsciencespace.com/2016/10/black-history-myth-mary-seacole/

358. McDonald L. Nursing the Enduring Myth of Mary Seacole [Internet]. Standpoint. 2019 [cited 2020 Oct 13]. Available from: https://standpointmag.co.uk/issues/may-2019/nursing-the-enduring-myth-of-mary-seacole/

359. McDonald L. Statue of 'Nurse' Mary Seacole Will Do Florence Nightingale a Disservice. The Guardian [Internet]. 2012 Jun 8 [cited 2020 Feb 13]; Available from: https://www.theguardian.com/commentisfree/2012/jun/08/mary-seacole-statue-florence-nightingale-disservice

360. McDonald L. Florence Nightingale: The Making of a Hospital Reformer. HERD. 2020 Apr 1;13(2):25–31.

361. Woolley S. Mary Seacole and Her Wretched Detractors [Internet]. 2013 [cited 2020 Oct 14]. Available from: https://www.obv.org.uk/news-blogs/mary-seacole-and-her-wretched-detractors

362. Yasmeh J. Leftist Student-Activist: Science Is Racist and Should Be 'Decolonized' [Internet]. The Daily Wire. 2016 [cited 2020 Sep 29]. Available from: https://www.dailywire.com/news/leftist-student-activist-science-racist-and-should-joshua-yasmeh

363. Goldberg J. This 'Anti-Racism Education' Sure Looks Awfully … Racist [Internet]. New York Post. 2020 [cited 2020 Oct 6]. Available from: https://nypost.com/2020/07/19/this-anti-racism-education-sure-looks-awfully-racist/

364. Yates C. Five Ways Ancient India Changed the World – with Maths [Internet]. The Conversation. 2017 [cited 2020 Oct 14]. Available from: http://theconversation.com/five-ways-ancient-india-changed-the-world-with-maths-84332

365. Brazier Y. Ancient Egyptian Medicine: Influences, Practice, Magic, and Religion [Internet]. Medical News Today. 2018 [cited 2020 Nov 12]. Available from: https://www.medicalnewstoday.com/articles/323633

366. Bergner D. 'White Fragility' Is Everywhere. But Does Antiracism Training Work? The New York Times [Internet]. 2020 Jul 15 [cited 2020 Jul 22]; Available from: https://www.nytimes.com/2020/07/15/magazine/white-fragility-robin-diangelo.html

367. Gunter M. Clemson Begs Profs to Sign up for $27,000 Diversity Training [Internet]. Campus Reform. 2017 [cited 2020 Jul 23]. Available from: https://www.campusreform.org/?ID=9034

368. Chait J. Is the Anti-Racism Training Industry Just Peddling White Supremacy? [Internet]. Intelligencer. 2020 [cited 2020 Aug 28]. Available from: https://nymag.com/intelligencer/2020/07/antiracism-training-white-fragility-robin-diangelo-ibram-kendi.html

369. Fine Maron D. 'Wet Markets' Likely Launched the Coronavirus. Here's What You Need to Know [Internet]. National Geographic. 2020 [cited 2020 Nov 12]. Available from: https://www.nationalgeographic.co.uk/science-and-technology/2020/04/wet-markets-likely-launched-coronavirus-heres-what-you-need-know

370. Webster RG. Wet Markets—a Continuing Source of Severe Acute Respiratory Syndrome and Influenza? The Lancet. 2004 Jan 17;363(9404):234–6.

371. Northam J. Calls Grow to Ban Wet Markets Amid Concerns Over Disease Spread [Internet].

NPR.org. 2020 [cited 2020 Nov 12]. Available from: https://www.npr.org/sections/coronavirus-live-updates/2020/04/16/835937420/calls-grow-to-ban-wet-markets

372. Lynteris C, Fearnley L. Why Shutting down Chinese 'Wet Markets' Could Be a Terrible Mistake [Internet]. The Conversation. 2020 [cited 2020 Nov 5]. Available from: http://theconversation.com/why-shutting-down-chinese-wet-markets-could-be-a-terrible-mistake-130625

373. BBC News. 'Mad Cow Disease': What Is BSE? BBC News [Internet]. 2018 Oct 18 [cited 2020 Nov 12]; Available from: https://www.bbc.co.uk/news/uk-45906585

374. NHS. Creutzfeldt-Jakob Disease [Internet]. NHS.UK. 2017 [cited 2020 Nov 12]. Available from: https://www.nhs.uk/conditions/creutzfeldt-jakob-disease-cjd/

375. BBC News. China Lifts Ban on Imports of British Beef. BBC News [Internet]. 2018 Jun 27 [cited 2020 Nov 12]; Available from: https://www.bbc.co.uk/news/business-44629275

376. Engber D. The Strange Case of Anna Stubblefield [Internet]. The New York Times. 2015 [cited 2020 Sep 30]. Available from: https://www.nytimes.com/2015/10/25/magazine/the-strange-case-of-anna-stubblefield.html

377. American Psychological Association. Facilitated Communication: Sifting the Psychological Wheat

from the Chaff [Internet]. https://www.apa.org. 2003 [cited 2020 Nov 23]. Available from: https://www.apa.org/research/action/facilitated

378. Hemsley B, Bryant L, Schlosser RW, Shane HC, Lang R, Paul D, et al. Systematic Review of Facilitated Communication 2014–2018 Finds No New Evidence That Messages Delivered Using Facilitated Communication Are Authored by the Person with Disability: Autism & Developmental Language Impairments. 2018 Dec 30;3:1–8.

379. Palfreman J. Prisoners of Silence [Internet]. 1993 [cited 2020 Sep 30]. (FRONTLINE). Available from: https://www.youtube.com/watch?v=CzCGux7qD1 c&app=desktop

380. Cerebral Palsy Alliance. Eye-Gaze Control Technology [Internet]. Cerebral Palsy Alliance. 2016 [cited 2020 Oct 1]. Available from: https://cerebralpalsy.org.au/our-research/about-cerebral-palsy/interventions-and-therapies/eye-gaze-technology-for-children-and-adults-with-cerebral-palsy/

381. Johnson Dm. RETRACTED: The Role of Communication in Thought. Disability Studies Quarterly [Internet]. 2011 Oct 25 [cited 2020 Nov 13];31(4). Available from: https://dsq-sds.org/article/view/1717

382. Stubblefield A. Sound and Fury: When Opposition to Facilitated Communication Functions as Hate Speech. Disability Studies Quarterly [Internet].

2011 Oct 25 [cited 2020 Sep 30];31(4). Available from: https://dsq-sds.org/article/view/1729

383. Engber D. The Strange Case of Anna Stubblefield, Revisited [Internet]. The New York Times. 2018 [cited 2020 Sep 30]. Available from: https://www.nytimes.com/2018/04/05/magazine/t he-strange-case-of-anna-stubblefield-revisited.html

384. Sherry M. Facilitated Communication, Anna Stubblefield and Disability Studies. Disability & Society. 2016 Aug 8;31(7):974–82.

385. Mintz K. Ableism, Ambiguity, and the Anna Stubblefield Case. Disability & Society. 2017 Nov 26;32(10):1666–70.

386. Stubblefield A. Living a Good Life...In Adult-size Diapers. In: Bickenbach JE, Felder F, Schmitz B, editors. Disability and the Good Human Life. Cambridge: Cambridge University Press; 2014. p. 219–42.

387. NIDDK. Health Risks of Overweight & Obesity [Internet]. National Institute of Diabetes and Digestive and Kidney Diseases. 2018 [cited 2020 Aug 27]. Available from: https://www.niddk.nih.gov/health-information/weight-management/adult-overweight-obesity/health-risks

388. Bacon L. Health at Every Size: The Surprising Truth About Your Weight. Revised. Dalas: BenBella Books; 2008.

389. Mitchell N, Catenacci V, Wyatt HR, Hill JO. Obesity: Overview of an Epidemic. The Psychiatric Clinics of North America. 2011 Dec;34(4):717–32.

390. Costanzo A. Want to Eat Better? You Might Be Able to Train Yourself to Change Your Tastes [Internet]. The Conversation. 2018 [cited 2020 Aug 27]. Available from: http://theconversation.com/want-to-eat-better-you-might-be-able-to-train-yourself-to-change-your-tastes-94914

391. Mills J. Cancer Research UK Accused of 'Fatshaming' Over Their Obesity Poster [Internet]. Metro. 2018 [cited 2020 Feb 23]. Available from: https://metro.co.uk/2018/03/01/cancer-research-uk-accused-fatshaming-obesity-poster-7353080/

392. Byrne C. The BMI Is Racist and Useless. Here's How to Measure Health Instead. [Internet]. HuffPost UK. 2020 [cited 2020 Jul 25]. Available from: https://www.huffpost.com/entry/bmi-scale-racist-health_l_5f15a8a8c5b6d14c336a43b0

393. Hicklin T. Factors Contributing to Higher Incidence of Diabetes for Black Americans [Internet]. National Institutes of Health (NIH). 2018 [cited 2020 Aug 27]. Available from: https://www.nih.gov/news-events/nih-research-matters/factors-contributing-higher-incidence-diabetes-black-americans

394. Center for Disease Control and Prevention. Faststats- Obesity and Overweight [Internet]. Center for Disease Control and Prevention. 2020

[cited 2020 Aug 27]. Available from: https://www.cdc.gov/nchs/fastats/obesity-overweight.htm

395. Beck S by J. The New Age of Astrology. The Atlantic [Internet]. 2018 Jan 16 [cited 2020 Sep 28]; Available from: https://www.theatlantic.com/health/archive/2018/01/the-new-age-of-astrology/550034/

396. Everyday Feminism. Astrology as Healing Work: How to Use Your Natal Chart for Self-Care and Self-Love [Internet]. Everyday Feminism. 2018 [cited 2020 Feb 26]. Available from: https://everydayfeminism.com/astrology-as-healing-work/

397. Beusman C. The Rise of the Queer Astrology Movement [Internet]. VICE. 2015 [cited 2020 Sep 28]. Available from: https://www.vice.com/en_us/article/evgg9a/the-rise-of-the-queer-astrology-movement

398. Matthews-King A. People Who Use Homeopathy and Alternative Remedies for Cancer Treatment Are Twice as Likely to Die from Disease [Internet]. The Independent. 2018 [cited 2020 Feb 27]. Available from: https://www.independent.co.uk/news/health/cancer-treatment-patients-acupuncture-herbal-medicine-homeopathy-death-rate-higher-a8454791.html

399. Johnson SB, Park HS, Gross CP, Yu JB. Complementary Medicine, Refusal of Conventional Cancer Therapy, and Survival

Among Patients With Curable Cancers. JAMA Oncology. 2018 Oct 1;4(10):1375.

400. Kale S. Blue Lips and Black Skin: Did a Standard 111 Question Help Cause Olufemi Akinnola's Death from Covid-19? [Internet]. The Guardian. 2020 [cited 2020 Sep 27]. Available from: http://www.theguardian.com/society/2020/sep/23/blue-lips-and-black-skin-did-a-standard-111-question-help-cause-olufemi-akinnolas-death-from-covid-19

401. Revesz R. Campaigners Demand Donald Trump Fully Divests from Empire [Internet]. The Independent. 2017 [cited 2020 Nov 24]. Available from: https://www.independent.co.uk/news/world/americas/donald-trump-business-conflicts-interest-divest-liquidate-blind-trust-campaigners-experts-ethics-a7522586.html

402. BBC News. Trump Boys Go Wild in the Emerald Isle. BBC News [Internet]. 2019 Jun 6 [cited 2020 Aug 23]; Available from: https://www.bbc.com/news/world-us-canada-48546443

403. Markay L, Suebsaeng A. Sinking in the Swamp: How Trump's Minions and Misfits Poisoned Washington. Viking; 2020.

404. Crockett Z. Donald Trump Is the Only US President Ever with No Political or Military Experience [Internet]. Vox. 2016 [cited 2020 Nov 24]. Available from: https://www.vox.com/policy-

and-politics/2016/11/11/13587532/donald-trump-no-experience

405. Voce A, Kommenda N, Leach A, Hulley-Jones F, Clarke S, Voce A, et al. Senate and House Elections 2020: Full Results for Congress. The Guardian [Internet]. 2020 Nov 13 [cited 2020 Nov 13]; Available from: https://www.theguardian.com/us-news/ng-interactive/2020/nov/09/senate-and-house-elections-2020-full-results-for-congress

406. Zeitz J. Why the Presidency Can't Just Go Back to 'Normal' After Trump [Internet]. POLITICO. 2020 [cited 2020 Nov 6]. Available from: https://www.politico.com/news/magazine/2020/02/15/why-presidency-cant-go-back-normal-trump-115362

407. Howell Jr. T. Trump Says Obamacare 'Already Essentially Gone' [Internet]. The Washington Times. 2020 [cited 2020 Oct 2]. Available from: https://www.washingtontimes.com/news/2020/sep/27/trump-says-obamacare-essentially-gone-after-ending/

408. Chen M. Opinion | Trump's Title X Rule, Like State Abortion Restrictions, Targets Poor Women [Internet]. NBC News. 2019 [cited 2020 Oct 15]. Available from: https://www.nbcnews.com/think/opinion/trump-s-title-x-rule-defunding-planned-parenthood-yet-another-ncna1045471

409. Rushe D. Trump's Tax Cuts Helped Billionaires Pay Less Than the Working Class for First Time [Internet]. The Guardian. 2019 [cited 2020 Nov 14]. Available from: http://www.theguardian.com/business/2019/oct/09/trump-tax-cuts-helped-billionaires-pay-less

410. Harvey F. Trump Exiting Paris Accord Will Harm Us Economy – LSE Research [Internet]. The Guardian. 2020 [cited 2020 Oct 2]. Available from: http://www.theguardian.com/environment/2020/aug/13/trump-exiting-paris-accord-will-harm-us-economy-lse-research

411. Irfan U. Trump's EPA Just Replaced Obama's Signature Climate Policy with a Much Weaker Rule [Internet]. Vox. 2019 [cited 2020 Oct 5]. Available from: https://www.vox.com/2019/6/19/18684054/climate-change-clean-power-plan-repeal-affordable-emissions

412. Borger J. Donald Trump Signs Executive Order to Keep Guantánamo Bay Open. The Guardian [Internet]. 2018 Jan 31 [cited 2020 Jul 14]; Available from: https://www.theguardian.com/us-news/2018/jan/30/guantanamo-bay-trump-signs-executive-order-to-keep-prison-open

413. Naughtie A. Executed Federal Prisoner Used Final Words to Plead Innocence [Internet]. The Independent. 2020 [cited 2020 Aug 16]. Available from: https://www.independent.co.uk/news/world/ameri

cas/daniel-lee-lewis-executed-prisoner-last-words-a9620466.html

414. Sampathkumar M. Trump Administration Will Withdraw US from UN Human Rights Council, Report Says [Internet]. The Independent. 2018 [cited 2020 Oct 5]. Available from: https://www.independent.co.uk/news/world/ameri cas/us-politics/trump-us-un-human-rights-council-nikki-haley-israel-north-korea-iran-a8401281.html

415. Dunlap DW. 1973 | Meet Donald Trump. The New York Times [Internet]. 2015 Jul 30 [cited 2020 Dec 20]; Available from: https://www.nytimes.com/times-insider/2015/07/30/1973-meet-donald-trump/

416. Rothman L. Trump's 1973 Discrimination Case Was Part of Larger Case [Internet]. Time. 2016 [cited 2020 Oct 5]. Available from: https://time.com/4508889/presidential-debate-1970s-bias-donald-trump/

417. O'Donnell JR, Rutherford J. Trumped!: The Inside Story of the Real Donald Trump-His Cunning Rise and Spectacular Fall. New York: Simon & Schuster; 1991. 348 p.

418. Pagliery J. Donald Trump Was a Nightmare Landlord in the 1980s [Internet]. CNNMoney. 2016 [cited 2020 Aug 21]. Available from: https://money.cnn.com/2016/03/28/news/trump-apartment-tenants/index.html

419. Baxter A. You've Been Trumped [Internet]. United Kingdom; 2011. Available from:

https://play.google.com/store/movies/details/You_ve_Been_Trumped?id=9M_StG5RpA4&hl=en_US&gl=US

420. Ward B. Trump Golf Course Partially Destroys Site of Special Scientific Interest [Internet]. Grantham Research Institute on Climate Change and the Environment. 2018 [cited 2020 Aug 22]. Available from: https://www.lse.ac.uk/granthaminstitute/news/trump-golf-course-partially-destroys-site-of-special-scientific-interest/

421. Davis K. Attorneys in Trump University Case Talk Strategy, Leaks and Deposing the Future President [Internet]. San Diego Union-Tribune. 2016 [cited 2020 Oct 6]. Available from: https://www.sandiegouniontribune.com/news/courts/sd-me-trumpu-lawyers-20161209-story.html

422. Winter T, Clark D. Federal Court Approves $25 Million Trump University Settlement [Internet]. NBC News. 2018 [cited 2020 Aug 5]. Available from: https://www.nbcnews.com/politics/white-house/federal-court-approves-25-million-trump-university-settlement-n845181

423. Cillizza C. Why the Trump Foundation Payout is a BIG Deal [Internet]. CNN. 2019 [cited 2020 Aug 5]. Available from: https://www.cnn.com/2019/11/07/politics/donald-trump-trump-foundation-2016/index.html

424. Dreams C. $2 Million and Compulsory Training for President's Children Called 'Poetic End' to

Trump Charity Abuse Case [Internet]. Raw Story. 2019 [cited 2020 Aug 18]. Available from: https://www.rawstory.com/2019/11/2-million-and-compulsory-training-for-presidents-children-called-poetic-end-to-trump-charity-abuse-case/

425. Trump ML. Too Much and Never Enough: How My Family Created the World's Most Dangerous Man. First. London: Simon & Schuster UK; 2020. 240 p.

426. Hurt III H. Lost Tycoon: The Many Lives of Donald J. Trump. Echo Point Books and Media; 1993.

427. Withnall A. All Donald Trump's Creepiest Comments About His Daughter Ivanka [Internet]. The Independent. 2016 [cited 2020 Oct 15]. Available from: https://www.independent.co.uk/news/world/americas/us-politics/donald-trump-ivanka-trump-creepiest-most-unsettling-comments-roundup-a7353876.html

428. Harper K. Donald & Ivanka Trump: The Throwback Family Photo That Has Everyone Freaked [Internet]. Hollywood Life. 2016 [cited 2020 Oct 15]. Available from: https://hollywoodlife.com/2016/02/02/ivanka-donald-trump-throwback-photo-daughter/

429. Newman OM. Unhinged: An Insider's Account of the Trump White House. First. New York: Gallery Books; 2018. 368 p.

430. Rosenthal MJ. Flashback: When Trump Called His Then 4-Year-Old Son, Trump Jr., a 'Loser' [Internet]. Mother Jones. 2020 [cited 2020 Oct 15]. Available from: https://www.motherjones.com/politics/2020/08/tru mp-files-when-trump-called-donald-jr-a-loser/

431. Trump Jr. D. Triggered: How the Left Thrives on Hate and Wants to Silence Us. New York: Center Street; 2019. 304 p.

432. Heimbrod C. Donald Trump Reportedly 'Slapped,' 'Knocked Down' Donald Jr After Son Did This [Internet]. International Business Times. 2020 [cited 2020 Dec 2]. Available from: https://www.ibtimes.com/donald-trump-reportedly-slapped-knocked-down-donald-jr-after-son-did-2905045

433. Fox EJ. Born Trump: Inside America's First Family. First Edition. Harper; 2018. 352 p.

434. Coppins S by M. The Heir. The Atlantic [Internet]. 2019 Oct [cited 2020 Sep 13]; Available from: https://www.theatlantic.com/magazine/archive/20 19/10/trump-dynasty/596674/

435. Holson LM. Donald Trump Jr. Is His Own Kind of Trump. The New York Times [Internet]. 2017 Mar 18 [cited 2020 Oct 15]; Available from: https://www.nytimes.com/2017/03/18/style/donal d-trump-jr-business-politics-hunting-twitter-vanessa-haydon.html

436. Van Meter J. Donald Trump's Children - The Real Apprentices [Internet]. New York Magazine. 2004

[cited 2020 Aug 8]. Available from: https://nymag.com/nymetro/news/people/features/10610/

437. Brooke J. The Real Story Behind Donald Trump's Infamous 'Best Sex I've Ever Had' Headline (Guest Column) [Internet]. Hollywood Reporter. 2018 [cited 2020 Oct 7]. Available from: https://www.hollywoodreporter.com/features/i-wrote-donald-trumps-infamous-best-sex-i-ever-had-story-guest-column-1101246

438. Trump I. Raising Trump. First Edition. New York: Gallery Books; 2017. 304 p.

439. Triggs C. Donald Trump Ex Marla Maples Talks Raising Tiffany Trump as a Single Mother [Internet]. PEOPLE.com. 2016 [cited 2020 Oct 15]. Available from: https://people.com/celebrity/donald-trump-ex-marla-maples-talks-raising-tiffany-trump-as-a-single-mother/

440. Linning S. Trump Says He's Proud of All His Kids but Tiffany 'to a Lesser Extent' [Internet]. Mail Online. 2016 [cited 2020 Oct 16]. Available from: http://www.dailymail.co.uk/~/article-3918806/index.html

441. Relman E. The 26 women who have accused Trump of sexual misconduct - Business Insider [Internet]. Business Insider. 2020 [cited 2020 Dec 20]. Available from: https://www.businessinsider.com/women-

accused-trump-sexual-misconduct-list-2017-
12?r=US&IR=T

442. Fahrenthold DA. Trump Recorded Having
Extremely Lewd Conversation About Women in
2005. Washington Post [Internet]. 2016 Oct 8
[cited 2020 Sep 30]; Available from:
https://www.washingtonpost.com/politics/trump-
recorded-having-extremely-lewd-conversation-
about-women-in-2005/2016/10/07/3b9ce776-
8cb4-11e6-bf8a-3d26847eeed4_story.html

443. Fox News. Pageant Contestants Claim Trump
Entered Dressing Rooms While They Were Half-
Naked [Internet]. Fox News. 2020 [cited 2020 Oct
15]. Available from:
https://www.foxnews.com/entertainment/pageant-
contestants-claim-trump-entered-dressing-rooms-
while-they-were-half-naked

444. Cillizza C. The Awful Reality That Donald
Trump's Attacks on John McCain Prove [Internet].
CNN. 2019 [cited 2020 Jul 19]. Available from:
https://www.cnn.com/2019/03/19/politics/donald-
trump-john-mccain-dead/index.html

445. Perez M. Report: Trump Called U.S. WWI
Veterans 'Suckers' And 'Losers' [Internet].
Forbes. 2020 [cited 2020 Oct 15]. Available from:
https://www.forbes.com/sites/mattperez/2020/09/0
3/report-trump-called-us-wwi-veterans-suckers-
and-losers/

446. West L. Fat People, Rise up! We Could Swing This
Election. The Guardian [Internet]. 2016 Sep 27

[cited 2020 Jun 2]; Available from: https://www.theguardian.com/commentisfree/201 6/sep/27/fat-people-rise-up-we-could-swing-this-election

447. Mazziotta J. Donald Trump's Fat Phobia Over the Years: from '400-Lb.' Hackers to 'Miss Piggy' [Internet]. Yahoo! 2016 [cited 2020 Oct 2]. Available from: https://www.yahoo.com/entertainment/donald-trumps-fat-phobia-over-181801015.html

448. Lopez G. Donald Trump's Long History of Racism, from the 1970s to 2020 [Internet]. Vox. 2016 [cited 2020 Jul 9]. Available from: https://www.vox.com/2016/7/25/12270880/donald -trump-racist-racism-history

449. Feinberg A. Mary Trump Has a Stark Warning About the Possibility of a Trump Political Dynasty [Internet]. The Independent. 2020 [cited 2020 Aug 4]. Available from: https://www.independent.co.uk/voices/trump-mary-cousin-ivanka-don-jr-family-dynasty-2020-election-a9653186.html

450. Solender A. Trump Sons Hint at 2024 Runs as President's Polling Looks Dire [Internet]. Forbes. 2020 [cited 2020 Nov 14]. Available from: https://www.forbes.com/sites/andrewsolender/202 0/10/24/trump-sons-hint-at-future-runs-as-presidents-polling-looks-dire/

451. Mastrangelo D. WATCH: Don Trump Jr. Met with Chants of '46' at New Hampshire Rally [Internet].

Washington Examiner. 2020 [cited 2020 Jul 23]. Available from: https://www.washingtonexaminer.com/news/watch-don-trump-jr-met-with-chants-of-46-at-new-hampshire-rally

452. Impelli M. Mike Pence Leads Donald Trump Jr. by 14 Points in 2024 Republican Primary Poll [Internet]. Newsweek. 2020 [cited 2020 Aug 18]. Available from: https://www.newsweek.com/mike-pence-leads-donald-trump-jr-14-points-2024-republican-primary-poll-1525110

453. Trump Jr. D. Liberal Privilege: Joe Biden and the Democrats' Defense of the Indefensible. New York: Donald Trump Jr; 2020.

454. Marritz J, Eisinger J, Elliott A, Bernstein I. Ivanka and Donald Trump Jr. Were Close to Being Charged with Felony Fraud [Internet]. ProPublica. 2017 [cited 2020 Aug 18]. Available from: https://www.propublica.org/article/ivanka-donald-trump-jr-close-to-being-charged-felony-fraud

455. New York State Attorney General. AG James Secures Court Order Against Donald J. Trump, Trump Children, And Trump Foundation [Internet]. New York State Office of the Attorney General. 2019 [cited 2020 Nov 14]. Available from: https://ag.ny.gov/press-release/2019/ag-james-secures-court-order-against-donald-j-trump-trump-children-and-trump

456. Reuters Staff. UK Had Europe's Highest Rate of Excess Deaths During Covid-19 Pandemic - Official. Reuters [Internet]. 2020 Jul 30 [cited 2020 Oct 15]; Available from: https://uk.reuters.com/article/uk-health-coronavirus-britain-deaths-idUKKCN24V1UK

457. Johns Hopkins University & Medicine. Mortality Analyses [Internet]. Johns Hopkins Coronavirus Resource Center. 2020 [cited 2020 Oct 15]. Available from: https://coronavirus.jhu.edu/data/mortality

458. BBC News. TalkTalk Hack: Boy, 15, Arrested in Northern Ireland Released on Bail. BBC News [Internet]. 2015 Oct 27 [cited 2020 Oct 15]; Available from: https://www.bbc.co.uk/news/uk-northern-ireland-34646196

459. BBC News. TalkTalk Boss Dido Harding to Step Down in May. BBC News [Internet]. 2017 Feb 1 [cited 2020 Oct 15]; Available from: https://www.bbc.co.uk/news/business-38824570

460. Campbell D. Dido Harding: Confident, Loyal – but with Precious Little Relevant Experience [Internet]. The Guardian. 2020 [cited 2020 Oct 15]. Available from: http://www.theguardian.com/uk-news/2020/aug/18/dido-harding-profile-institute-health-protection

461. NHS England. NHS England» Board members [Internet]. England.NHS.UK. [cited 2020 Nov 24]. Available from:

https://www.england.nhs.uk/about/board/nhs-improvement-board/board-members/

462. White N. Johnson and Hancock Are Being Sued for Appointing Dido Harding [Internet]. HuffPost UK. 2020 [cited 2020 Nov 24]. Available from: https://www.huffingtonpost.co.uk/entry/governme nt-sued-dido-harding-test-and-trace_uk_5f9ff885c5b65662bcc91ecd

463. Anonymous. Why I Quit Working on Boris Johnson's 'World-Beating' Test-and-Tracing System [Internet]. The Guardian. 2020 [cited 2020 Oct 15]. Available from: http://www.theguardian.com/commentisfree/2020/ may/30/boris-johnsons-test-and-tracing-system-britain-lockdown

464. Taylor J. Government Faces Ridicule After 'Spreadsheet Glitch' Causes Huge Testing Figures Error [Internet]. Indy100. 2020 [cited 2020 Oct 15]. Available from: https://www.indy100.com/article/boris-johnson-dido-harding-test-and-trace-spreadsheet-excel-glitch-9718241

465. Phung V-H, Asghar Z, Matiti M, Siriwardena AN. Understanding How Eastern European Migrants Use and Experience UK Health Services: A Systematic Scoping Review. BMC Health Services Research. 2020 Mar 6;20(1):173.

466. Sippitt A. What Impact Does Immigration Have on School Places? [Internet]. Full Fact. 2015 [cited 2020 Oct 3]. Available from:

https://fullfact.org/education/what-impact-immigration-school-places/

467. Robineau D. Ageing Britain: Two-Fifths of NHS Budget Is Spent on Over-65s. The Guardian [Internet]. 2016 Feb 1 [cited 2020 Nov 14]; Available from: https://www.theguardian.com/society/2016/feb/01/ageing-britain-two-fifths-nhs-budget-spent-over-65s

468. Millar P. What's All This About the EU's 'Democratic Deficit'? [Internet]. The Guardian. 2013 [cited 2020 Nov 15]. Available from: http://www.theguardian.com/commentisfree/2013/may/20/eu-democratic-deficit

469. European Commission. EU Position in World Trade [Internet]. European Commission. 2019 [cited 2020 Nov 15]. Available from: https://ec.europa.eu/trade/policy/eu-position-in-world-trade/

470. Kentish B. 10 Ways the EU Protects British Workers' Rights [Internet]. The Independent. 2017 [cited 2020 Nov 15]. Available from: https://www.independent.co.uk/news/uk/home-news/brexit-latest-news-10-ways-eu-protects-british-workers-rights-danger-european-union-a7531366.html

471. Elliott L. EU's Funding for UK's Poorest Areas 'Must Be Matched After Brexit'. The Guardian [Internet]. 2020 Jan 17 [cited 2020 Nov 30]; Available from:

https://www.theguardian.com/politics/2020/jan/17/eus-funding-for-uks-poorest-areas-must-be-matched-after-brexit

472. Ipsos MORI. How Britain Voted in the 2016 EU Referendum [Internet]. Ipsos MORI. 2016 [cited 2020 Oct 1]. Available from: https://www.ipsos.com/ipsos-mori/en-uk/how-britain-voted-2016-eu-referendum

473. Hannam P. There's Nothing Marxist About Black Lives Matter [Internet]. Spiked! 2020 [cited 2020 Jul 8]. Available from: https://www.spiked-online.com/2020/07/08/theres-nothing-marxist-about-black-lives-matter/

474. Christina G. Yes, The Left Needs to Keep Infighting – Here Are 6 Reasons Why [Internet]. Everyday Feminism. 2017 [cited 2020 Jun 8]. Available from: https://everydayfeminism.com/2017/02/why-left-needs-to-keep-infighting/

475. Three Rivers Green Party. General Election 2019 [Internet]. Three Rivers Green Party. 2019 [cited 2020 Nov 15]. Available from: https://threerivers.greenparty.org.uk/local-elections.html

476. Parsons V. There Isn't a Single Trans or Non-Binary Voice at the Top of UK Politics, but This Green Party Activist Wants to Change All That [Internet]. PinkNews. 2020 [cited 2020 Sep 25]. Available from: https://www.pinknews.co.uk/2020/08/06/tom-

pashby-green-party-deputy-leadership-election-non-binary-trans-environment/

477. Hill R. The Green Party's Leadership Gender Balancing Rules Aren't Fit for Purpose [Internet]. Bright Green. 2020 [cited 2020 Sep 26]. Available from: http://bright-green.org/2020/07/24/the-green-partys-leadership-gender-balancing-rules-arent-fit-for-purpose/

478. Pashby T. It's Time to Improve the Green Party's Gender Balancing Rules [Internet]. Bright Green. 2020 [cited 2020 Oct 7]. Available from: http://bright-green.org/2020/10/05/its-time-to-improve-the-green-partys-gender-balancing-rules/

479. Freshwater P. Green Election Candidates Struggle to Answer 'What Is a Woman?' GrimsbyLive [Internet]. 2020 Jul 20 [cited 2020 Sep 25]; Available from: https://www.grimsbytelegraph.co.uk/news/uk-world-news/what-is-a-woman-greens-4347697

480. West P. Why so Many BLM Ultras Are White [Internet]. Spiked! 2020 [cited 2020 Jul 6]. Available from: https://www.spiked-online.com/2020/07/03/why-so-many-blm-ultras-are-white/

481. Clements T. Autism Is a Disability, Not an Identity [Internet]. Spiked! 2019 [cited 2020 Oct 7]. Available from: https://www.spiked-online.com/2019/11/11/autism-is-a-disability-not-an-identity/

482. Wharmby P. Pete Wharmby's Autism and Teaching Blog: My letter to The Guardian [Internet]. Pete Wharmby's Autism and Teaching Blog. 2019 [cited 2020 Nov 15]. Available from: https://petewharmby.blogspot.com/2019/08/my-letter-to-guardian.html

483. Downs J. Peter Thiel Shows Us There's a Difference Between Gay Sex and Gay [Internet]. Advocate. 2016 [cited 2020 Sep 30]. Available from: http://www.advocate.com/commentary/2016/10/1 4/peter-thiel-shows-us-theres-difference-between-gay-sex-and-gay

Index